MINERVA SERIES OF STUDENTS' HANDBOOKS No. 20

General Editor
BRIAN CHAPMAN

The British System of Government

THE MINERVA SERIES OF STUDENTS' HANDBOOKS

The British System of Government

by ANTHONY H. BIRCH
University of Victoria, British Columbia

London
GEORGE ALLEN & UNWIN
Boston   Sydney

George Allen & Unwin (Publishers) Ltd,
40 Museum Street, London WC1A 1LU, UK

George Allen & Unwin (Publishers) Ltd,
Park Lane, Hemel Hempstead, Herts HP2 4TE, UK

Allen & Unwin Inc.,
9 Winchester Terrace, Winchester, Mass 01890, USA

George Allen & Unwin Australia Pty Ltd,
8 Napier Street, North Sydney, NSW 2060, Australia

First published in 1967
Second edition 1968
Second impression 1969
Third edition 1973
Third impression 1978
Fourth edition 1980
Second impression 1980
Fifth edition 1982

British Library Cataloguing in Publication Data

Birch, Anthony H.
    The British system of government. – 5th ed. –
(Minerva series of student's handbooks; no. 20)
1. Great Britain – Politics and government – 1964–
I. Title   II. Series
354.41   JN234
ISBN 0–04–320149–0

Set in 10 on 11 point Times
and printed in Great Britain
by Biddles Ltd, Guildford, Surrey

To Peter and Tanya

by the same author

REPRESENTATION (*Macmillan*)

REPRESENTATIVE AND RESPONSIBLE GOVERNMENT

POLITICAL INTEGRATION AND DISINTEGRATION
IN THE BRITISH ISLES

SMALL-TOWN POLITICS (*OUP*)

FEDERALISM, FINANCE AND SOCIAL LEGISLATION (*OUP*)

Contents

Preface to the Fourth Edition

In the seven years since I prepared the third edition of this book, Britain has gone through an unhappy and difficult period. Inflation has reached unprecedented levels; unemployment has reached levels not known since the 1930s; a government has been brought down as a result of trade union action; political violence of various kinds has increased; and the unity of the kingdom has been challenged by the growth of the Scottish and Welsh nationalist movements. The political system has shown considerable resilience in the face of these developments, but it has nevertheless changed in numerous ways which I have discussed. Almost half of this edition consists of new material, and I must, as ever, thank my wife Dorothy for her invaluable help and unfailing support in its preparation.

Vancouver Island,   A.H.B.
1979

Part I

The Social Basis

Chapter 1

British Society and the British People

This book is concerned with the nature of British political institutions and the way in which they operate. Both the institutions and their mode of operation have been shaped to a large extent by the nature of the society in which they have developed, and they reflect and embody the habits and assumptions of the people who operate them. This is a general truth about political systems which applies not only to the government of Britain but also to the government of other nations; and not only to the government of nations but also to the government of small societies within nations. It can be seen as clearly as anywhere in the government of voluntary societies. Thus, student organisations tend to be ultra-democratic because students dislike authority, and to have elaborate rules of order because of the ingenuity with which student politicians exploit any ambiguity or loophole in the rules. Church organisations, on the other hand, tend to be dominated by a few leading personalities and to have very loose rules of procedure which reflect the belief that relations between members should be characterised by mutual trust and good faith. Nations are similar to voluntary societies in this respect: how they are governed depends to a large extent on the beliefs and habits of their citizens and the social relations between them. The most appropriate introduction to a study of British government is therefore a short discussion of some of the salient characteristics of British society and the British people.

THE COMPONENT PARTS OF BRITISH SOCIETY

The term 'Britain' is slightly ambiguous, being used sometimes as a shorthand equivalent of the political entity called the United Kingdom of Great Britain and Northern Ireland, sometimes as a short version of the social entity called Great Britain, and frequently (by the English) as a synonym for England. As 83 per cent of the people of the United Kingdom live in England, the whole political system is heavily influenced by the character of English society, but it is nevertheless appropriate to begin by saying a word about Ireland, Wales and Scotland.

Ireland is best regarded as England's oldest colony, having been invaded by the English in the twelfth century and governed in colonial fashion until 1800, with a Governor responsible to London and a local Parliament (in the eighteenth century) composed almost entirely of Anglo-Irish landowners and merchants. Between 1800 and 1922 Ireland was legally part of the United Kingdom, and subject to laws passed by the Westminster Parliament. In the latter year, after a limited but bitter campaign of guerilla warfare, the greater part of Ireland became an independent country known first as the Irish Free State and now as the Irish Republic, leaving the six north-eastern counties as a partially self-governing province of the United Kingdom.

Irish society and Irish politics have always been very different from English society and English politics, and strictly speaking they are outside the scope of this book. However, the political violence which broke out in Northern Ireland in 1969 has been kept within bounds only by a large contingent of British troops, and since 1972 the Belfast Parliament has been suspended and the Province has been governed directly from London. In view of these developments the political character and problems of Northern Ireland will be summarised briefly in an appendix.

Wales, like Ireland, was invaded by the English in the twelfth century. It was politically integrated with England in 1536, and from then onwards the two countries were governed as one, with no significant differences between their political institutions until a measure of decentralisation was introduced in 1964.

The social integration of Wales and England has inevitably been a more gradual process than their political integration. Until the nineteenth century the Welsh language was spoken by the great majority of people, although English had been the language of government since 1536 and the Welsh middle classes had adopted both the English language and many aspects of English culture. During the nineteenth century the development of coal mining and industry in south Wales brought a large influx of English workers, while the development of state education was accompanied by an official campaign to establish English as the universal language of discourse. By 1971 only 21 per cent of the people of Wales claimed any knowledge of Welsh, and it is only in rural areas and a few small towns that the language is actually used. Traditional Welsh culture has declined along with the language, and it would be easy to conclude that Welsh society will be completely integrated with English society within two or three generations.

Such a conclusion may not be warranted, however. For one thing, a vigorous campaign is being promoted to revive the Welsh language and culture, and the Welsh nationalist party, Plaid Cymru, has had some significant electoral successes since 1967. Secondly, there are in fact subtle differences between Welsh and English society, quite apart from the language and the traditional culture of rural Wales. Lacking their own aristocracy, the Welsh tend to be more egalitarian than the English and are considerably more reluctant to vote Conservative. Since the franchise was extended to most working-class men in 1867, the Conservative Party has always had difficulty in winning more than a handful of the Welsh parliamentary constituencies. (In the 21 elections held between 1900 and 1979, excluding 1918, Conservatives gained an average of 5·6 Welsh seats out of a total that varied between 34 and 36.) Until 1922 Wales was overwhelmingly Liberal in sentiment and since then it has been overwhelmingly Labour. In addition, Welsh people tend to show more emotion than the English, and this affects their political attitudes and behaviour. A leading student of Welsh politics has observed that 'Welsh political culture is . . . shot through with Welsh cultural and national values and is thus inherently conducive to anger and conflict'.[1]

The position of Scotland is different again. For several centuries Scotland was an independent state, and when it joined in political union with England and Wales in 1707 it did so by agreement, not by conquest. Moreover, although the Scottish Parliament voted itself out of existence, other Scottish institutions remained intact, including a distinctive legal system, a distinctive (and rather advanced) educational system, and the Presbyterian Church of Scotland. With this history, it is not surprising that the Scottish people have a secure sense of national identity, which has survived two and a half centuries of political union with England and is now the basis of a flourishing nationalist party which seeks to regain Scottish independence.

It follows that there is a real sense in which British society is multi-national. However, the differences between England, Wales and Scotland are limited in extent. The Industrial Revolution has had a similar impact on each, and they are all highly urbanised. The proportion of male workers engaged in agriculture in 1971 was 3 per cent in England, 5 per cent in Wales, and 5 per cent in Scotland, compared with 8 per cent in West Germany and the United States of America, 12 per cent in Canada and the Netherlands, and over 20 per cent in France, Italy and Switzerland. There is a high level of personal mobility between the various parts of Britain, and communication statistics reveal an exceptionally high degree of integration between England and Wales and a rather high degree between England and Scotland.[2] The centralised nature of British government has further reduced the social differences between the various parts of the country. It is therefore reasonable (in a brief treatment) to outline the characteristics of British society as if it were one society, even though occasional reservations have to be made to allow for Welsh and Scottish differences.

SOME CHARACTERISTICS OF BRITISH SOCIETY

As the resolution of conflicts is one of the main functions of government, the nature of the divisions and cleavages in society has a major influence on the character of the political system. Cleavages vary in kind, and one of the most important lessons to be drawn from a study of politics is that conflicts deriving from linguistic, religious or racial cleavages are usually more difficult to resolve than conflicts deriving from economic cleavages, whether the latter be between regions of the country or classes within society. There are two reasons for this difference. The first is that people are locked into their linguistic, religious and racial groups, usually having no wish to change even if they could, whereas people can hope to escape from a depressed region or class by individual mobility. If they themselves cannot escape, they can hope that their children will do so. The second reason is that it is easier for governments to mitigate economic conflicts, by a process of incremental adjustment, than it is for them to mitigate linguistic, religious or racial conflicts.

The contemporary world provides ample evidence for these generalisations. Linguistic conflicts have created constitutional crises in both Belgium and Canada. Religious conflicts have led to prolonged violence in Northern Ireland. Racial conflicts have led to riots in American cities, to bloodshed in many African and Asian states, and to warfare in the Middle East. Economic conflicts, though present in all countries, are normally resolved peacefully by bargaining, wage increases, price controls, and adjustments to the tax system.

In this perspective, Britain can be counted as fortunate in that modern British society is relatively free from the most troublesome kinds of cleavage. There is no linguistic cleavage in Britain except in some parts of Wales, and as the Welsh-speakers comprise only 1 per cent of the British population (and can virtually all speak English as well) this does not pose a serious threat to political stability. Religious divisions are no longer of any general significance, largely because of the decline of religious conviction. Less than 10 per cent of the population attend church on a normal Sunday, and the attitude of the great majority of people towards religion is one of indifference. There are a few constituencies in and around Glasgow and Liverpool where the concentration of Roman Catholic voters is so great that the Labour

Party, at least, normally nominates a Catholic candidate; but these are areas of heavy Irish immigration, so that the religious dimension to political life there can be regarded as an importation from across the water. In the remainder of Britain the great majority of voters neither know nor care what religious views (if any) are held by candidates for political office.

The question of race is rather more delicate. For many centuries Britain has had a high degree of ethnic homogeneity, with immigrants arriving only in a trickle and thus easily assimilated. Between 1881 and 1960 only 149,000 certificates of naturalisation were issued, amounting to only one-third of 1 per cent of the total population at the latter date. In the nineteenth century the arrival of large numbers of Irish settlers sometimes created tension in industrial areas, but did not lead to any permanent social problems. Since 1955, however, the situation has been changed by the arrival of very considerable numbers of Pakistani, Indian and West Indian immigrants, who until 1962 had unrestricted right of entry to Britain as citizens of Commonwealth countries. As soon as this development came to the attention of the general public, opinion polls showed that over 80 per cent of the public were opposed to it, and in 1962 immigration of this kind was restricted by the Commonwealth Immigrants Act. Subsequent measures have tightened the controls, but by 1979 Britain had 1·8 million Commonwealth immigrants and it is officially estimated that by the end of the century the number will be between 3·5 and 4 million.

The appearance of these new ethnic minorities, unlikely to be assimilated easily, and largely concentrated in a few cities, has given rise to widespread concern. Many people fear that British cities may experience the race riots that have affected cities in the United States and other countries with sizeable racial minorities. Up to 1979 this had not happened, and it may be avoided by the generous provision of welfare and housing services, combined with extensive legislation to discourage racial discrimination and the generally enlightened behaviour of the British police. The promotion of good race relations is a matter on which all major parties are agreed, even though the control of immigration has been a hot political issue. The immigrants themselves, though well represented by group spokesmen, have so far shown little disposition to join political parties or take an active role in the electoral process. But there is a clear possibility that racial cleavages will be a source of political conflict in the years to come.

Economic divisions with a geographical (as distinct from a class) basis fall into two categories: divisions between urban and rural areas, and divisions between more and less prosperous regions. Divisions between urban and rural areas are relatively unimportant in Britain because the country is more highly urbanised than any other country in the world apart from city states like Kuwait and Singapore. International comparisons are complicated by the problem of local government boundaries, but two American social scientists who have tried to overcome this problem estimate that in 1965 72 per cent of the British people lived in sizeable urban areas compared with 51 per cent in the United States, 43 per cent in Canada, 34 per cent in France, and 52 per cent in West Germany.[3] One of the consequences is that in British politics there is no sharp clash between representatives of urban and rural interests. The farming industry is an important pressure-group, but its influence depends on the goodwill of the Government and the fact that the country could not easily afford to increase its imports of food, not upon the voting power of people dependent on agriculture for their livelihood.

Regional disparities in prosperity are inevitable in any sizeable country, and in Britain they have been accentuated since the 1920s by the decline of several older staple industries such as coalmining, shipbuilding and textiles. These industries are mainly situated in Wales, Scotland and the north of England, so that the interwar period saw a sizeable migration of people towards the more prosperous Midlands and south-east. Since 1945, however, all major political parties have subscribed to the view that it is the Government's duty to divert industrial growth to areas of relatively high unemployment, with the object of minimising this kind of migration. This policy has met with only partial success, and the losses to the areas of potentially high economic growth have almost certainly exceeded the gains of poorer regions. However, the fact that this has not become an issue between the parties has prevented regional economic differences from having as much impact on the political process as they do in some countries.

Another factor that reduces the impact of regional issues is the centralisation of the mass media. There is no other country of Britain's size in which the press is so dominated by a handful of national newspapers. Two of these, *The Times* and the *Guardian,* have a considerable influence but fairly small circulations, these being about 330,000 each during 1974. The five other national dailies had a combined circulation of 13·8 million in the same year, and it is estimated that 75 per cent of the population over the age of 16 read one or more of these seven papers. With a handful of exceptions, Welsh and provincial papers are read in addition to national papers rather than as alternatives to them, and people tend to look to the national press for political news and to their local papers to find out what is on at the cinema. The only papers that can be regarded as alternatives to the national press are the *Yorkshire Post,* with a circulation of 105,000, the *Western Mail* (circulation 95,000), the *Liverpool Daily Post* (99,000), and the *Birmingham Post* (60,000). It will be seen that their combined circulation is insignificant compared with that of the national dailies. The Sunday press is similarly central-ised, and a 1972 readership survey showed that 87 per cent of the population over the age of 16 read one or more of the seven national Sunday papers, which had a combined circulation of just over 21 million in 1974.

However, Scotland is an exception to this general rule. It has three important daily papers of its own in the *Scotsman,* the *Glasgow Herald* and the *Daily Record,* as well as several smaller independent dailies and the Scottish editions of British national papers. Statistics show that the total circulation of the Scottish-owned daily papers is about the same as that of the London-owned papers, and the Scottish editions of the latter contain a high proportion of Scottish news even though they are now all edited in England.

It is, of course, also important that the national radio network is owned by the Government and that the two television news program-mes are produced by national agencies, one by the BBC and the other by an independent organisation which provides a news service for all the commercial television companies. The television networks are to some extent regionalised and they put on short magazine programmes of local interest, but there is not much by way of local news.

The consequence of all these factors is that political news is much the same all over the country. In the United States, where sectional differences are considerable, and all newspapers and radio stations are local, it often happens that at any one time people in different parts of the country are concerned with quite different political issues. In the south-western states a prominent issue might be the position of Mexican immigrants; in Texas the politics of the oil industry; in the mid-west the federal government's policy towards agriculture; in the north-east it might be foreign policy. As a result, in an election the fortunes of the parties may vary between regions, the Democrats gaining in one part of the country and the Republicans gaining elsewhere.

In Britain, the combined effect of the smallness of the country, the absence of marked sectional differences, and the existence of national newspapers is that political localism of this American kind rarely occurs except in Scotland. Local issues do not often make newspaper headlines, and when they do they usually make headlines all over the country – at any rate in England and Wales. This state of affairs is partly responsible for the fact that since 1945 movements of political opinion have been remarkably uniform over the whole country. If the government of the day loses popularity, the general tendency, as indicated by the public-opinion polls, is for it to lose popularity almost everywhere. If one of the main parties loses support to the other in a general election, this is apt to be reflected in the results in all regions.

This last point emerges very clearly from the statistics compiled by D. E. Butler and his colleagues at Nuffield College, Oxford. They have calculated the swing of votes between the Conservative and Labour parties in each constituency in each postwar election, and grouped the constituencies into areas.[4] Between 1945 and 1950 there was a swing from Labour to Conservative of 3·4 per cent over the whole of Britain, and of the fifty-five areas no fewer than fifty-three experienced a swing in the same direction. Between 1950 and 1951 the movement of opinion was equally uniform. Fifty-one areas experienced a slight swing to the Conservative Party, and in thirty-six of these (that is, two-thirds of the country) the swing was between 1 per cent and 2 per cent.

In 1955 the story was repeated, and only in 1959 was there any real sign of regional variation. In this election forty-six areas registered a swing to the Conservative Party, but nine areas went the other way. These nine included all five areas of Scotland, which had become aware that its economic development was lagging behind that of England and Wales, and three areas in the north-west which had been affected by the decline of the cotton industry in the late 1950s. In 1964 the swing to Labour was general but rather uneven in magnitude, but in 1966 the variations were largely ironed out. Even in 1964 the range of variation between areas was very small compared with what is common in many other countries. In 1970 the swing was again very even: over the whole country the Conservatives gained 4·7 per cent and in England and Wales the regional swings all fell between 3·9 per cent (in the extreme north) and 5·9 per cent (in the East Midlands). However, in Scotland the swing to the Conservatives was a little lower at 2·9 per cent, and it is noticeable that in the fifteen years between 1955 and 1970 there was a 5 per cent swing away from the Conservatives in Scotland although in the country as a whole there was a swing to the Conservatives of 0·1 per cent.

The three elections of the 1970s provided dramatic evidence of the increasing gap between political attitudes in Scotland and those in the rest of the country. The Conservative Party continued to lose ground north of the border, but the beneficiary in 1974 was not the Labour Party but the Scottish National Party, which gained 22 per cent of Scottish votes in February and 30 per cent in October. However, in England and Wales the regional variations in voting behaviour continued to be very small. In the February 1974 election there was a small swing to Plaid Cymru in Wales and a large swing to Labour in the West Midlands, but all the other areas of the country saw a large increase in Liberal support and a small net swing to the Labour Party (which lost fewer votes than the Conservative Party). Between February and

October 1974 all areas but one registered swings to Labour of between 1·1 per cent and 3·5 per cent. In 1979 there was an overall swing of 5·2 per cent to the Conservatives, the variation in England ranging only from 6·6 per cent in the south and west to 4·5 per cent in the north. In Wales there was a swing to the Conservatives of 4·8 per cent, but in Scotland there was actually a swing of 0·1 per cent to the Labour Party.

THE CLASS SYSTEM

It has often been observed that the British are more obsessed by considerations of social class in their relations with each other than the citizens of any other modern industrial country, and some account of the class system is essential to any discussion of the characteristics of British society. However, we have to consider not just the existence of class differences and rivalries but their exact nature, and here it is easy to be led astray. The problem is not only that the subject is intrinsically complicated but also that there exist various doctrines and myths about it which influence the way people discuss it.

Like other aspects of society, the class system is constantly changing, and at any given time the popular view of the system is apt to be somewhat out of date. Thus, in the middle of the last century people were still talking of orders and ranks in society, a terminology which had been appropriate in the eighteenth century but which the growth of industry had made obsolescent in many parts of the country by the 1850s. In rural areas it was still reasonable to assume that class was a matter of a man's station in life, with the lower orders deferring to their social superiors but sharing with them a common interest in the land and its produce. In the industrial areas, however, the social scene was increasingly dominated by the new men of wealth and influence, the manufacturers and middlemen and merchants. These groups had already won a notable political victory in their campaign for the repeal of the Corn Laws, but in the old language of ranks and orders they could hardly even be described.

In the latter part of the century this way of discussing the class system was largely replaced by another one, in which class distinctions were assumed to be based not mainly on birth or rank, but on economic power. People adopted Disraeli's expression and began to talk of 'the two nations', by which they meant the rich and the poor. Some socialists adopted Marx's ideas and wrote of the exploitation of the proletariat by the capitalists. Others, more numerous, campaigned in more moralistic terms for the rights of the working class. The inhumanity of industrial conditions was captured in a little ditty which one labour leader used to repeat on public platforms:

> The golf course lies beside the mill
> And on a sunny day
> The little children at their work
> Can see the men at play.

This new view of the class system, which was a natural reflection of social conditions in mid- and late-Victorian England, led to the creation in 1900 of the Labour Representation Committee, founded in the belief that working-class conditions would not be substantially improved until working-class MPS were sent to Westminster. The representation of the workers in Parliament was the only official aim of the Labour Party, which succeeded the Committee in 1906, until the Party adopted a new constitution in 1918. In the same period trade unions and employers clashed in bitterly fought strikes, and Conservative and Liberal writers warned the country of the danger that class conflict might transform the British system of government.

This view of the class system was always oversimplified, and in the last fifty years the social structure has become increasingly complex. In the lower half of the social hierarchy it is possible to discern at least three groups with differing interests and attitudes. First, there are the dockers, miners and shipyard workers and their families, who live in close-knit communities in the older industrial areas and whose style of life has not greatly changed in the last three decades. Their incomes are much higher than they were, but they live in depressing surroundings and face the threat of unemployment because of the progressive decline of their industries. Their unions are militant, and they give solid support to the Labour Party. In some parts of the country railway workers and steel workers are in a similar position.

A second group consists of workers in the industries that have expanded in recent decades, such as electrical engineering, the motor and aircraft industries, oil, chemicals, plastics and man-made fibres. The standard of living of these workers has been transformed by the rapid economic growth of the postwar period, and their horizons have been expanded by cars and foreign holidays. Their incomes are higher than those of many white-collar workers, and some social scientists have used the term 'embourgeoisement' to predict a consequent change in their social and political attitudes.

This was a not unreasonable prediction in view of the fact that, in economic terms, British society is now very egalitarian. The after-tax income of the average doctor or business executive is only about twice that of skilled manual workers in these modern industries, a much smaller gap than exists in most Western countries. However, social attitudes change rather slowly, status gradations remain important, and there is still a marked gap between skilled workers and middle-class people in terms of accent, tastes, eating habits and leisure-time activities. The public awareness of class differences remains acute, and the prediction of embourgeoisement was premature.

There is, however, a third group of workers who do seem to have broken through to a different style of life. The prototypical member of this group is the computer operator, and it includes all kinds of people in high-technology industries and service trades who exercise individual skills and do not have their pace of work determined by a production line. The size of this group is expanding rapidly, and the social and political attitudes of its members are apt to be volatile. They look at political parties with a critical eye and are less likely than members of the other two groups to vote automatically for the party favoured by their parents or their trade union.

Social relations and attitudes in the upper half of the social spectrum also reflect the influence of earlier periods of history. As in other industrial societies, the middle classes have become more numerous, more mobile and more cosmopolitan since the Second World War. What is truly distinctive about British society, however, is the continuing importance of the traditional upper classes. Whereas in most European countries these groups have lost all but a vestige of their former influence, in Britain (and particularly in England) they have retained much of their influence and perpetuated many of their values by opening their ranks to the more successful members of the bourgeoisie. The main agents of socialisation are the public schools, nearly all located in rural areas, concerned to develop the character of their pupils as well as to train their minds, and more in demand than ever in spite of astronomical fees. (It is common for parents to enter their son for Eton as soon as the mother becomes pregnant, withdrawing the entry if the baby turns out to be a girl.)

To a greater or lesser extent, all the public schools transmit the social values of the upper classes. These values include a preference for amateurs rather than professionals and a dislike for the materialistic attitudes of the self-made businessman. The qualities of loyalty, integrity, and devotion to duty are valued more than those of efficiency and success. Competition in debate and in sport is regarded more highly than competition in salesmanship.

Needless to say, these attitudes have had their greatest political influence in the Conservative Party, which has never been a party of business and whose leaders' attitudes to the poorer sections of the community have generally been paternalistic rather than harsh. The self-help philosophy of Samuel Smiles crossed the Atlantic to find a natural and enduring home in the Republican Party, but Smiles was never a Conservative and the *laissez-faire* liberalism which he advocated did not survive beyond the early years of the twentieth century in

Britain. The influence of upper-class attitudes has permeated the other parties by way of the public schools and the older universities. In the years from 1940 to 1963 the main political parties had eight leaders between them, of whom seven (all but the Welsh Liberal, Clement Davies) had been educated at one of the top public schools followed by Oxford, Cambridge or Sandhurst – an educational background enjoyed by less than half of 1 per cent of the population. The emergence in the mid-sixties of party leaders educated at state grammar schools, which in a social sense may be regarded as a democratic development, has been accompanied by a desperate search for greater efficiency in government, by a more abrasive style of party conflict, and (though for a variety of reasons) by a sharpening of class rivalries and divisions.

POLITICAL ATTITUDES AND VALUES

The British system of government is determined not only by the history and social characteristics of the country but also by the political attitudes and values of the British people. Some of these have been mentioned already and many others will emerge during the course of the book. However, one or two of them have played such an important part in shaping political institutions that they merit a special place in this opening chapter.

The first of these is a very strong attachment to personal liberty. This is so well known that it hardly needs explanation, but a few contemporary examples may reinforce the point. The British would never accept the widespread security checks that are taken for granted in the United States. The authorities see no need for them except in regard to a handful of sensitive posts involving access to military secrets, and the public would not put up with them as Americans do. The British would not agree to a proposal to ban extremist parties in times of peace, as communist and fascist parties are banned in West Germany. If it were revealed that the British police had conducted several hundred illegal break-ins, a British Prime Minister would not feel able to tell Parliament that such actions were justified in the campaign against potential terrorists and criminals, as the Canadian Prime Minister did in 1978. If any British minister were to make such a statement, it would be followed by a storm of public protest, which simply did not happen in Canada. Equally, it is inconceivable that a British government would instruct the security police to compile files on the political affiliations and activities of all candidates for political office, irrespective of party, as the Canadian Government has done. Nor would British citizens accept the peacetime identity cards, and the need to register addresses with the police, which are a routine feature of life in France.

Even in minor matters of everyday life, similar contrasts can be found. British licensing laws are odd enough; but people would never accept the situation of many Canadian provinces, in which it is a legal offence to consume alcoholic beverages in the open air, and a glass of beer at a picnic can lead to prosecution. British motorists would not easily accept the 55 mph speed limit which is obeyed in docile fashion all over the United States, together with regulations which make it a legal offence for a motorist to adjust the carburettor on his own car. British housewives would not tolerate the regulations regarding refuse that exist in many parts of Switzerland, where rubbish has to be enclosed in plastic bags before being deposited in the dustbin, and a housewife can be fined if she fails to do this or if she puts rubbish of one type in bags designed for another type. British swimmers would hardly put up with the situation on American beaches, where the provision of life guards is immediately followed by rules making it an offence to swim anywhere except in a small roped enclosure in front of the life guard. British yachtsmen would be appalled by the detailed regulations about safety equipment which French yachtsmen have to cope with. In all kinds of ways Britain is still a land of freedom, and any readers who doubt this should move overseas and find out for themselves.

Another common observation about British political attitudes is that they are 'deferential' in character. Dennis Kavanagh has analysed the usages of this omnibus term and shown it to be confusing rather than helpful.[5] It is, however, relevant to mention three rather different propositions that have often been (wrongly) grouped under this heading. One of these, which used to be very popular with American scholars, is that British manual workers exhibit deference towards their social superiors and tend to vote Conservative as a consequence of this. However true this may possibly have been in the past, its explanatory value has not been very great since 1945, and its significance is now rapidly approaching vanishing-point.

A quite different proposition is that the British public place a relatively high degree of trust in their public servants. This is undoubtedly true. To be sure, confidence in the efficiency and wisdom of the higher civil service has somewhat declined since it became evident in the 1960s that British economic growth was slower than that of most other industrial countries. Nevertheless, British public officials and police are still generally regarded as honest, considerate, trustworthy, and willing to respond to public pressure. A survey of contemporary attitudes would probably reveal a pattern not very different from those of the 1959 'civic culture' survey, some figures from which are given in Table 1.1.

Table 1.1   *Attitudes to Public Officials*

Nation	Proportion of citizens expecting serious consideration for their point of view from		Proportion confident of their ability to do something about an unjust regulation	
	Bureaucrats	*Police*	*Local regulation*	*National regulation*
	%	%	%	%
Britain	59	74	78	62
United States	48	56	77	75
West Germany	53	59	62	38
Italy	35	35	51	28
Mexico	14	12	52	38

Source: Gabriel Almond and Sidney Verba, *The Civic Culture* (Little, Brown, 1965), pp. 72 and 142.

A third fairly common proposition is that the British value stable government and strong leadership. The evidence for this proposition is rather ambiguous, however, and recent developments have tended to cast doubt upon its validity. One thing that can certainly be said is that most British politicians believe in the virtues of firm leadership. In the early years of Victoria's reign Sir Robert Peel made the following comment on this topic:

> I could not admit any alteration in any of these bills. This was thought very obstinate and very presumptuous; but the fact is, people like a certain degree of obstinacy and presumption in a minister. They abuse him for dictatorship and arrogance, but they like being governed.[6]

That was a long time ago, but in 1967 Harold Wilson displayed a similar attitude when he was interviewed by John Mackintosh (a political scientist who had become a Labour MP). When Mackintosh put a list of possible cases of backbench influence on policy to his leader, the Prime Minister did not say – as government leaders in many other democracies would have done – that he had taken account of the views of his party colleagues and the movements of public opinion they represented. On the contrary, he went through each example carefully 'to demonstrate that on no occasion was he consciously deflected from his original purpose, even over mode of presentation or timing, by any estimate of what dissident groups on his backbenches might say'.[7]

That this kind of attitude is shared fairly widely among the political

élite is su⟨   ⟩ctive support that ministers normally give
to Cabine⟨   ⟩rength of party discipline, and by the
infrequency⟨   ⟩s. However, the other side of the coin
is that moderi⟨   ⟩nts have shown little disposition to
take bold decisio⟨   ⟩cies have been vacillating and have
been greatly influ⟨   ⟩erations of electoral popularity.
Compromise is the n⟨   ⟩ture of government policies.

Moreover, on those⟨   ⟩when a bold initiative has been
taken, the Government i⟨   ⟩to modify or withdraw its policy
in the face of widespread o⟨   ⟩on. In 1969 the Labour Government
had to abandon its plan to reform the House of Lords. A few months
later it had to give up its proposal to regulate industrial relations. The
Conservative Government's decision in 1970 to give no more public
subsidies to declining industries was abandoned within two years. The
1971 Industrial Relations Act was effectively sabotaged by trade
union opposition. The several plans to build a new airport for London
were all given up in the face of public hostility. The record suggests that
the ease with which British governments in the twentieth century have
usually been able to get their policies accepted by Parliament and
people depends on the fact that governments have usually avoided
bold initiatives. If this is so, then what is valued in Britain is not stable
government combined with strong leadership but stable government
combined with cautious leadership.

This leads to the final point that has to be emphasised in this chapter,
namely the pragmatic character of British government and its tendency to produce piecemeal reforms rather than radical changes. A
compromise is always preferred to a clean break. An adaptation of an
existing situation is always preferred to a fresh start. Institutions are
modified out of all recognition, but are rarely abolished. Largely
because of this, an institutional map of British government would be
complex and a chart of public administration would be labyrinthine.
To understand the institutional framework of British government it is
necessary to stand back and appreciate its outlines and functions,
rather than to plunge into details about its structure and the legal
relationships between its parts. The following three chapters are based
on this assumption.

NOTES

1 See P. J. Madgwick, 'Linguistic conflict in Wales: a problem in the design of
   government', in Glyn Williams (ed.), *Social and Cultural Changes in Contemporary
   Wales* (Routledge & Kegan Paul, 1977), pp. 236–7.
2 For details, see A. H. Birch, *Political Integration and Disintegration in the British
   Isles* (Allen & Unwin, 1977), ch. 3.

3 C. L. Taylor and M. C. Hudson, *World Handbook of Political and Social Indicators*, 2nd edn (Yale University Press, 1972).

4 The following statistics are taken from D. E. Butler and Richard Rose, *The British General Election of 1959* (Macmillan, 1960), and from subsequent volumes in the same series.

5 Dennis Kavanagh, 'The deferential English: a comparative critique', in *Government and Opposition*, vol. 6 (1971).

6 Quoted in Lord Rosebery, *Sir Robert Peel* (Cassell, 1899), p. 67.

7 John P. Mackintosh, *The Government and Politics of Britain*, 4th edn (Hutchinson, 1977), p. 85.

Part II

The Constitutional Framework

Chapter 2

The Nature of the Constitution

Of the 140 or more nations which at the time of writing are members of the United Nations Organisation, all but one have written constitutions which set out the nature and powers of their institutions of government. These constitutions may be short or they may be long; they may be helpful guides to the operation of the political systems concerned or they may be seriously misleading; but from the point of view of the student they at least have the advantage of serving as a point of departure and a point of reference. The only nation which does not have such a constitution is the United Kingdom.

Of course it does not follow from this either that Britain lacks a body of constitutional law or that this law is based entirely on custom and precedent. There are numerous statutes concerning the composition and powers of particular institutions. Thus, the powers of the monarchy are limited by the Bill of Rights of 1689 and the Act of Settlement of 1701; the powers of the House of Lords are defined by the Parliament Acts of 1911 and 1949; and the modern electoral system is regulated by the Representation of the People Acts of 1948 and 1949. There is no lack of statutory provisions regarding the various institutions of government, considered individually. What is lacking is a documentary and authoritative statement of the relations between these institutions.

The consequence of this lack is that when writers and speakers describe the British constitution they produce accounts which are often significantly different from one another. And these differences are so deeply rooted that it often appears that the participants in a discussion on constitutional matters are using different languages.

The predominant language at the present time is best called the 'liberal language', not because it has anything to do with the modern Liberal Party but because it embodies a number of ideals associated with the liberal reform movement of the nineteenth century. In this language one of the central concepts is 'the sovereignty of Parliament'. It is said that in the British system of government supreme power lies with Parliament, which has direct and exclusive control over legislation and indirect control over the actions of the executive and the central administration. In respect of legislation, Parliament is said to be both omnipotent and omni-competent: there is no constitutional restriction on its authority; the courts are bound to enforce without question any laws that it passes; and other law-making bodies in the country (such as local councils) exercise their poweis only so long as Parliament authorises them to do so. In respect of administration, Parliament is said to have ultimate control by virtue of the convention that ministers are responsible to Parliament both for their own decisions and for all the actions of their departments. Government policy may be framed in the Cabinet, but Cabinet ministers have to answer to Parliament for all that they do and may be forced to resign by a vote of no confidence in Parliament if their actions do not meet with parliamentary approval.

It is of course accepted, and indeed emphasised, that within Parliament the House of Commons is now the centre of power, and that the members of that House have to answer to the electorate. Those points are sometimes expressed in another concept known as 'the sovereignty of the people'. It is said that while Parliament is legally sovereign the growth of representative institutions since the 1860s has transferred the ultimate power over issues of policy from Parliament to the people. Ministers have to answer to Parliament between general elections, but at elections the Government and all its parliamentary supporters have to answer to the electorate, who either endorse their policies by returning them to power or reject them and give a mandate to the rival party.

In this view of the constitution our political life is dominated by a chain of command which leads from the electorate to the House of Commons, from the Commons to the Cabinet and other ministers, and from the ministers to the civil servants who carry out their instructions. Since civil servants have some authority over citizens, the chain of command eventually completes a circle, as is illustrated in Figure 2.1. The system is said to be democratic because it ensures that government policies reflect 'the will of the people'.

This is a crude and over-simplified version of the view of the constitution that appears to command most general acceptance and to underlie most of the comments on political affairs that are to be found in the popular press. It is by no means universally accepted, however. If the average middle-grade civil servant were asked to comment on it, he would probably say that it gives an unrealistic picture of the flow of power. The British civil servant does not see the role of the departments as being confined to the implementation of policies that are made by politicians, bending to the will of the electorate. He knows that policy and administration are intimately related and that many, perhaps most, changes of policy are initiated in the departments as the result of memoranda written by civil servants, not by politicians. He might even suggest that the diagram would illustrate the situation more accurately if the arrows pointed in the opposite direction.

Figure 2.1   *The Liberal Model*

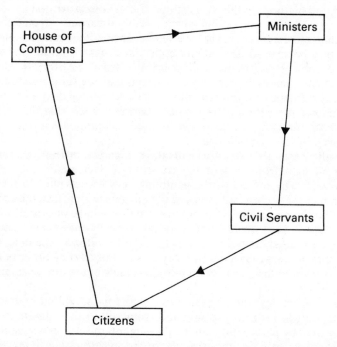

A good example to support this bureaucratic view of the constitution is afforded by the reform of the gambling laws in 1960. This major reform, which permitted the establishment of betting shops, involved issues which many people regarded as issues of moral or political principle. It was proposed immediately after a general election and had clearly been in the pipeline before the election, but the Government had carefully refrained from raising it as an electoral issue. The movement for the reform was in fact generated within the administration, using this term in a wide sense to include the police.

Until 1960 the law had prohibited off-the-course betting on horse races for cash, although this was permitted on credit. Since most manual workers were unable to secure credit, the consequence was that a large-scale illegal industry had developed, with an annual turnover of tens of millions of pounds. The unsuccessful efforts of the police to stamp out this industry took time which the police thought could better be devoted to other purposes and also tended to bring the law (and possibly the police) into disrepute with the betting public. Chief Constables had therefore frequently pointed out to officials in the Home Office that there was a case for the reform of this law, and when a reforming Home Secretary in the person of R. A. Butler was appointed he took up this suggestion. The next step was the appointment of a Royal Commission which consulted various affected interests and mustered the evidence for reform; after that the Home Secretary persuaded his Cabinet colleagues that a reform was both administratively desirable and politically feasible; officials in the Home Office made the first draft of a new law on the subject; and then, but only then, the Government informed Parliament of their intentions. It remained for ministers to persuade backbench MPs that the reform was desirable and for the MPs to defend the proposal when it was criticised by their constituents.

It will be seen that this story puts the democratic process in a rather different light from that of the constitutional view summarised in Figure 2.1. The reform of the gambling laws was certainly a reform which met the wishes and needs of the citizens most affected by these laws, but these wishes were not expressed through the electoral system and Parliament. Instead, they were taken up by the administration, which persuaded the politicians of the case for reform. The main role of backbench MPs in this whole story was that of fending off criticisms by citizens who disapproved on moral grounds of the liberalisation of the gambling laws.

Other examples could be cited to support the view that in practice many political reforms are initiated from within the administration rather than by party politicians in Parliament, but it is unnecessary to give them because the liberal model of the constitution is in fact open to objections that are far more radical than this. The most important of these is its failure to depict the role of the Crown in the British system of government. In the liberal language there is no indication that ministers are appointed by the monarch (on the advice of the Prime Minister), and that both ministers and civil servants are servants of the Crown, not of Parliament. Nor is there any indication that the House of Commons can meet only when it is convened by the Crown (again acting on the advice of the Prime Minister). It is true that the House must be convened at least once every twelve months, but a great deal can happen in twelve months and a body which lacks the power to convene itself cannot properly be described as the centre and source of authority. In 1963, when Lord Home took office as Prime Minister, he advised the Queen to postpone the opening of Parliament until he had had time to divest himself of his title, fight a by-election, and take a seat in the House of Commons. The Opposition were annoyed by this, but had no power to do anything about it.

Equally, the liberal view of the constitution fails to take account of the independence enjoyed by the executive in the conduct of foreign policy and the making of war. There are other countries (notably the

United States) in which treaties are made subject to ratification by the legislative assembly, and if the British Parliament were really as powerful as the liberal language implies it would be reasonable to assume that this situation obtained in Britain. In fact treaties are concluded by ministers in the name of Her Britannic Majesty; they are not subject to ratification by Parliament; and they cannot be disowned by Parliament. Declarations of war are made in a similar fashion, and Parliament is told that war has been declared, not asked whether war should be declared.

A further weakness of the liberal view is that it ignores or virtually ignores the position of the House of Lords in the British constitution. It is true that the power of the House of Lords has greatly diminished in recent decades, since the Parliament Act of 1911 abolished its power to veto legislation. But the House exists, its powers are not negligible, and it cannot properly be ignored simply because it cannot be fitted into the chain of command which the liberal view assumes to be the central feature of the constitution.

People who are conscious of these features of the constitution, including most ministers, top civil servants and constitutional lawyers, rarely use the liberal language when discussing constitutional matters. Instead, they use a language which may for convenience be called 'the Whitehall language', both because many of those who use it are connected with the departments in Whitehall and because in this language it is Whitehall rather than Parliament that is depicted as the centre of government.

The Whitehall language emphasises the importance of the Crown in the British constitution and the fact that ministers and civil servants are servants of the Crown, responsible for governing the country according to their view of the public interest and not obliged by law (though to some extent they are by convention) to take account of opinions expressed in Parliament. In this language Parliament appears not as a corporate entity wielding power but as a pair of debating chambers in which public opinion is aired and grievances are ventilated. It is noted that Parliament is convened and prorogued by the Queen, acting on the advice of her ministers, and it is suggested that the political process consists in part of a debate or conversation between Parliament on the one hand and the Government on the other. Parliament has the right to criticise the actions of the administration, to withhold assent to legislation, and in the last resort to pass a motion of no confidence in the government of the day. But it does not have the right to participate in or to control the administration. In this view of the constitution, which is illustrated in Figure 2.2, there is clearly something like a separation of powers between Parliament and the executive, and there is no chain of command except that within the administration itself. It will be seen

Figure 2.2   *The Whitehall Model*

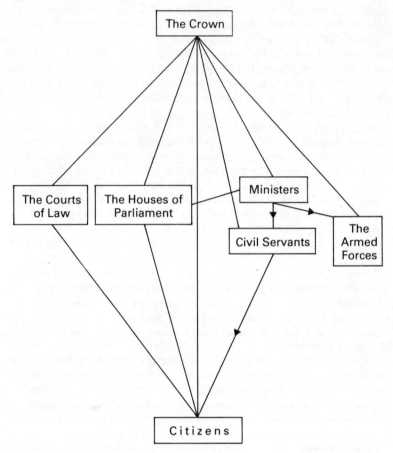

that in this model of the constitution there are also clear places for the courts of law and the armed forces, which cannot easily be fitted into the liberal model.

The co-existence of these different views of the constitution raises two questions which must now be answered. The first question is: should one view be regarded as right and the other as wrong, or do both views contain aspects of the truth? If the answer to this is that both views contain aspects of the truth, as will be suggested, a second question follows. This is: how can we account for the fact that an adequate explanation of the British system of government apparently requires the use of two rather different languages?

It is suggested that both views of the constitution embody aspects of the truth. Taking the second view first, it is certainly true, as a matter of constitutional principle, that the monarch (acting on the advice of the Prime Minister) decides when and when not to convene Parliament, that ministers are servants of the Crown, not of Parliament, and that Parliament does not have the right to control the activities of the executive or even to probe into them in the way that Congressional committees probe into the actions of the American administration. In 1958 a Select Committee on Procedure considered a proposal that the House of Commons should establish a specialised committee to deal with colonial affairs. In rejecting this proposal the Select Committee (which consisted of MPs of all three parties) made the following comment on the constitutional position:

> There is little doubt that the activities of such a committee would ultimately be aimed at controlling rather than criticising the policy and actions of the department concerned. In so doing, it would be usurping a function which the House itself has never attempted to exercise. Although the House has always maintained the right to criticize the executive and in the last resort to withdraw its confidence, it has always been careful not to arrogate to itself any of the executive power.[1]

This view of the constitution is not only correct as a matter of principle but is also a helpful guide to practice. The British administration conducts its affairs in substantial independence of Parliament, not only in respect of defence and foreign relations but also in respect of domestic matters. An example which will affect the lives of many readers of this book is the revolution in policy for higher education which followed the publication of the Robbins Report in the autumn of 1963. The first point to note about this is that the Report was not made available to Members of Parliament until the Government had considered its contents and formulated a policy in regard to its recommendations. This policy was in fact announced by the Prime Minister the day after the Report was published. The second point to note is that the implementation of this policy was and is entirely a matter for executive action. The amount of money made available for university expansion is decided by the Treasury and the ministry responsible for higher education, with the Cabinet acting as arbiter in case of dispute. It is true that Parliament has to authorise this expenditure, but Parliament has no power to increase the estimates presented to it and has never been known to decrease them. When new universities are established they are created by royal charter, no parliamentary action being required.

In this whole process Parliament has no real function save to act as a forum for criticism and debate. Certainly the discussions in Parliament may have an influence on government policy, but this influence is not necessarily any greater than that of discussions in the correspondence columns of *The Times* and is almost certainly less than that of private discussions between the universities and the departments. It would seem that Figure 2.2 gives a fairly accurate illustration of the role of Parliament in regard to policy for higher education.

On the other hand, this view of the constitution is clearly incomplete. Its most crippling omission is that it takes no account of the fact that the composition of the House of Commons determines which party or parties will form the Government. In the twentieth century the normal situation has been for one party to have an absolute majority of seats in the Commons and for members of this party to fill all ministerial appointments. There were exceptions during both world wars, when coalition governments were formed for the sake of national unity even though the majority party could have kept its monopoly of ministerial posts had it chosen to do so. There were also exceptions in 1923–4 and 1929–31, when no single party had a majority of seats in the Commons. In both these periods the country was ruled by Labour governments which depended for their parliamentary majorities on the support of the Liberal Party. In 1924 the Liberals withdrew their support over one particular issue, as a consequence of which the Prime Minister advised the King to dissolve Parliament and Labour was defeated at the ensuing election. Until 1979 this was the only occasion in the present century on which a defeat in Parliament brought about the downfall of a government. In 1931 the Labour Cabinet split and the Government was replaced by a Liberal–Conservative coalition which included a few Labour leaders, though it was opposed by the bulk of Labour MPs.

For much of the period 1974–9 there was again a minority Labour government, supported normally by Plaid Cymru and in many divisions by the Scottish National Party and the Liberal Party. In consequence the Government had to accept defeat on a number of legislative issues, but it did not make them issues of confidence and did not feel obliged to resign when defeated. However, in March 1979 it was defeated in a vote of confidence and had to call an election.

A corollary of this weakness in the Whitehall view of the constitution is that no adequate account is given of the importance of elections in the British political system. A general election is not simply a way of choosing the people who will conduct debates in one of the Houses of Parliament, it is the institution which determines which party or parties will govern the country. And the prospect of the next general election is rarely far from the minds of politicians and has an influence on government policy as well as on parliamentary debates.

The other weaknesses of the Whitehall view of the constitution flow from the fact that, by focusing attention on the conduct of administration, it tends to underestimate the role of Parliament in the political life of the country. In the first place, Parliament is the training-ground for political leaders. The great majority of ministers achieve ministerial office because they have made a mark in parliamentary debates, and as a consequence of this they tend to remain 'Parliament men', with a special sensitivity to parliamentary criticism even though they know there is no danger of it leading to an adverse vote. Then again, the attention of the press is focused on Parliament and for this reason parliamentary criticism of the Government may have an effect on public opinion that is out of proportion to the real weight of the criticism. And, even if it does not have such an effect, ministers, being human, may sometimes fear that it will do so, and may moderate their actions accordingly. The behaviour of civil servants is also affected by their wish to avoid provoking parliamentary questions about their departments.

It follows that both these views of the constitution embody aspects of the truth, and that both are necessary to a balanced account of how government is conducted in Britain. The question of why these two different views exist side by side must now be answered. This question can be dealt with very briefly, though the answer to it falls into two parts.

In the first place, each view of the constitution incorporates a set of political values. Each purports to be an objective description, but in fact each is based upon a particular way of looking at politics. The Whitehall view is based upon the values of the administrator, who sees government as a way of providing public services and promoting the public interest, and tends to regard party conflict as a distraction which may be necessary but which is somewhat irrelevant to the main business in hand. The liberal view is based on the values of the democratic theorist, who thinks that the essential criteria of good government are that all shades of opinion should be reflected in public discussion and that in the end the will of the majority should prevail. There is no necessary contradiction between these views, but they emphasise different aspects of the political process. To some extent they reflect differing values of different actors on the political stage, with backbench champions espousing the liberal view and senior civil servants thinking in terms of the Whitehall view. But this difference in values only emerges occasionally as a conflict between groups because most people, including most politicians, embrace both sets of values, emphasising the one or the other according to the situation in which they find themselves. Thus any Cabinet minister is likely to think mainly in terms of the Whitehall view, knowing as he does that the Cabinet is responsible for governing the country and that Parliament is normally a place where decisions have to be justified and only occasionally a place where they are made. But a minister is also a former backbencher and a future member of the Opposition, and in these roles he will be conscious of the importance of Parliament and the need to maintain its influence over the government of the day. So he may speak with two voices about the role of Parliament in the constitution, each voice reflecting legitimate views about what the role should be.

The other part of the answer is that each view has a basis in British history. To put the matter in its simplest form, the Whitehall view reflects those features of the constitution which have remained fairly constant from the eighteenth to the twentieth centuries while the liberal view reflects the ambitions and achievements of nineteenth-century reformers who transformed the political system from one of oligarchy to one of democracy. Both views remain valid because the reformers did not abolish institutions but merely changed their nature to a greater or lesser degree. To understand the present constitution it is therefore necessary to know something of both eighteenth-century institutions and nineteenth-century reforms, and these will be discussed in the following two chapters.

NOTE

1   *Report from the Select Committee on Procedure,* HC 92–1 of 1958–9, p. xxv.

FURTHER READING

The liberal view of the constitution was given its most influential expression in A. V. Dicey, *The Law of the Constitution* (Macmillan, 1885); the Whitehall view of the constitution is to be found in numerous official reports, a good example being the *Report and Minutes of Evidence of the Select Committee on Procedure, 1958–9,* HC 92–1 of 1959; a High Tory view which resembles the Whitehall view is presented in L. S. Amery, *Thoughts on the Constitution* (Oxford University Press, 1947); an analysis of these and other views of the constitution will be found in A. H. Birch, *Representative and Responsible Government* (Allen & Unwin, 1964); a commentary on recent constitutional changes is given in Peter Bromhead, *Britain's Developing Constitution* (Allen & Unwin, 1974).

Chapter 3

The Development of Liberal Institutions

As everyone knows, the central institutions of British government are extremely old. The monarchy has an almost unbroken history dating from before the Norman conquest, and the two Houses of Parliament both have medieval origins. The development of these (and other) institutions in the medieval and early modern periods is a subject for historians; the student of modern politics can safely begin at the end of the seventeenth century.

In this period three events of great importance took place in quick succession. The first was the revolution of 1688, in which a group of politicians invited William of Orange to bring an invading army to England in order to depose James II from the throne. It was a bloodless revolution because when it came to the point James's lieutenants would not fight, but it was a revolution nevertheless. The success of this venture greatly strengthened Parliament's position in relation to the monarchy, and it was immediately followed by the Bill of Rights of 1689. In this Bill it was declared, among other things, that henceforth the monarch could neither make nor suspend laws without the consent of Parliament; that he could not raise money except by parliamentary grant; that he could not maintain a standing army without parliamentary authority; and that neither he nor anyone else could restrict the right of free speech within Parliament. A few years later the Act of Settlement of 1701 decided the immediate succession to the throne, declared that no future monarch could either be or marry a member of the Roman Catholic Church, and deprived the monarch of the power to dismiss judges, who henceforth could be removed from office only by an address of both Houses of Parliament.

THE EIGHTEENTH-CENTURY CONSTITUTION

This Revolutionary Settlement inaugurated a period of stable government and gradual constitutional evolution that continued without any major legislative change until the great Reform Act of 1832. The eighteenth-century constitution was one in which the mass of the people had little direct influence; it was a system of government by a small ruling class. However, it was distinguished from the autocratic systems of Continental Europe (and of England under the Tudors) by some vitally important features.

First, and of most importance to the ordinary man, it gave its citizens a considerable degree of liberty. True, punishments were harsh and a man could be hanged for stealing a sheep. But he could not be punished except for a clear offence against the law; he was entitled to a fair trial; and, most important of all in terms of its political effects, he was free to criticise the Government as much as he pleased so long as he kept within the laws relating to libel and sedition. Only those who value political liberty but do not enjoy it can appreciate just how much it means. It is not surprising therefore that some of the most eloquent praise of the eighteenth-century British constitution came not from Britons but from foreigners who visited the country. One of these was Voltaire, who wrote in the following terms of the rights of the subject in Britain:

> To be secure on lying down that you shall rise in possession of the same property with which you retired to rest: that you shall not be torn from the arms of your wife, or from your children, in the dead of night, to be thrown into a dungeon or buried in exile in a desert; that when rising from the bed of sleep you will have the power of publishing all your thoughts; and that, if you are accused of having either acted, spoken, or written wrongly, you can be tried only according to law. These privileges attach to everyone who sets his foot on English ground.[1]

The explanation of this liberty lay partly in the nature of British society, which was both more tolerant and less rigidly hierarchical than that of France and many other Continental countries. But another French observer, Baron Montesquieu, suggested that a good part of the explanation was to be found in the structure of the central government. The basis of British liberty, he declared, was the separation and balance of powers between the executive, the legislature, and the judiciary. In France the King dominated all three and the result was despotism; in Britain the executive was restricted on the one hand by the fact that it did not control Parliament and on the other by the independence of the judiciary, and the result was freedom.[2] The same view was put forward by the English constitutional lawyer, Sir William Blackstone, who made the following comment on the independence of the judiciary:

In this distinct and separate existence of the judicial power in a peculiar body of men, nominated indeed, but not removable at pleasure, by the crown, consists one main preservative of the public liberty; which cannot subsist long in any state, unless the administration of common justice be in some degree separated both from the legislative and also from the executive power.[3]

And elsewhere in the same treatise Blackstone noted that 'the total union' of the executive and legislature 'would be productive of tyranny' and commended the balanced nature of the British constitution, in which the executive was a part of the legislature but was not identical with it.[4]

At the time when Blackstone wrote the executive consisted of the King and six or seven ministers. The ministers were chosen, and could be dismissed, by the monarch, so that he was able to exercise a good deal of influence over government policy if he chose to do so. On the other hand, neither he nor his ministers could control Parliament. They could influence its behaviour through the distribution of patronage and the formation of cliques and parties, but MPS were jealous of their independence and were not willing to be dominated by the executive. And of course neither the executive nor the legislature could control the actions of the courts, in which judges held office for life once they were appointed.

This system of government could be described as both constitutional and parliamentary. It was not, of course, in any sense democratic. Parliament in the eighteenth century was based on the medieval principle that consent to taxation and legislation should be given by representatives of the three 'estates of the realm', the nobility, the clergy, and the commons. The nobility and clergy had their representatives in the House of Lords while the rest of the population were represented by the 'knights of the shires' and the members for 'parliamentary boroughs' who sat in the House of Commons. The House of Commons was elected on a very narrow franchise, and until the 1832 Act less than 5 per cent of the adult population enjoyed the right to vote. This franchise was based on property qualifications which varied from one area to another, and the constituencies themselves were wildly unequal in size and number of electors. There was no machinery for the redistribution of seats to take account of population movements, with the result that some constituencies retained the right to send representatives to Parliament even though their population had dwindled so that only a handful of electors lived there. These constituencies were known as 'rotten boroughs'. Such a representative system was easily manipulated by those who possessed social influence and wealth, and their task was made easier by the absence of any effective laws against bribery and other corrupt practices at elections.

Wealthy landowners could put their nominees into seats which were normally uncontested, and it has been estimated that in 1793 about 150 landowners (many of whom were themselves in the House of Lords) controlled almost half the seats in the House of Commons. The Duke of Newcastle alone controlled eleven seats. Moreover, the Treasury could control up to 100 seats by the careful distribution of patronage, so that the governing group at the time of a general election was normally safe from defeat. Ministries were brought to an end as the result of intrigue among the ruling élite, intervention by the monarch, or failure to get parliamentary support for their policies, but not by the verdict of the electorate.

This system of government was democratised during the course of the nineteenth century. However, no legislative change was made in the powers of the monarch, the two Houses of Parliament, and the judiciary. The representative system was transformed by successive extensions of the franchise, and the result was to transform the working of the governmental system without changing its structure, which remains today very similar to that of the eighteenth-century constitution.

THE MOVEMENT FOR REFORM

The changes brought about by the Industrial Revolution were the basis of the movement for political reform that developed in the last two decades of the eighteenth century and eventually resulted in the Reform Act of 1832 and the numerous other reforms that followed the Act. The development of industry led to the growth of classes whose fortunes depended on industry, notably mill-owners and manufacturers but also including merchants, tradesmen and skilled artisans. These groups grew in numbers, in wealth, and in social influence, but the political system denied them both adequate representation in Parliament and influence over local administration. Their under-representation in the House of Commons was thrown into relief by the growth of large industrial towns that had no parliamentary representative of their own, including Manchester, Birmingham, Leeds and Sheffield.

The campaign for political reform was waged by a number of largely unrelated groups who differed in both their arguments and their methods. There were spokesmen for the industrial and commercial interests who advocated a redistribution of parliamentary seats to take account of population movements and the establishment of franchise qualifications which would be uniform over the whole country, though it was assumed that a property qualification would be retained. There were middle-class societies devoted to political reform who proposed changes of a more sweeping nature, using arguments drawn from the writings of intellectual reformers like Joseph Priestley, Richard Price and Jeremy Bentham. And there were the new political unions, composed mainly of skilled workers, who adopted the revolutionary ideas that Tom Paine had advanced in his pamphlets and in his book *Rights of Man.*

This is not the place to discuss the differences between these arguments and the relations (such as they were) between these groups. It must suffice to say that their discussions and activities were largely responsible for the generation of a reform movement which was to transform the British political system from an oligarchy to a democracy in the sixty years following 1830, and was also to professionalise the central administration and to create the modern system of local government. The intellectual leaders of this movement were the legal reformer Jeremy Bentham, his friend and associate James Mill, the latter's son, John Stuart Mill, and the great Victorian administrator, Edwin Chadwick. Their political ambitions can be sketched in a few sentences.

In the first place, they wanted the representative system to be reformed so that the House of Commons would reflect all the interests and classes of the nation. Some reformers advocated the rapid adoption of universal suffrage while others thought that a gradual extension of the franchise would be both more appropriate and more practicable. But they all insisted that Parliament should represent the nation rather than simply the upper classes. Secondly, the reformers wanted the executive to be fully accountable to Parliament. They were the first to insist (in the 1830s) that the new habit of Cabinet ministers of accepting collective responsibility for their policies should be regarded as a principle of the constitution, and a very important principle at that. Thirdly, the reformers wanted to see the administrative system organised in a more efficient and professional way, with sinecures abolished, recruitment based on merit rather than on personal connections, and each department controlled by a political head who could be held individually accountable to Parliament for its work rather than by a board which was not accountable to anyone.

The reformers won their first and most crucial victory in the passage of the Reform Act of 1832. This Act increased the electorate from 5 per cent of the adult population to 7 per cent, which in itself was hardly a revolutionary change. However, this quantitative change in the franchise was less important than two other features of the Act. One of these was that the Act abolished the system of local franchises, which varied from one constituency to the next, and replaced it by a uniform national franchise. The implication of this was that representation was being granted not to areas and municipal corporations but to individuals. The change made further demands for reform inevitable and also deprived the opponents of reform of some of their more persuasive arguments. Until 1832 they had been able to produce the familiar British argument that, although the system might not be logical, it was hallowed by tradition. It would be wrong to deprive boroughs of a right to parliamentary representation which they had long enjoyed; since nobody wanted to increase the size of the House this made it difficult to give direct representation to the new industrial towns; and in any case the residents of these towns should regard themselves as 'virtually represented' by the members for older industrial towns which had similar interests. After 1832 these points lost all their force, and the opponents of further reform had no firm ground on which to take their stand.

The other feature of the Act which was of considerable significance was the way in which it was passed. In the election of 1831 the proposed reform was the only important issue, and in constituencies up and down the country reformers demanded that the candidates pledge themselves to support it if they were returned. The result was a sweeping victory for the reformers, and the subsequent Parliament was the first one whose members could claim that they had been given a mandate by the electors to pursue a specific policy. Strengthened by this development, the Prime Minister persuaded the King to agree to create sufficient new peers to secure the passage of the Bill through the House of Lords. The threat proved sufficient and the Lords eventually let the Bill go through. The potential supremacy of the people over the Commons was thus made clear for the first time in the election of 1831, and the supremacy of the Commons over the Lords was asserted for the first time just twelve months later. It was this that led Disraeli to remark that 'the aristocratic principle has been destroyed in this country, not by the Reform Act, but by the means by which the Reform Act was passed'.[5]

The immediate effects of the Act on the working of the political system were important even though they were not dramatic. The main consequence was that the choice of government was effectively placed in the hands of the Commons. Some discretion remained with the monarch but the limits within which it could be exercised were narrowed. When a ministry was defeated in the Commons on an issue of confidence, the Prime Minister felt obliged to resign or to ask for a dissolution. If he resigned, the monarch rarely had any choice but to offer the post to the leader of the largest opposition group. In case of a dissolution the question of who should form a government was effectively settled by the votes taken in the first few meetings of the newly elected House. In short, the convention that the Government should be collectively responsible to Parliament, and in particular to the House of Commons, was firmly established as a principle of the constitution.

This principle assumed considerable prominence in the middle years of the nineteenth century because the nature and distribution of party loyalties resulted in a series of government defeats. The Irish party consisted of a group of about eighty MPs on whose support no government could rely with any confidence; the Conservatives were split by the repeal of the Corn Laws in 1846 and for many years after were divided into protectionists and free traders; and the Liberal Party had Whig and Radical wings whose differences were occasionally reflected in the division lobbies. Most governments in this period had to depend on more than one group for support, and in any case the discipline within groups was very slack. The consequence was that in the thirty-five years between the first and second Reform Acts ten governments were brought to an end by defeat in the Commons and no government succeeded in staying in office for the entire life of a Parliament, from one general election to the next.

It was in this period that writers with liberal sympathies laid stress on the supremacy of Parliament in the British constitution. Gladstone described the House of Commons as 'the centre of our system' and said that the supremacy of the Commons over the administration was 'the cardinal axiom of the constitution'. Walter Bagehot described the Cabinet as 'a committee of Parliament'. The Duke of Devonshire said that Parliament 'can dismiss a ministry if it is too extravagant, or too economical; it can dismiss a ministry because its government is too stringent or too lax. It does actually and practically, in every way, directly govern England, Scotland and Ireland.'[6] Certainly it seemed in this period as if the reformers' aim of parliamentary control of the executive had been achieved. Not only were ten governments brought down in thirty-five years, but also it was established as a convention that each minister should answer to Parliament for the blunders of his department, the first ministerial resignation for this reason occurring in 1855. However, with the franchise extended to less than 10 per cent of the adult population, it could not be said that the House of Commons yet represented anything like the whole nation. In the late 1850s and 1860s the attention of liberals was therefore focused on the need for a further reform of the electoral system.

This reform came in 1867, when Disraeli introduced an Act which almost doubled the electorate in one stroke. For a Conservative leader to seize the initiative in reform in this way was a surprise, and it was said that he 'stole the Liberals' clothes when they were bathing'. It was also an extremely shrewd and far-sighted move: Disraeli realised that the progressive extension of the franchise was inevitable, and that it would relegate his party to the position of a permanent minority unless something could be done to attract lower-class voters to the Tory banner. Few of his colleagues had much confidence in this possibility, but Disraeli 'saw the working-class Tory in the British proletariat as the sculptor sees the angel in a rough lump of stone'.[7] History has triumphantly vindicated his judgement.

Besides extending the franchise, the 1867 Reform Act deprived the House of Commons of the right to decide on the validity of elections in cases of protest, and put questions of this kind within the jurisdiction of the courts. This was a move towards the elimination of corrupt practices in elections, which was carried a great deal farther by the adoption of the secret ballot in 1872 and the establishment of effective controls on electoral expenditure, and sanctions against bribery, by the Corrupt Practices Act of 1883.

In 1884 there was yet another extension of the franchise, which increased the electorate by 67 per cent and gave the vote to the great majority of adult men. Perhaps equally important, the Redistribution Act of the following year was the first important step towards the equalisation of territorial constituencies. Before this Act the electorates in the most populous constituencies in England were over forty times as big as those in the smallest constituencies; after the Act the ratio was only seven to one.

The result of this second wave of reform, when five major Acts were passed in eighteen years, was an electoral system that could reasonably be called democratic. True, it was not until many decades later that the liberal reformers' objective of 'one man, one vote; one vote, one value' was finally achieved. Complete manhood suffrage did not come until 1918. Women acquired the vote in two instalments, those over thirty being grudgingly given the rights of full citizenship in 1918 and their younger sisters getting the same privilege ten years later, when it had become clear to even the most suspicious male that they were not likely to subvert the constitution. The second vote enjoyed by university graduates and some business proprietors was not abolished until 1948. But these later changes, important as they were to the groups concerned, made relatively little difference to the working of the representative system. After 1885 this system ensured that Members of Parliament, and therefore the Government, had to keep the support of the greater part of the population if they wished to stay in office, just as the system before 1832 had made it necessary only for them to keep the support of the aristocracy and the country gentry. The whole transformation had occurred during the lifetime of William Gladstone and his contemporaries.

THE DEVELOPMENT OF PARTY MANAGEMENT

Liberal reformers had assumed that the extension of the franchise would make the House of Commons more representative of the nation without in any way diminishing its influence over the administration. Indeed, many reformers thought that the authority and the power of the House would be enhanced if it could claim to reflect all sections of society. However, at this point there occurs a twist in the story. The assumptions of the reformers were not borne out by events, because the most significant political development in the years following the 1867 Reform Act was one which few had foreseen. This was the development of large-scale party organisation and a form of party management which made it possible for the government of the day to ensure that its parliamentary supporters would toe the party line on all important issues.

Up to 1867 the political parties were simply parliamentary group-ings, with some organisation inside Parliament but without mass memberships or branches in the constituencies. Elections were fought by individual candidates, not by a party organisation. To some extent the candidates gained or lost support according to the popularity of their parties, but generally speaking the main determinants of a candidate's fortunes at the polls were his popularity in the constituency and the success of his personal campaign. It followed that party leaders had very little power over their parliamentary supporters, who could be sure of keeping their seats so long as they kept control of the situation in their constituencies. The sanctions for party discipline did not exist, and backbench revolts were common.

This situation changed after the reforms of 1867 and 1872. The extension of the franchise meant that the more populous constituen-cies contained several thousand voters, too many for the personal appeal and influence of the candidate to be sufficient to carry the day. The limitations placed on electoral expenses made it impossible for candidates to go on buying large numbers of votes by bribery, lavish entertainment and free beer all round. And the adoption of the secret ballot in 1872 made even the more discreet forms of corruption less effective, since the candidate had no clear way of checking that the voters had honoured their side of the bargain.

These changes created a clear need for party organisation, at any rate in the urban areas, and as it happened the move in this direction was given extra impetus by a direct consequence of the reforms that had not been foreseen. Before the redistribution the city of Birming-ham had been a two-member constituency, with each elector having two votes. In 1868 its representation was increased to three members, but the electors were still limited to two votes each. The Liberals had a majority in the city, and it immediately became clear to a group of shrewd local politicians that careful organisation was necessary to ensure that this majority resulted in the election of all three Liberal candidates and not just the two most popular. They thereupon created a representative organisation of Birmingham Liberals with an annual subscription of a shilling, a committee in each ward, a general committee for the whole city, and an executive committee to take charge of electoral tactics. This organisation located Liberal voters and persuaded one-third of them to vote for each of the three possible combinations of Liberal candidates in the 1868 election. The result was entirely successful, and the Birmingham caucus (as it came to be called) was subsequently taken as a model by local party organisers up and down the country.

This development of party organisation in the constituencies might have led to the growth of local party bosses, as in the United States. In fact, for a variety of reasons (of which one was that the political scene happened at that time to be dominated by the two outstanding party leaders of the century, Gladstone and Disraeli) the development led to the emergence of national party organisations in the shape of the National Liberal Federation and the National Union of Conservative Associations. These organisations came to acquire a strategic place in the political system as parliamentary candidates became increasingly dependent on organised support for their election campaigns.

The relationship between these new national party organisations and the parliamentary leaders was not immediately settled. In both parties there was an attempt by ambitious politicians (Joseph Chamberlain on the Liberal side and Lord Randolph Churchill among the Conservatives) to build up the power of the organisations in order to promote their own political aims. But both these attempts failed, and their failure settled the question in favour of the parliamentary leaders. The same period, namely the twenty years following the 1867 Reform Act, also saw the development of efficient party bureaucracies, staffed with professional organisers and propagandists and under the direct control of the parliamentary leaders. It was these bureaucracies, by name the Conservative Central Office and the Central Liberal Association, that undertook to find candidates for local party organisations in need of them, and so were able to hold out the promise of a tangible reward (in the shape of a safe seat) for the loyal party man.

These developments laid the foundation of the party loyalty that has been so conspicuous a feature of the British political scene in the twentieth century. While MPs were entirely dependent on their own efforts and popularity for re-election, they could vote against their party leaders without risking their seats. When they became dependent on organised support for re-election, and the organisations which provided this support were controlled (directly or indirectly) by the party leaders, the independence of backbenchers was sharply diminished.

As it happened, the strength of the Government in relation to backbenchers in the House of Commons was also increased by the procedural reforms of the early 1880s, which were introduced in order to frustrate the attempts of the Irish MPs to disrupt government business. The most important of these reforms was the introduction of the Closure, which gave the Government effective control over parliamentary time. All these developments, taken together, transformed the relationship between Parliament and the Government in the last third of the century, and the nature of the change is indicated by the figures in Table 3.1. These show, first, the total number of divisions in the Commons in which governments were defeated in the years 1851–1903 and, secondly, the number of amendments to government Bills (excluding estimates) carried against government opposition in the same years. The figures in the first line are for five parliamentary sessions and those in each subsequent line are for six sessions.[8]

Table 3.1　*The Growth of Party Loyalty in Parliament*

Parliamentary sessions	Number of government defeats	Number of amendments to government Bills
1851–5	59	29
1856–61	52	24
1862–7	60	26
1868–73	50	27
1874–9	8	1
1880–5	62	11
1886–91	13	5
1892–7	9	2
1898–1903	2	1

These figures give a fairly clear picture of the development of party loyalty in the House of Commons. If the table were continued into the present century it would show that government defeats and amendments to government Bills have continued to be extremely rare.

CONCLUSION

The democratisation of the House of Commons did not therefore strengthen the position of the House in relation to the executive, as might have been expected. Instead, it was the main cause of developments in the party system which gave the executive the means of controlling the House of Commons. The executive remains responsible to Parliament, but since Parliament has become fully representative of the nation the practical significance of this responsibility has changed. The nature and significance of ministerial responsibility to Parliament in the twentieth century will be examined in later chapters, but it must not be assumed that it can be summarised in terms of the 'chain of command' implied by liberal views of the constitution.

NOTES

1 From *Dictionnaire philosophique,* published in 1764.
2 These ideas were put forward in Montesquieu's book, *De l'esprit des lois,* published in 1748.
3 W. Blackstone, *Commentary on the Laws of England* (first published 1765; 15th edn, Clarendon Press, 1809), Vol. I, p. 268.
4 ibid., p. 153.
5 See *What Is He?* (1833), reprinted in *Whigs and Whiggism,* ed. W. Hutcheson (John Murray, 1913), p. 19.
6 From a speech on the Home Rule Bill of 1893.
7 R. T. McKenzie, review in the *Listener,* 19 Nov 1959.
8 These figures are adapted from those in A. L. Lowell, *The Government of England* (Macmillan, 1919) Vol. I, p. 317, and Vol. II, pp. 79–80.

FURTHER READING

The relations between Parliament and the executive in the eighteenth century are summarised in J. P. Mackintosh, *The British Cabinet,* 3rd edn (Stevens, 1977), ch. 2; the ideas of the reformers are analysed in A. H. Birch, *Representative and Responsible Government* (Allen & Unwin, 1964), chs 3–5; extracts from the speeches and writings of the reformers will be found in S. Maccoby (ed.), *The English Radical Tradition: 1763–1914* (Nicholas Kaye, 1952), and in Alan Bullock and Maurice Shock (eds), *The Liberal Tradition* (A. & C. Black. 1956); an account of changes in the electoral system up to 1885 is given in C. S. Seymour, *Electoral Reform in England and Wales* (Yale University Press, 1915); the changing relations between Commons, Lords, Cabinet and monarch are discussed in Mackintosh, chs 3–9; the development of party organisation in the country and party management in Parliament is discussed in A. L. Lowell, *The Government of England* (Macmillan, New York, 1919), pt II, and in H. J. Hanham, *Elections and Party Management: Politics in the Time of Disraeli and Gladstone* (Longmans, 1959).

Chapter 4

The Survival of Medieval Institutions

The development of liberal institutions changed the British political system without completely transforming it. The 'chain of command' concept of government was superimposed on the older system of balance, but the old institutions were not abolished. It is not part of the British political tradition to do away with established institutions, and the modern constitution abounds with practices and offices which have survived from medieval times. Some of these are symbolic and perhaps picturesque but have little or no practical importance: a good example is the procedure by which members of the House of Commons are summoned to the House of Lords for certain formalities by a gentleman dressed in medieval clothes who bears the title of Black Rod. It is not our purpose to discuss formal procedures of this kind, so practices and institutions which no longer play a significant role in the working system of government will be ignored in this book.

But there are, of course, two surviving medieval institutions which are of considerable importance in the political system. One is the House of Lords, much less powerful than it was but still playing an active part in government. The other is the monarchy, the existence of which affects the whole pattern of government even though the personal powers of the reigning monarch are a pale shadow of what they used to be. The role of these two institutions in the modern political system will now be considered.

THE MONARCHY

American commentators and students often think that there is something incongruous about the existence of monarchical institutions within a democratic system of government. In fact many (by some definitions, most) of the world's stable democratic systems are monarchical in form, and this is understandable both in historical and in political terms. Historically, nearly all European states were monarchies in the past and the monarchical institutions have survived where they have not been overthrown by revolutions. Politically, the convenience of a monarchical system in a democracy is that it provides a head of state who has been insulated from party politics since childhood and can thus be accepted as neutral between the contending parties.

The roles of the British monarch may be categorised as symbolic, social and political. The first two need not concern us in this book. The political role of the monarch has changed dramatically since the beginning of the nineteenth century, though without any legislative measure or other overt action to which a date can be given. To explain how this change took place it will be helpful to distinguish the nature of the Royal Prerogative from the personal discretion enjoyed by the reigning monarch.

The Royal Prerogative is a term which denotes the authority which rests with the Crown, as distinct from that which rests with Parliament or the courts. Thus, it is within the Royal Prerogative to enter into diplomatic relations with other states and to conclude treaties with them; to command the armed forces, to declare war and to make peace; to appoint judges, to initiate criminal prosecutions, and to pardon offenders; to summon, to prorogue and to dissolve Parliament; to appoint ministers, including the Prime Minister; to confer honours, to create peers, and to appoint bishops of the Church of England. All these acts, and others, are acts performed in the name of the Crown, and the way in which they are performed cannot be questioned or controlled by the courts. Most of them are equally free from parliamentary control, though some of them are now subject to the influence of parliamentary opinion because ministers themselves are subject to that influence.

The extent of the Royal Prerogative has not diminished appreciably during the last 200 years. What has happened is that, whereas 200 years ago the reigning monarch performed many or most of these acts at his own discretion, today the monarch performs the acts on the advice of ministers or other persons. The acts are performed in the name of the Crown, but except in a few special cases the decision is no longer taken by the monarch. The conduct of foreign affairs is in the hands of the Prime Minister and the Cabinet, as are decisions about defence policy; judges are appointed by the monarch on the advice of the Prime Minister or the Lord Chancellor; ministers are appointed on the advice of the Prime Minister, and on his advice alone; honours are conferred and other appointments are made on the advice of a variety of persons.

These changes have not come about as the result of crises or been marked by formal declarations, but have simply emerged over the course of the years. It is not easy to give precise dates for them because the monarch's powers have not been taken away, but have merely fallen into disuse. Thus, with the advantage of hindsight we can now say that the royal power to veto Bills passed by both Houses of Parliament was last used in 1707, but in the 1720s it was not known that this power would never be used again. Equally, we can say that during the latter part of Queen Victoria's reign the monarch lost the power to exercise a positive influence on the Prime Minister's choice of ministers, but Queen Victoria would not have acknowledged that this was the case. At the present time there remain one or two powers of the Royal Prerogative of which the exercise is surrounded by a penumbra of doubt, at any rate in the popular mind, and these will be discussed in the following section.

THE POWERS OF THE MONARCH TODAY

An understanding of the position of the monarch today may possibly be helped by drawing on the analogy of the position of a referee at a football match. In one sense the referee is in charge of the match: he tosses the coin to decide which captain shall have choice of ends, he determines the start and finish of the game, and only he can declare that a goal has been scored. But the referee exercises this control within strict rules which he did not make and cannot influence. He has the power to give orders to players, but in his exercise of this and other powers he has less freedom of action than anyone else on the field. There are three indiscretions which the referee must at all costs avoid. The first is interfering with the natural course of the game, except when some rule has been violated. The second is partiality to one of the teams, or even the appearance of it. The third is involvement in disputes between players. If a referee fails to avoid these mistakes, he will find himself in difficulties, and serious failures of this kind will result in the termination of his career as a referee.

This is, of course, a very crude analogy, but it may serve to focus attention on some of the difficulties of the monarch's position. He (or she) is expected to play a daily part in the government of the country without ever showing the slightest sign of partiality towards one party rather than another or one policy rather than another. Action by him is required at most crises and turning-points of politics, but he must never be thought to be interfering with the natural course of political events. The task of the monarch is clearly one of extreme delicacy and it is only by the strict observance of convention that it is possible to keep the monarchy from becoming involved in political controversy. One important convention is that normally only the Prime Minister has access to the monarch, their discussions naturally being entirely secret. When a Prime Minister resigns other conventions are brought into play which result in the appointment of a successor.

To delineate the role of the monarch more precisely it will be helpful to give examples of events in recent years which have led to public speculation about the extent of his discretion. The royal powers which have been under discussion in this way in the twentieth century are the power to create large numbers of peers, the power to dissolve Parliament, and the power to appoint a Prime Minister. After the questions arising from these have been dealt with it will be a fairly simple matter to outline the normal pattern of royal activities in relation to government.

The power to create sufficient new peers to change the majority in the House of Lords is one that has been used once and invoked on two other occasions. It was used in 1712 when Queen Anne created twelve Tory peers to secure a majority in the House of Lords which would support her government's proposals to end the war with France. It was next invoked in 1832, when the King agreed to accede to the Prime Minister's request to create sufficient new peers to swamp the House of Lords if that House refused to pass the Reform Bill. A similar pledge was given by the King in 1910 in connection with the proposal to restrict the powers of the upper chamber over legislation. The government of the day was successful in an election which turned on the issue and once again, as in 1832, the threat of the creation of a large number of new peers was sufficient to induce the House of Lords to pass the Bill.

It could be said, therefore, that there is a convention that if the government of the day asks the monarch to overcome the opposition of the Lords to a constitutional reform (or possibly to any important reform) in this way the monarch is entitled (and perhaps ought) to insist that a general election be held to test the popularity of the government but should accede to the request if the government is successful in the election. In practice, however, this convention is unlikely to be used again. The Parliament Act of 1911 contained its own procedure for overcoming the opposition of the Lords to a legislative measure, after a delay of two years, and the Parliament Act of 1949 (which was passed under the provisions of the 1911 Act) reduced the period of delay to one year. It is difficult to envisage a measure that would be so urgent that it could not wait twelve months, and for this reason it is now unlikely that any government will find it necessary to invoke the threat of swamping the House of Lords with new members.

The existence of the royal power to dissolve Parliament raises two possible questions: whether the monarch could dissolve against the advice of his Prime Minister and whether he could refuse to accede to a Prime Minister's request for a dissolution. The answer to the first question is, in all conceivable circumstances, in the negative. In the crisis over Home Rule for Ireland between 1912 and 1914 several Conservative leaders argued that the King had the right, and even the duty, to dissolve Parliament and call for a general election before letting the Government proceed with a measure which would put some of His Majesty's loyal subjects under the rule of a government which they would regard as alien. King George V made no public comment on this suggestion, though he wrote to the Prime Minister at length about the prospect of civil war in Ireland and suggested that it would be desirable for a general election to be held before the Home Rule Bill was put through Parliament. The Prime Minister could not accept this suggestion, and it is clear from the correspondence that the King, though extremely anxious about the course of events, did not feel that he could dissolve Parliament any more than he could dismiss his ministers or refuse assent to the Home Rule Bill. If he had done any of these things, he would have provoked a constitutional crisis which would have jeopardised the position of the monarchy itself. Since it is difficult to envisage a situation in which the arguments for royal intervention would be stronger than they were in regard to Home Rule, it is reasonable to conclude that dissolution against the advice of the Prime Minister is not a practical possibility.

The question of whether a monarch can refuse to dissolve when asked to do so is slightly more complex. The key to the question lies in the need for the monarchy to retain its reputation for impartiality between the parties. If the monarch were to refuse a dissolution and the Prime Minister were to resign, it would presumably be necessary to ask the Leader of the Opposition to form a government. If this government were quickly defeated in Parliament, dissolution would be the only possible way out of the ensuing crisis. But this would mean that the monarch would be granting to one Prime Minister what he had refused to another, which would inevitably tend to damage the esteem in which the monarch was held by supporters of the original government. It follows that the practical rule is that the monarch can only refuse to grant a dissolution if he knows that a viable alternative government can be formed. This situation will obtain only when no one party has a majority in the House of Commons, so that there is the possibility of varying coalitions. If one party has an absolute majority and the leader of that party, being Prime Minister, asks for a dissolution, the most that the monarch can do is to express his opinion that the move might be unwise and ask the Prime Minister to give the proposal further consideration. If the Prime Minister adheres to his position, the monarch has no real choice but to accede to the request.

These points were illustrated by the events of 1923 and 1924. The general election of 1922 had given the Conservative Party a parliamentary majority, and Bonar Law had become Prime Minister. In 1923 Bonar Law became ill and Stanley Baldwin, who succeeded him, wished to call a general election after only a few months in office. The King was unhappy at the prospect of an election when Parliament was only about a year old and he asked the Prime Minister if he would think about the matter further and discuss it with his colleagues. But Baldwin insisted on a dissolution, and the King therefore agreed to his request.

The result of this election was that no one party had a majority in the Commons, and a minority Labour government was formed with the support of the Liberals. Ten months later the Liberals withdrew their support and J. Ramsay MacDonald, the Prime Minister, asked the King for a dissolution. On this occasion the possibility existed of a viable alternative government being formed with Liberal and Conservative support, and the King (anticipating MacDonald's request) had consulted the Liberal and Conservative leaders to see if they would be willing to join in a coalition. As they were not so willing, MacDonald's request was accepted, but it is to be assumed that if a Liberal–Conservative government had been possible the King might have refused to dissolve Parliament and would have been entitled to do so.

The third royal power which has sometimes led to uncertainty about the role of the monarch is the power to appoint a Prime Minister. As both main parties now have settled procedures for the election of their leaders no problem can arise if the leading party has a secure majority in Parliament. If the Prime Minister should retire or die in these circumstances, the monarch would simply wait until the governing party elected its new leader, who would then be invited to form a government. However, if a political crisis should develop when no party had a parliamentary majority, it might still fall to the monarch to exercise a degree of initiative, as happened in the difficult circumstances of 1931.

In 1931 no party had a majority in the House of Commons and the Labour Government was dependent on Liberal support. This government had to deal with the most serious economic crisis of modern times. Two million workers were unemployed, and as the economic difficulties of the year increased it became clear that a major financial crisis, likely to be crippling in its effects, could only be averted if the Bank of England could secure a large loan from New York. American bankers would not make such a loan unless the Government made a serious attempt to reduce its budgetary deficit; to do this involved cuts in public expenditure, including unemployment benefits; and several members of the Cabinet were known to be unwilling to continue in office if unemployment benefits were cut. As the crisis developed the Prime Minister therefore faced the probability that if he reduced unemployment benefits the Government would fall apart, whereas if he did not do so it would be defeated by the withdrawal of Liberal support, and in either case he would have to resign.

When he informed the King of this probability the King thought the proper constitutional course was to consult the leaders of the Liberal and Conservative Parties, who were clearly in a position to form an alternative government which would command a parliamentary majority. The Liberal leader, Sir Herbert Samuel, advised the King that as the necessary economies were likely to prove unpopular with workers and trade unions it would be in the national interest for them to be imposed by a Labour government. If the Prime Minister were unable to carry his party with him on the matter, the next best course, in Samuel's view, would be the creation of a national government with members from all three parties, but with MacDonald as Prime Minister, for the purpose of dealing with the financial crisis. Stanley Baldwin, the Conservative leader, agreed that a national government was desirable and expressed his readiness to serve under MacDonald.

In the evening of the same day a telegram arrived from New York confirming that the very large loan required could not be granted unless economies in public expenditure were made on at least the scale indicated in the provisional plan prepared by the Treasury. When the Prime Minister proposed that this plan should be adopted eleven of his Cabinet colleagues supported him but eight disagreed. He then told the Cabinet that in view of this division he would have to inform the King of the situation and to advise the King to arrange a conference between the leaders of the three major parties to decide what should be done. The members of the Cabinet told him that he could let the King know that they were prepared to resign.

When the three party leaders met at Buckingham Palace the following morning they quickly agreed that the best way to meet the emergency would be to form a national government, with MacDonald at its head, on the understanding that the King would grant a dissolution as soon as the crisis was over. However, when MacDonald reported this to the Cabinet, and invited his colleagues to join the new government, only three signified their readiness to do so, and the result was a split in the leadership of the Labour Party. The great majority of the Party went into opposition and MacDonald was subsequently expelled from its ranks.

This story has been recounted in some detail because the events caused a storm of controversy and it has sometimes been suggested that the King acted improperly in encouraging the formation of a national government. This suggestion cannot be upheld. It is possible to criticise MacDonald or other politicians for their behaviour, but the King acted with complete propriety. Faced with the possibility that the leader of a minority government would resign, he naturally consulted the leaders of the other two parties, and thereafter he acted upon their advice. Samuel has testified in his memoirs that at no stage did the King advance his own personal opinions: he simply consulted the party leaders, called them together when it became apparent that they wished to co-operate with each other, and gave them words of encouragement in their efforts to reach agreement.[1]

Every political crisis is slightly different, and we are unlikely ever to see an exact repetition of the events of 1931. Their relevance lies in the fact that they illustrate the conventions which guide the behaviour of the monarch when he is called upon to exercise political initiative. These conventions are well understood by the monarch, by the staff at Buckingham Palace, and by the leading members of the parties. By observing them the monarch is able to play an infrequent but important part in the process of government without jeopardising the modern reputation of the Crown for impartiality as between politicians and parties.

THE NORMAL ROLE OF THE MONARCHY IN GOVERNMENT

The preceding section has outlined the role of the monarch at the various turning-points of politics: when a Prime Minister dies or resigns; when a dissolution of Parliament is proposed; and in cases of acute conflict between the two Houses of Parliament. In addition the monarch plays a small but continuous part in the normal process of government. He opens and closes Parliament each year and delivers the 'speech from the throne' setting out the legislative policy of the Government at the beginning of each session. He assents to Bills after they have been passed by both Houses, his assent marking the formal completion of the legislative process. He receives ambassadors from foreign countries. He confers honours of varying degree. And as Head of State and Head of the Commonwealth he occasionally makes state visits to foreign or Commonwealth countries.

In none of these activities does the monarch have much personal discretion. The Prime Minister will always listen respectfully to the monarch's views, but the effective decisions are made by members of the Government. The speech from the throne, for instance, is written by the Prime Minister even though it is read by the monarch. It is in this way that the ancient institution of monarchy has been adapted to meet the requirements of a democratic age.

Of course, in private discussion the monarch has an opportunity to present his views to the Prime Minister. It is the custom of the monarch to be sent copies of Cabinet papers and to have a brief weekly meeting with the Prime Minister to discuss current issues. The rights of the monarch in these discussions were summarised about a century ago by Bagehot as 'the right to be consulted, the right to encourage, and the right to warn'. But the monarch is not a politician and it should not be thought that the government of the day is likely to be deviated from its chosen course by royal influence.

It is evident that in the twentieth century the monarch is a figurehead rather than an active political force. However, it does not follow that the existence of the monarchy should be regarded as a formality which makes no difference to the political process. On the contrary, the institution of monarchy is extremely important in two quite different ways.

First, the existence of the Royal Prerogative gives the British Government a substantial degree of independence of Parliament in some fields, without giving it so much independence that it cannot be called to account. Thus, the conclusion of international treaties is within the Royal Prerogative, and British diplomats can conduct negotiations and reach agreements without any fear that their work might be undone and their future position undermined by a refusal on the part of Parliament to ratify the agreements made. At the same time Parliament has the right to question the Foreign Secretary and the Prime Minister about their conduct of foreign policy so that these ministers have to explain and justify their actions in public – and to suffer a loss of reputation if their justifications fail to convince.

The institution of monarchy is also important in that it provides a Head of State who constitutes a symbol of the identity and unity of the nation. There is no evidence that a monarchical system of government is in any objective sense better than a republican system, but there can be no doubt that the continued existence of the British monarchy symbolises in a direct and personal way the continuity and stability of the British political community, and by so doing acts as a focus for the loyalty of British citizens.

THE HOUSE OF LORDS

While the monarchy has been criticised only rarely and its political role has been changed only by convention, and with the agreement of successive monarchs, the House of Lords has been the subject of frequent criticism in the twentieth century and has been stripped of its major powers by legislation passed contrary to its wishes.

The House has in fact been in a weakened position ever since the passage of the 1832 Reform Act, to which it had agreed only under duress. The fact that the House of Commons could claim to be based on a national suffrage after 1832 gave it a degree of moral and political superiority over the Upper House. The accepted convention after 1832 was that the Government was collectively responsible to the Commons but not to the Lords. Ministers had, of course, to answer questions put to them by peers, but the Government was not expected to resign if it was defeated in the Lords.

It was recognised that the House of Lords retained the right to reject Bills sent to it by the Lower House, but it was argued by Whigs and Liberals that the Lords ought not to exercise this right so as to obstruct legislation that was repeatedly passed by the Commons. Bagehot (himself a Liberal but by no means a Radical) put the matter in the following terms in 1867:

> Since the Reform Act the House of Lords has become a revising and suspending House. It can alter Bills, it can reject Bills on which the House of Commons is not yet thoroughly in earnest – upon which the nation is not yet determined. Their veto is a sort of hypothetical veto. They say: We reject your Bill for this once, or these twice, or even these thrice; but if you keep on sending it up, at last we won't reject it.[2]

The behaviour of the House corresponded fairly closely to this description during the middle decades of the century, but after the second Reform Act of 1867 the conflict between the two major parties sharpened and on several occasions the Conservatives used their majority in the Upper Chamber to reject measures which had been promoted by a Liberal administration. Liberal measures which were either rejected or mutilated in this way included the Irish Land Bill of 1887, the first version of the Reform Bill of 1884, the Home Rule Bill of 1893 and the Education Bill of 1906. All these actions by the Lords were regarded by Liberal politicians as a misuse of power, and by the early years of the present century Liberal leaders had determined to reduce the constitutional powers of the Upper Chamber as soon as an issue arose on which the reformers could be sure of popular support.

Such an issue arose in 1909, when the House of Lords flouted precedent and outraged Liberal opinion by rejecting Lloyd George's Budget. The Government secured a dissolution of Parliament, won the ensuing election, and announced that they proposed to introduce a Bill which would curtail the legislative powers of the Upper House. Since that House could not be expected to pass such a Bill voluntarily, it was necessary for the Prime Minister to ask the King if he would be willing to create sufficient new peers to swamp the House. The King's answer was that he would be willing to do this, if it proved necessary, provided a further general election was first held at which the proposed reform could be canvassed; a government victory in the election would be taken by the King to indicate popular endorsement of the Government's policy. This election was duly held and the parties supporting the Government were returned with an almost identical majority.[3] The King's threat to create new peerages then proved sufficient to carry the day, and in 1911 the House of Lords reluctantly passed the Act which abolished its own right to veto legislation.

The Parliament Act of 1911 contained three main provisions. First, it removed the power of the House of Lords to amend, delay or reject Bills certified by the Speaker as money Bills. Secondly, it provided that any other public Bill (except a Bill to extend the life of the House of Commons) would become law if it were passed by the Commons in three successive sessions, over a period of at least two years. Thirdly, the maximum period between general elections was shortened from seven years to five years.

This Act drastically weakened the position of the Upper House, which could henceforth do no more than delay legislation for two years. Inevitably, this power is more likely to be used when Liberal or Labour governments are in power than during the life of a Conservative government. On one or two occasions, the delaying power has made a significant difference to events. Thus, in 1912 the Lords rejected the Bill to establish the Church in Wales. After a delay of two years the Bill was passed under the provisions of the Parliament Act, but by this time the war had begun and the measure did not come into force until 1920. Another example was the 1913 Bill to abolish the right of business proprietors to vote both in the constituency of their residence and in the constituency of their business premises. This was similar in terms to the Bill which had been passed by the Commons but rejected by the Lords in 1906. The 1913 Bill met a similar fate, and as the war broke out before the provisions of the Parliament Act could be applied this Bill never reached the Statute Book. Since the opposition of the Lords to the abolition of the business franchise also prevented the enactment of the Bill introduced by the Labour Government in 1931, the actions of the Upper House actually delayed this electoral reform for forty-two years, from the rejection of the 1906 Bill to the passage of the Representation of the People Act of 1948.

As the hereditary principle ensures a large and permanent Conservative majority in the House of Lords, its ability to delay reforms is inevitably unpopular with the Labour Party. In view of this, it has to be asked why the Labour Government of 1945 did not use its large parliamentary majority to abolish the Lords and replace it by a more representative second chamber.

The Question of Reform since 1945

The answer to the question posed above falls into three parts. First, it was generally agreed that a second chamber of some kind was necessary to give legislation a closer scrutiny than time permitted in the House of Commons. Simple abolition of the Lords would not have been a feasible solution in itself.

Secondly, the Labour Party had no agreed plan for a reformed or new second chamber, and it was clear that any proposal would be highly controversial and would take up a great deal of time. As the new Government had a full programme of social and economic legislation to introduce, and it quickly became clear that the Lords did not intend to delay measures of this kind, the Government had a strong incentive to put the issue of constitutional reform on one side for the time being.

The third answer is that Labour politicians who contemplate a radical reform of the Lords have to face the probability that a reformed House would have more prestige and more influence than the existing House. Since most Labour politicians feel that parliamentary power should be concentrated in the hands of the Commons, they jib at the prospect of creating a second chamber that might be an effective rival to the Commons. This dilemma was stated very clearly by Herbert Morrison, who was Lord President of the Council in the 1945 Labour Government and had a general responsibility for steering legislation through Parliament:

> The Labour Government was not anxious for the rational reform or democratisation of the second chamber, for this would have added to its authority and would have strengthened its position as against that of the House of Commons. Changes which gave the House of Lords a democratic and representative character would have been undemocratic in outcome, for they would have tended to make the Lords the equal of the Commons. . . . The very irrationality of the composition of the House of Lords and its quaintness are safeguards for our modern British democracy.[4]

The Labour Government of 1945–51 therefore made no attempt to change the composition of the Lords, though the 1949 Parliament Act reduced its power of delay from two years to one year. It was in fact a Conservative Government which made the first attempt to modernise the composition of the House, in the form of the Life Peerages Act of 1958. This measure enabled the Prime Minister to appoint (or more strictly to advise the Queen to appoint) persons of either sex to peerages which are not hereditary. By 1978 the House contained just over 250 life peers, compared with about 800 hereditary peers, many of whom rarely attend. The life peers are mostly men and women who have enjoyed distinguished careers in other walks of life and they have improved the quality of debates. As most of them are Labour supporters or crossbenchers, the party bias of the House has also been partially corrected.

Another reform that affected the composition of the House was the Peerage Act of 1963, which enables peers to disclaim their peerages (providing they do so within a limited time) and thus to stand for election to the Commons. The first to take advantage of this opportunity was Lord Stansgate, whose individual campaign was largely responsible for the reform and who resumed his career in the House of Commons as Anthony Wedgwood Benn. Within a year he was followed by Lord Hailsham, who hoped to succeed Harold Macmillan as Prime Minister, and by the Earl of Home, who in fact succeeded Macmillan. The latter could not have become Prime Minister had it not been possible for him to renounce his earldom and acquire a seat in the Commons. In the first ten years after the passage of this Act twelve peers disclaimed their peerages. The Act also admitted all Scottish peers (instead of only a proportion of them) to membership of the House and permitted women holding hereditary peerages to enter the House for the first time.

These reforms, although welcomed by all parties, did nothing to change the central anomaly of the House, namely the right of hereditary peers to vote on legislative proposals for no better reason than that one of their ancestors was included in a royal honours list. In 1969, however, a radical reform was proposed by the Labour Government and was actually passed by the House of Lords. This Bill provided for a House that would contain about 250 working members, all of whom would be appointed, and for a process whereby the hereditary peers would gradually be phased out. In outline, the proposals were as follows.

(1) The voting members of the House would be life peers and would initially comprise:
    105 supporters of the Government
    80 supporters of the main Opposition party
    15 supporters of other parties
    30 independents
    5 bishops
    9 Lords of Appeal
(2) After a general election which resulted in a change of government, additional members would be appointed to ensure that the governing party had a small majority over the Opposition parties but not a majority of the House as a whole.
(3) Life peers would be paid a salary and would have to retire at 72.

(4)   Existing hereditary peers could continue as members of the House, with the right to speak but not to vote. If they preferred to withdraw, they could do so without losing their titles.

(5)   After the reform, succession to a hereditary peerage would not carry the right to a seat in the House, though such peers would not be debarred from appointment as life peers.

(6)   The delaying power of the House would be reduced from twelve months to six months.

This ingenious scheme had been partially worked out in confidential talks between representatives of the main parties. However, some time before the Bill was drafted the Prime Minister had broken off these talks and in consequence the reform was sponsored by the Government alone, so that although the Conservative front bench gave it tacit support they did not feel under any obligation to use their Whips to assist its progress. The Bill was given a Second Reading by 287 votes to 137, but at the Committee Stage in the Commons it ran into an unexpected and determined campaign of obstruction from backbenchers on both sides of the House. Labour left-wingers like Michael Foot joined in an unprecedented alliance with Conservative right-wingers like Enoch Powell to frustrate a plan which they disliked for contrasting reasons. For ten days the business of the House was held up by protracted manœuvres, skilfully planned and executed, until the Government simply gave up in disgust and withdrew the Bill. Parliament had not seen a backbench revolt on this scale since the turn of the century, and its success came as a shock to ministers and lobby correspondents alike. It also undermined some of the generalisations political scientists had been making about Parliament for the previous thirty years.

Since this débâcle there have been no more attempts at reform. Many members of the Labour Party have moved towards the view that the House should be abolished entirely, and in 1977 Labour's National Executive Committee voted to include abolition as a proposal in the Party's next election manifesto. This creates a new situation in which it is relevant to outline the work of the House briefly, with a view to answering the question of whether a second chamber is really necessary.

The Present Role of the House

The functions of the House of Lords are of four main kinds. First, it revises Bills sent to it by the Commons, which rarely has sufficient time to give legislation the detailed consideration it deserves. Secondly, it saves the time of the Commons by giving a first hearing to non-controversial Bills which subsequently go through the Commons with a minimum of discussion. Thirdly, it occasionally refuses to pass Bills which it thinks do not have the support of public opinion. Fourthly, it constitutes a forum in which large issues of national policy can be debated without the sense of urgency which necessarily affects debates in the Lower House.

The revision of legislation has become increasingly important in the twentieth century as the activities of the State have been extended. Legislation has become more voluminous and more complex without any commensurate increase in the amount of time which the House of Commons can devote to it. Many Bills are necessarily pushed through the Commons with far less discussion than they need and reach the Lords in a somewhat untidy condition. Detailed consideration of such measures by the Upper House is usually welcomed by the Government, by the Commons, and by the various organisations which represent interests likely to be affected by the legislation in question.

Sometimes the Lords make amendments which the Commons subsequently strike out or revise again, but in the great majority of cases amendments in the Upper House are accepted by the government of the day and are endorsed by the Commons when the Bill is referred back to the Lower House. In many cases the amendments are initiated by the Government, using debates in the second chamber as an opportunity to present its own second thoughts on the matter. Thus, in 1947 the House of Lords made no fewer than 310 amendments to the Town and Country Planning Bill, of which 55 were amendments of substance and the other 255 were amendments on points of drafting. Of these 310 amendments all but six were accepted by the Labour Government and endorsed by the Commons. In the same year the Lords made 240 amendments to the Transport Bill, of which 42 were rejected by the Commons but the other 198 were accepted and welcomed. A number of these amendments gave effect to agreements that had been reached in the final stages of the Bill's first passage through the Commons, or in discussions between the Government and affected interests.

There can be no question about the value of this work of revision. Discussions on the floor of the House of Commons are short, highly partisan, and normally intended to score debating points rather than to improve legislation. Discussions in committees of the Commons tend also to be highly partisan, and are frequently too brief to cover all the sections of a Bill. It follows that unicameral government could only work if the committee system of the Commons were radically reformed, with MPs working longer hours than they do at present and more ready to suspend their partisan feelings while they consider the practicality of legislative proposals. It is very difficult to envisage either of these conditions being met. Most MPs complain that they are already overworked, and committee work tends to be unpopular because in committee Members have no chance to make an impression on party leaders, on whom they depend for political advancement. It is also somewhat unrealistic to expect Members who have been exchanging vitriolic abuse on the floor of the House one evening to work constructively together in a committee room the following morning. For the detailed consideration of legislation some kind of second chamber seems almost essential.

The second function of the Lords is to give a first hearing to non-controversial Bills, which saves a certain amount of time in the Commons. Since 1945 something like a quarter of all government Bills have had their first hearing in the Lords, and in a fair number of cases this has resulted in an appreciable saving of time in the Commons. The procedure is particularly appropriate when the legislation is complex in a technical sense, recent examples being a Bill dealing with company law and a Bill amending the law of copyright.

The third and most controversial function of the Lords is that it occasionally rejects Bills sent to it by the Commons, or amends them in ways unacceptable to the Commons. Since the House has an in-built Conservative majority, there is a natural temptation for it to reject Bills promoted by a Labour government. This problem was discussed in 1945, and the Conservative leader in the House at that time (Lord Salisbury) persuaded his colleagues to accept the convention that they would not reject measures for which the Government had a clear electoral mandate. It was in accordance with this convention that the House agreed to all the major economic and social reforms of the period 1945–51, though in 1949 it insisted on an amendment which had the effect of postponing the nationalisation of the steel industry by a few months. The same attitude was taken to measures promoted by the Labour Government of 1964–70.

What measures, then, have been rejected by the House since 1945? One was the Parliament Bill of 1948, which had the effect of halving the maximum period of delay that the Lords could impose, and which was passed in 1949 under the provisions of the 1911 Parliament Act. On two occasions the Lords rejected measures for the abolition of capital punishment which were passed by a free vote in the Commons against the advice of the government of the day. The first occasion was in 1947, under a Labour government, and the second was in 1956 under a Conservative government. As public-opinion polls showed that abolition was unpopular at both these times, the Lords could claim that they had public opinion on their side. In 1969 the Lords rejected a government Bill which would have freed the Home Secretary from his legal obligation to lay the report of the Electoral Boundary Commissions before Parliament, a decision which was justified on the grounds that the Government was attempting, for partisan purposes, to fight the forthcoming general election with outdated constituency boundaries.

After 1974 the House felt more free to attack government Bills, as the Labour Party secured the support of only 29 per cent of the electors at the October 1974 election and it was possible to argue about whether it had a popular mandate for its policies. In practice, however, in the period 1974–8 only one Bill was seriously delayed and another mangled by an amendment. The Bill subjected to delay was the Bill to nationalise shipbuilding, which was held up because the Lords wanted to exclude ship repair work from its provisions. This was a somewhat partisan action by the Lords which angered many members of the Labour Party. The other measure involved was one which proposed to extend the monopoly over manual employment which the dockers' union enjoys in British docks to all packing and shipping establishments located within five miles of the dock gates. This was a blatant concession to a sectional interest which was unpopular with the general public and would never have passed the Commons on a free vote. The Lords amended it by reducing the geographical limit from five miles to half a mile. When the Government tried to secure the rejection of this amendment in the Commons, they failed to do so because of the defection of two Labour backbenchers.

It follows that since 1945 the Lords have used their power of rejection very sparingly. No impartial observer could criticise their actions, except possibly in the case of the Bill to nationalise shipbuilding. It might, of course, be argued that the power to reject has been used so seldom that it is unimportant. But a safety device does not lose its importance because it is rarely brought into play, any more than fire alarms or insurance policies lose their importance because they are rarely activated. It has to be remembered that the United Kingdom has no written constitution, no Bill of Rights, and no supreme court with the power to challenge legislation. In these circumstances it would seem only prudent to retain some institution – though not necessarily the present House of Lords – which has the power to delay legislation so that public opinion about a controversial measure can have time to express itself.

The fourth function of the House is to stage debates on general issues of national policy. The Lords can discuss issues in a broader frame of reference than is possible in the Commons and can conduct their debates in a less partisan way. As the House includes peers with a wide range of valuable experiences, the level of debate is often rather high. However, these debates are poorly reported and it is not clear that they have very much practical influence, either on public opinion or on the government of the day.

Most impartial observers would agree that a second chamber of some kind is highly desirable, with the ability to perform at least the first and third of these four functions. The problem is to devise a second chamber that would not only be efficient but would also be regarded as a legitimate component in a democratic system of government. In 1977 the Conservative leader in the House of Lords, Lord Carrington, said in a recorded interview that he believed a second chamber would only be regarded as legitimate if its members were elected by popular vote. He therefore suggested the creation of a chamber that would represent the regions of the United Kingdom, its members being elected by proportional representation in large regional constituencies. Such a chamber would reflect public opinion in a somewhat different way from the Commons, as the basis of representation, the method of election and the date of election would all be different. Its membership would be less distinguished than that of the House of Lords, as the retired diplomats, top industrialists and leading surgeons who now get peerages could not be expected to stand for election. However, Lord Carrington (himself a hereditary peer) felt that the loss of distinction would be a price worth paying for the establishment of a second chamber which could be regarded as legitimate in a democratic age.

The device of representing the regions of the country in a second chamber has been used successfully in the United States, Australia, West Germany and several other countries. Moreover, it can be argued that the case for a solution along these lines has been strengthened by the growing devolution of power to Scotland and Wales and by the discussions that have taken place in the 1970s about the merits of some devolution to the English regions. All possible reforms involve problems, but this one is certainly plausible. To say that it is plausible is not to say that it is likely to be adopted, however. The Conservative Party is not committed to it and in any case the present Conservative government will have other priorities, notably labour relations and the economy. At the time of writing it is impossible to predict what will happen to the House of Lords. However, major changes to this venerable institution are now under discussion in both major parties.

NOTES

1   See Harold Nicolson, *King George V,* ch. 27, for a careful and full account of the whole affair.
2   *The English Constitution* (first published 1867; World's Classics edn, Oxford University Press, 1928), p. 88.
3   Liberals and Conservatives each returned 272 Members, but the Liberals were supported by 42 Labour and 84 Irish MPs.
4   Herbert Morrison, *Government and Parliament* (Oxford University Press, 1954), p. 194.

FURTHER READING

W. Ivor Jennings, *Parliament*, 2nd edn (Cambridge University Press, 1957), contains a standard account of the role of the House of Lords; P. A. Bromhead, *The House of Lords in Contemporary Politics* (Routledge & Kegan Paul, 1958), goes into greater detail; J. P. Mackintosh, *The British Cabinet*, 3rd edn (Stevens, 1977), ch. 9, provides a concise summary of relations between the monarch and the Cabinet; and the best way of acquiring a fuller understanding of the role of the monarch is to read Harold Nicolson's superb *King George V* (Constable, 1952).

Part III

The Actors and Their Roles

Chapter 5

Electors and Voters

Michael Oakeshott has defined politics as 'the activity of attending to the general arrangements' of a society. It is not a specialised activity, of concern only to a section of the population. It concerns us all, because it affects all our lives. And in a political system like that of Britain all adult citizens have the opportunity to engage in politics and the chance to play their part, however small, in the shaping of political decisions. Naturally, people are active in differing degrees and when they participate they fill a variety of roles. Most people vote, many people subscribe to a pressure group or a political party, some people seek election to political office or seek jobs in the administration.

The object of this part of the book is to provide a brief discussion of the main roles which people fill in the political system and to say something about the type of people who fill them and the way in which these people behave. A relevant consideration is that while some roles are mutually exclusive, other roles are not. Thus nobody can be both a Member of Parliament and a civil servant, but MPs can represent pressure groups as well as their constituencies and their parties. When people fill two or more roles simultaneously they are often subject to the pull of conflicting loyalties and interests, and the incidence of 'role conflict' of this kind will be exemplified in the chapters which follow.

In a system of liberal democracy the first political role of the citizen is that of elector. Manhood suffrage is not a sufficient condition of democracy but it is invariably regarded as a necessary condition. Of course, the physical act of voting occupies the elector for only a few minutes a year, and the role cannot be said to be a demanding one. But possession of the right to vote transforms the great mass of citizens from being a captive audience of the political drama to being occasional participants themselves. Audience they may be for most of the time, but when their turn comes they have the power to replace the entire cast if the performance is found wanting, and the knowledge of this power is bound to make the full-time actors more sensitive to audience reactions.

In Britain the extent of the franchise has been the most important constitutional issue of the past 150 years, and the successive liberalisations of the franchise have transformed the political system and made the general election the most significant date in the political calendar.

Before the Reform Act of 1832 a general election was simply an occasion on which a very small proportion of citizens had the opportunity to select MPs to represent their interests in the House of Commons. Nowadays it is the occasion on which the public choose which party will govern the country for a period of up to five years.

The franchise is no longer a political issue in Britain, since it may be assumed, here as in most other advanced countries, that the principle of 'one man, one vote' is now a settled and unchangeable feature of the constitution. However, it is a condition of liberal democracy not only that all citizens should have the right to vote but also that the electoral system should provide freedom of choice, should avoid the grosser forms of corruption, and should secure general acceptance as a fair way of choosing between rival claimants to political office. Whether this condition is fulfilled depends partly on the nature of the electoral machinery established, and the first topic to be considered in this chapter will be the electoral machinery in Britain and the way in which it operates. This will be followed by a discussion of the nature and effects of election campaigns and then by a discussion of the way in which electors participate in the process and the factors which influence their decisions about voting.

ELECTORAL MACHINERY

The way in which an electoral system works will depend partly upon the methods adopted of dealing with certain practical problems of electoral organisation which arise in every country. It will help readers to understand the British system if the main problems are outlined before the British way of dealing with them is described.

(1) The first problem is that of compiling the electoral register. The main question here is whether the initiative and responsibility should rest with electors or with the Government. If electors are made responsible, and they have to do it in advance, those people who are ignorant, idle or forgetful will find themselves unable to vote at the time of the election, when their interest might be awakened by the campaign. If the Government is made responsible, it is essential to ensure that the Opposition parties have no reason to think that the politicians in power are taking more care over the registration of their own supporters than they take over the registration of their opponents. In either case there is the administrative problem of ensuring that the name of every qualified elector appears once on the register but not more than once, and of keeping the names of dead and imaginary electors off the list. This last problem tends to loom large in countries where a high proportion of electors are illiterate, and it is not unknown

for it also to cause concern in advanced countries where politics is tinged with corruption. The number of dead men who have been on the register and voted in New York and Chicago has often been considerable.

(2) The second problem is that of dividing the country into constituencies in a way that will be accepted as fair and impartial. This is an administrative task which is fraught with minor difficulties. Any division is likely to benefit one party rather than another so that the charge of 'gerrymandering' – arranging the constituency boundaries to suit the interests of the party in power – can be avoided only if conspicuous care is taken to ensure that the decisions are made in an impartial way. The demand for constituencies of roughly equal population means that boundaries have frequently to be redrawn to adjust the system to population movements, yet frequent boundary changes are certain to be unpopular both with candidates who have been representing or 'nursing' a constituency and with local communities who suddenly find themselves divided in two, or joined to a dissimilar area, for purposes of parliamentary representation.

(3) The third problem is that of deciding how the votes are to be counted and the result arrived at. There are many systems of election, ranging in complexity from the British system of simple plurality through the present French system of a second ballot in constituencies where no candidate secures an absolute majority on the first ballot to the various systems of proportional representation that have been devised and put into operation. Each system translates a given distribution of votes between parties into a rather different distribution of seats, and for this reason it is not surprising that in some countries the system of election is a constant source of controversy. A notable example is France, where four different systems have been used since 1945, each designed to benefit a particular party or group of parties at the expense of others.

(4) The fourth problem is that of agreeing upon rules for the nomination of candidates. In countries where the names of the parties are printed on the ballot papers, this matter may be quite complicated if it becomes necessary for the State to define what constitutes a political party and to establish rules for the resolution of conflicts between rival candidates, each claiming to be the official candidate of the same party. In the United States the need to resolve disputes of this kind has led the state governments to lay down procedures for the nomination of candidates by parties and thus to pass legislation regulating the internal organisation of the parties. However, in Britain this particular problem has so far been avoided and the main purpose of the rules is to eliminate frivolous nominations.

(5) The fifth main problem with which electoral laws have to deal is

that of controlling expenditure by or on behalf of the candidates. The concept of a free and fair contest implies the elimination of bribery, lavish entertainment and 'free beer all round'. It also implies that some steps should be taken to limit the advantages that a candidate with wealth at his disposal would have over a poor candidate in respect of propaganda. Countries vary in their approach to this matter, but in most societies some effort is made to bar certain kinds of electoral expenditure and in many societies a further effort is made to limit the advantages of wealth, either by placing a ceiling on the total expenditure permitted or by making certain facilities available to candidates without charge.

These are the basic problems with which electoral laws have to deal. In countries where electoral systems are created *de novo,* either after a revolution or as a step towards colonial self-government, it may be necessary for a self-conscious effort to be made to devise solutions to these problems. However, the British electoral system, like many other British institutions, has its roots in the past: it has been subject to piecemeal revision on many occasions, but the task of reformers has always been to improve an existing system rather than to invent a new one. Largely because of this, Britain has avoided some of the controversies over electoral arrangements that other democratic countries have experienced: the debates have occasionally been heated but they have been confined to a relatively narrow range of issues.

(1) The register

The first of the problems outlined above has been met in Britain since 1918 by placing the responsibility for compiling the register on the State. In each county or borough the clerk to the council, acting in his capacity as Registration Officer, has the duty of canvassing the area each year to ensure that all adult citizens are registered. In practice time is saved by sending a registration form to each householder with the request that he complete it and return it by post, and a door-to-door canvass is necessary only for the small minority who do not comply with this request. The register is compiled afresh each autumn and is a record of those qualified to vote on 10 October. It is normally published in January and comes into force on 16 February for a period of twelve months. This means that the register may be as much as sixteen months old when the election is held, but the effects of this are mitigated in two ways: persons within eight months of their eighteenth birthday at registration day are placed on the register even though they are not allowed to vote until they reach eighteen; and persons moving out of the constituency can vote by post (as can invalids). It may be noted in passing that this provision for postal voting (which was made a regular feature of the electoral system in 1948) has had the effect of helping the Conservative Party, which has been more successful than the Labour Party in persuading its supporters to take advantage of the arrangement. It has been estimated that the greater success of the Conservatives in this respect probably gained their party six seats in 1970 and possibly gained them as many as eight.[1]

This system of registration works smoothly and efficiently; 97 or 98 per cent of eligible electors are normally included in the register; and since 1918 there have been no suggestions in Britain of corrupt practices or party bias in the registration process. But, of course, this is only the case because of the absence of corruption in British local administration, and it should not be assumed that the system would work equally well in other conditions.

(2) Constituency boundaries

The problem of dividing the country into constituencies caused a good deal of controversy in Britain from the early part of the nineteenth century until 1944, when an attempt was made to take the matter out of politics by establishing permanent Electoral Boundary Commissions. Until that time boundaries were revised only by occasional Acts of Parliament, each one the focal point of a great deal of political bargaining. Inequalities in the size of constituencies were drastically reduced by each Act, but movements of population tended constantly to reverse this effect. Thus, after the 1918 Act the largest of the normal constituencies (i.e. excluding the outer islands) had about three times as many electors as the smallest, but by 1944 the proportion had grown to about twelve to one. The Boundary Commissions which were set up in that year (one each for England, Wales, Scotland and Northern Ireland) have the task of surveying the country as a whole at periodic intervals and of making reports and recommendations to the House of Commons. The first reports of the Commissions were adopted (with some amendments) in 1948 and changed the boundaries of over 80 per cent of the constituencies.

The impartiality of the Boundary Commissions has never been questioned. They are instructed to take into account a number of social and geographical factors, including the desirability of making constituency boundaries co-terminous with local authority boundaries wherever possible. But they take no account of political factors and their proposals tend to irritate members of all parties. This was certainly the case in 1954, when the Commissions published their second reports and recommended that about a third of all constituencies should suffer further alterations to their boundaries before the next election. The proposals were adopted, but the reaction from all sides was so vigorous that amending legislation was subsequently passed (in 1958) to lengthen the periods between review. Whereas the

Commissions had been obliged by the 1944 legislation to make
national surveys at intervals of between three and seven years, the new
rule is that the intervals should be not less than ten or more than fifteen
years. This neatly illustrates one of the inherent difficulties in adjusting
constituency boundaries: a system of infrequent changes is convenient
for politicians and administrators but results in inequalities of size
which grossly violate the principle of 'one vote, one value'; on the
other hand, a system of constant adjustment would be highly inconvenient to all concerned. The art here, as so often in politics, is to find the
most appropriate compromise.

The third report of the Boundary Commissions was due to be
published and implemented at some time between 1964 and 1969.
However, after the report was published it gradually became clear that
the Labour Government was unwilling to implement it. The reason for
this was the simple one that the changes would benefit the Conservative Party. The main movement of population since 1954 had been
from the centres of large cities to the outskirts, so that the population
of largely Labour seats in the city centres had fallen below the electoral
quota while the population of largely Conservative seats on the
outskirts had grown above the quota. It was estimated at the time that
the boundary changes recommended to correct this state of affairs
would have helped the Conservatives to the tune of between five and
twenty seats.

Some government action was essential since the Home Secretary
was legally obliged to 'lay the report before Parliament together with
the draft of an Order in Council for giving effect whether with or
without modifications to the recommendations contained in the
report'. The Government met this by introducing a Bill which would
free the Home Secretary from this obligation until after the next
election and which proposed, as an interim measure, that changes
should be made affecting somewhat less than 100 constituencies,
compared with the 410 that would have been affected by the Commissions' proposals. This Bill was totally unacceptable to the Opposition
and, although it was passed by the Commons, it was rejected by the
Lords. Amid mounting uproar, the Home Secretary then resorted to
the device of laying the Commissions' proposals before the House in
the form of draft Orders but announcing that he would advise all his
Labour colleagues to vote against them. The Orders were duly
rejected, and the 1970 election was fought in outdated constituencies
which varied in size from Birmingham Ladywood with 18,309 electors
and Manchester Exchange with 18,643 to Billericay with 113,452.
However, the Boundary Commissions' proposals were adopted in full
in November 1970.

In view of this little gerrymander it cannot be said that the Boundary

Commissions have entirely succeeded in removing the question of constituency boundaries from the field of controversy. If politicians wanted to make a fuss about constituency boundaries, there are two other issues that could well be raised. One is the permanent over-representation of Wales and Scotland in the House of Commons, as compared to the representation of England and Northern Ireland. If Scotland had the same ratio of seats to electors as England, it would be entitled to 57 seats, whereas in fact it has 71 seats. The other (less explicable) anomaly in the system is the failure of the Boundary Commission to get very near to equality of representation within England. In the first general election to be fought after the redistribution of 1970, the size of the English constituencies ranged from 25,023 electors to 96,380 electors. The average electorate in the 516 constituencies was 64,134, but 49 constituencies had over 80,000 electors and 58 had under 50,000. In the United States, maldistribution on this scale would probably be declared an unconstitutional violation of the principle of equal democratic rights. It would seem that the Boundary Commissioners have opted for a quiet life by making concessions to all kinds of local interests, at the expense of the general interest in equal representation.

(3) The voting system

The basic system of counting votes in Britain has not been changed since Parliament was established in the Middle Ages, though it has sometimes been criticised. It is the simplest system of all, known sometimes as 'simple plurality' and sometimes as 'first past the post'. Each constituency returns one Member, each elector has one vote, and the candidate receiving the largest number of votes is elected. Under this system each party has only one candidate in a constituency, so there is no problem of determining the order of priority between candidates of the same party; there is only one ballot, so the elections can be held simultaneously throughout the country and the results declared immediately; and the elector has to do nothing more complicated than put a cross against the name of the candidate he prefers. The overall effect of the system is to exaggerate the success of the winning party, as is shown by Table 5.1.

It will be seen that when the result is balanced on a knife-edge, as in 1964 and February 1974, the number of seats won by the two main parties is roughly (though not exactly) proportional to the relative number of votes cast for them. The more usual situation is for the most successful party to gain a majority in Parliament that is inflated when compared with the distribution of votes. At all times the Liberal Party comes off very badly indeed. The fate of other small parties depends on how far their support is geographically concentrated. Those with a

Table 5.1   *General Election Results: 1959–79*

Date	Party	No. of votes .000	% of votes	No. of seats won	% of seats won
1959	Conservative	13,750	49·4	365	57·9
	Labour	12,216	43·8	258	41·0
	Liberal	1,639	5·9	6	1·0
	Others	275	0·9	1	0·1
1964	Conservative	12,001	43·4	304	48·3
	Labour	12,206	44·1	317	50·3
	Liberal	3,093	11·2	9	1·4
	Others	349	1·3	0	–
1966	Conservative	11,418	41·9	253	40·1
	Labour	13,065	47·9	363	57·6
	Liberal	2,328	8·5	12	1·9
	Others	463	1·7	2	0·3
1970	Conservative	13,145	46·4	330	52·4
	Labour	12,179	42·9	287	45·6
	Liberal	2,118	7·5	6	1·0
	Others	903	2·2	7	1·1
Feb 1974	Conservative	11,869	37·9	297	46·8
	Labour	11,639	37·1	301	47·4
	Liberal	6,063	19·3	14	2·2
	Others	1,762	5·6	23	3·6
Oct 1974	Conservative	10,465	35·8	277	43·6
	Labour	11,457	39·2	319	50·2
	Liberal	5,347	18·3	13	2·1
	Others	1,920	6·6	26	4·2
1979	Conservative	13,698	43·9	339	53·4
	Labour	11,510	36·9	268	42·2
	Liberal	4,314	13·8	11	1·7
	Others	1,700	5·5	17	2·7

small following dispersed around the country find the electoral system disadvantageous, but this is not necessarily true of local parties such as the Ulster Unionists, Plaid Cymru or the Scottish National Party.

Since at least 1968 there has been an intermittent campaign for the replacement of the existing electoral system by some form of proportional representation. The main arguments for this proposed reform are: (*a*) that the present system is unfair to minor parties; and (*b*) that the present system turns parliamentary politics into an adversarial battle between left and right, which does not reflect the wishes of the electorate and may be unhealthy for British democracy.[2] The main argument against reform is that the present system usually produces a safe majority in the House of Commons for the governing party, whereas proportional representation would usually result in coalition governments. It is claimed that majority government gives a clear line of responsibility to the electorate, who know whom to blame when things go wrong, whereas coalition government enables the politicians to blame each other.

In practice, this debate is greatly influenced by the fact that the Liberal Party would be the only certain beneficiary of such a reform. Whereas the present system results in the permanent underrepresentation of the Liberal Party, proportional representation might well put it into a position in which it normally held the balance of power in Parliament and would thus decide which of the other parties joined it in government. For this reason, the Liberals have favoured electoral reform ever since the emergence of the Labour Party as a major force after the First World War. For this reason also, the Labour and Conservative Parties are opposed to change. The period since 1974 has seen the emergence of a small reforming group within the Conservative Party known as CAER (Conservative Action for Electoral Reform), but the Liberal Party's decision to form a pact with the Labour Party in 1977 has strengthened the opposition to reform on the part of most Conservative leaders without producing any support for reform among Labour leaders. It can therefore be predicted that proportional representation will not be introduced for parliamentary elections unless the Liberals and the other minor parties gain sufficient political leverage to be able to insist upon it. It is worth noting that the rise of the Labour Party demonstrates that the present system does not prevent a third party from becoming successful if it can command enough support among the electorate to achieve a breakthrough.

(4) Nominations of candidates
As noted above, legal complications are inevitably involved if candidates stand as the official nominees of their parties. Britain has avoided these problems because candidates stand simply as individuals, requiring the support of only ten local citizens to be nominated. There is therefore no need for rules about what constitutes a political party, how parties should be organised, or how they should nominate candidates. And until 1969 there was no provision for the names of parties to be printed on the ballot paper.

When the Representation of the People Bill 1968–9 was introduced the Home Secretary proposed to change this state of affairs by allowing party labels to be printed on ballot papers and requiring that all political parties register with the Chief Registrar of Friendly Societies as part of the machinery for controlling the labels. Perhaps it was because the Home Secretary represented a constituency in Wales, where there is a certain paucity of surnames, that he thought the inconvenience of this proposed machinery would be less than the inconvenience caused when two competing candidates have the same surname. However, Parliament did not agree and at the Report Stage this proviso was replaced by a simple clause which gave candidates permission to add any slogan of their choice after their names, provided it did not exceed six words. The chief beneficiary of this provision in the 1970 election was Edward Heath, who was able to describe himself as 'Leader of the Conservative Party' to distinguish his line on the ballot from that of another candidate who had adopted the same name by deed poll in the hope of causing confusion. The 1979 election produced a plethora of eccentric slogans, including 'Liberal dog lover', 'Committee for Prevention of Police State', 'Anti Common Market on any terms' and 'Democratic monarchist public safety white resident'.

The rules regarding nomination provide simply that candidates must be themselves eligible to vote, that they must be nominated by ten local citizens, and that they must pay a deposit of £150, which will be forfeited if the candidate fails to secure one-eighth of the votes cast. There is no 'locality rule', and in practice the majority of candidates come in the first place from outside the area, though if they are elected they may acquire a house or flat in the constituency. The object of the deposit is to discourage frivolous candidates whose inclusion would lengthen the ballot paper to no good purpose.

The requirement of a relatively small deposit is much more convenient than the requirement that is made in some American states, namely that candidates for parties not previously included on the ballot have to be supported by a petition signed by so many thousand electors. That kind of arrangement is both administratively complicated (because signatures can be forged) and open to political objections (in that it may be a difficult hurdle for new parties to surmount). However, the effectiveness of the deposit as a deterrent has been steadily decreasing in Britain. In the seven interwar elections an average of 36 candidates lost their deposits; in the elections between 1945 and 1959 the average was 71; in the elections of the 1960s the average was 121; in the first three elections of the 1970s the average was 250; and in 1979 the number was 1,002. This trend has occurred largely because the deposit has not been increased to take account of inflation and the growth of affluence since 1918. In that year £150 was equivalent to about twelve months' wages for a manual worker, whereas in 1979 it was equivalent to about two weeks' wages. If a deterrent is still thought desirable, there is clearly a strong case for increasing the size of the deposit.

Before last elect.
only 10 people to supt candidate +
£1000. deposit.

(5) Control of expenses

In Britain electoral expenses were first regulated in 1883 as part of an attempt to stamp out corruption, and the control has been progressively tightened since then with the object of preventing wealthy candidates or parties from having an untoward advantage over others. The machinery of control is simple but extremely effective: each candidate is required to appoint an official election agent; all expenditure designed to promote the interests of the candidate during the campaign has to be authorised by the agent; and at the end of the campaign the agent has to submit a statement of accounts showing that the total sum expended does not exceed the permitted maximum. The maximum allowed is determined by a formula and works out at something like £2,000 per candidate. This is a very small sum compared with election expenditure in many other countries, but British election campaigns are short and simple, and in practice most candidates spend appreciably less than the maximum: in October 1974 the average Conservative candidate spent £1,275, the average Labour candidate spent £1,163, and the average Liberal £725.

THE CAMPAIGN

Election campaigns in Britain are short and quiet in comparison with campaigns in most other democratic countries. Polling takes place only seventeen working days after the Proclamation summoning a new Parliament, which is made by the monarch on the advice of the Prime Minister. The approximate date of the election may be guessed or even announced some time in advance of this if a Parliament is permitted to enjoy something approaching its maximum life of five years, as were the Parliaments of 1945–50, 1959–64 and 1974–9. But this is not usually the case. The Government of the day has some tactical advantage in being able to fix the date of the election, and it is the normal practice, not regarded as in any way improper, for the Government to make the most of this by calling the election at fairly short notice some time before the end of Parliament's term. It may be noted in passing that the development of public opinion polls has increased the importance of this advantage.

The campaigns are quiet for a variety of reasons. The restrictions on local expenditure make it difficult for the candidates to do very much except circulate election addresses, hold a few public meetings, and get their party workers to conduct a house-to-house canvass. Until 1969 the regulations specifically forbade payment for music and for flags or banners which might enliven the contest. As posters displayed in a constituency are chargeable to the local candidate, one of the paradoxical signs of the beginning of the official campaign is the removal of many of the posters that have previously filled the hoardings, though they may be replaced by smaller ones which are displayed in house windows without charge. Then again, the radio and television programmes carefully control political news and features during the campaign. They provide free time for party speakers according to a formula arranged by agreement between broadcasting authorities and the parties, but they ration comment regarding party politics in order to avoid the possibility or appearance of bias.

The justification for the quietness of British elections is the modern British concept of the function of the campaign period. It is not generally regarded, as it is in the United States, as an occasion for interest groups to press their views on politicians, for parties and leaders to formulate attitudes and policies, and for candidates to meet the people and subject themselves to cross-examination regarding their records and ambitions. Instead, it is regarded as essentially an occasion when the parties should be given a fair and equal opportunity to rally their followers and persuade them to go to the polls, it being assumed that both the policies of the parties and the allegiance of most of the electors are established before the campaign opens.

These assumptions are largely valid. Whatever the character of the party programmes, and they may range from a generalised promise to continue on the lines that have already been followed to a detailed plan of proposed reforms, the programmes are generally prepared well in advance of the campaign and are rarely changed during it. And the surveys that have been made of voting intentions and behaviour show that the great majority of voters also make up their minds in advance of the campaign. For instance, a 'before and after' survey of two constituencies in the Leeds area in 1959 showed that 80 per cent of the voters were quite certain how they would vote before the campaign was launched.[3]

The voting behaviour of the minority who are uncertain may, of course, be of crucial importance, as the two main parties are now so evenly balanced that a change in the votes of only 3 or 4 per cent of the electorate is enough to throw one party out of office and install the other in its place. If it were possible for the parties to design propaganda specially calculated to influence these 'floating voters', this would doubtless be done, and the nature of election campaigns might thereby be transformed. If the floating voters were mainly women, or pensioners, or white-collar workers, the campaign might be dominated by propaganda directed particularly at these groups. However, the surveys that have been made show that, broadly speaking, floating voters are a cross-section of the electorate, not distinguished from their fellow-citizens by any particular social characteristics. In these circumstances

pecial appeal to the floating voters is possible: the only sensible way
he parties to seek their support is to direct their appeals to as wide a
s-section of the community as possible.

ne effects of election propaganda on political opinions and
iviour appear to be very slight indeed. Surveys show that very few
ple feel they have been influenced by it: thus, in a Bristol consti-
cy in 1955 only 4 per cent of the electors interviewed cited any
of propaganda source when explaining why they had voted the
they had, and this includes both those who cited local election
literature and those who mentioned any of the mass media of communication.[4] In 1959 an elaborate study of the influence of television
on political attitudes also produced results which were largely negative. The study showed that watching television programmes enlarged
people's knowledge of party politics and election issues, but had no
effect whatever on their attitudes to the parties or to party policies. The
other sources of information, including radio, the press and the local
campaign, had even less influence than television. They had no direct
effect on people's political attitudes or on their knowledge of party
politics. Radio broadcasts and the local campaign had no measurable
effect at all, and the only effect of the press was that as people read
more they tended to become slightly more sceptical of the message that
was being presented to them. The authors of the study summarised
their findings by saying that 'What is established here is not merely an
absence of cause and effect but a definite and consistent barrier
between sources of communication and movements of attitude in the
political field at the general election.'[5]

No similar study has been made of the effects of poster advertising,
nor would this be easy to do, but if voters remain impervious to
television propaganda in the home, with all its immediacy and liveli-
ness, it is difficult to envisage their opinions being changed by the sight
of a few words on a hoarding. Political parties devote a large and
increasing amount of effort to election propaganda, and television
techniques have become more sophisticated since 1959, but there is no
statistical evidence that it influences the opinions of voters.

In these circumstances the main objects of local party organisers in
the campaign are, first, to make sure that as many as possible of the
party's supporters turn out to vote and, secondly, to make sure that
their supporters know the name of the candidate. Canvassers concentrate almost entirely on supporters and try to avoid being drawn into
argument by opponents or floating voters. Local political meetings are
now no more than a ritual which candidates are expected to perform.
The personality and views of the candidate himself have little direct
effect on the result, except sometimes in the case of candidates for the
smaller parties. The attitude of most voters was neatly summarised by

the elector in Birmingham who said: 'I'd vote for a pig if my party put one up'; and statistics have confirmed the dictum of an experienced agent for one of the main parties that 'no candidate is worth more than 500 votes' (out of about 50,000). It remains true, of course, that a good candidate or Member may advance his cause by promoting the growth of a lively and active local party, and this is particularly true of the smaller parties.

Election campaigns conducted in this manner are quite effective in getting out the vote. In postwar general elections between 72 and 84 per cent of the electorate have voted, and in assessing these figures it has to be remembered that, because the register is always somewhat out-of-date and some electors are always ill or away from home, a 90 per cent turnout is about the maximum possible.

VOTING BEHAVIOUR

The way most British people vote is not determined to any considerable extent by these short election campaigns. The campaigns affect the level of turnout and occasionally have a significant effect on the result, as may have happened in 1970 and February 1974. But the great majority of party preferences are formed and maintained over a longer period.

To explain British voting behaviour two questions have to be asked, as follows. First, how is voting behaviour influenced by social factors such as family background, sex, religion and occupation? Secondly, how is voting behaviour influenced by political factors such as opinions on issues and public perceptions of the relative abilities of the political parties?

In considering social factors which influence voting behaviour it is appropriate to begin with family background, for young people do not live in a political vacuum until the age of eighteen and then consider the question of how to vote with unbiased minds. Instead, they are brought up in the knowledge that their parents have a preference for one of the parties and they tend to retain this family allegiance unless they have some specific reason to abandon it. The figures in Table 5.2 are based on nationwide surveys conducted between 1963 and 1966. The figures should be treated with caution, since people's ability to recall the past is far from perfect and there was undoubtedly a tendency for respondents to credit their parents with views similar to their own in cases of doubt. But when all reasonable allowance is made for errors of this kind, it does look as if there is a clear tendency for people to follow the political views of their parents.

Two other basic social factors are sex and religion. There is a tendency for women to be slightly more Conservative than men, but the difference is very small. In the 1964 election male voters for the two main parties divided in the proportion 46 per cent Conservative, 54 per cent Labour, while the respective figures for female voters were 48 per cent and 52 per cent.[6] The reason for this slight difference is to be found in differences in daytime environment, with many young women working in offices while their brothers enter industrial jobs, and older women keeping house in the suburbs while their husbands are working on the shop floor.

Table 5.2   *The Relationship Between Parents' Views and Party Preferences*[7]

Respondent's own present preference	Parents' partisanship		
	Both Conservative	Divided Con./Lab.	Both Labour
	%	%	%
Conservative	75	37	10
Labour	14	49	81
Liberal	8	10	6
None	3	4	3
	100	100	100

The political significance of religion appears to be greater, as in 1964 nominal members of the Church of England were divided 50/50 between the Conservative and Labour Parties while other voters split 60/40 in favour of Labour.[8] However, part of this difference is to be explained in terms of a correlation between religion and social class while another part of it has ethnic origins, since Welsh voters are overwhelmingly Labour and mostly Methodist while Irish voters (of whom there are over a million living in Britain) are overwhelmingly Labour and mostly Catholic. The residue of the relationship between religion and voting has historical origins, is still significant among voters who were born before 1918, but is only of marginal importance among younger generations.

The relationship between occupation and party preference is rather strong, which is not surprising since categorising voters according to the type of occupation they (or their spouses) follow is broadly equivalent to categorising them according to their life experiences in material terms. Some people are fortunate or successful in their encounters with the educational system, are able to find secure employment, and earn enough to satisfy their material expectations. Others are inadequately educated, face insecurity in their employment, and find that their lives are dominated by a struggle to maintain acceptable living conditions for themselves and their families. The

Table 5.3   *Occupation and Voting in Great Britain: 1951*[9]

Occupational group	No. of Conservative voters (millions)	No. of Labour voters (millions)	Conservative % age of two-party vote
Business and professional	3·6	1·0	78
White-collar and intermediate	2·7	1·6	63
Manual	6·2	11·3	35
Total	13·4	13·9	49

former group tend to support the Conservative Party because the general image of the Party is that it is in favour of maintaining the existing pattern of economic and social relations rather than of modifying it. The latter group tend to vote Labour because the general image of the Party is that it is in favour of social change and of measures designed to increase the security of the less fortunate sections of the community. The figures in Table 5.3 show the relationship between occupation and voting in the 1951 election, when the two main parties were evenly balanced. Votes for the smaller parties are omitted from this table because there is no significant relationship between occupation and voting for those parties.

Three points emerge from this table. First, the relationship between occupation and voting is appreciably stronger among business and professional people than it is among the remainder of the electorate. Secondly, the preponderance of manual workers among the electorate makes it advantageous for the Labour Party to stress class rivalries and advantageous for the Conservatives to play these rivalries down in favour of issues which do not divide electors on class lines. The ideological predispositions of the two parties are thus reinforced by electoral interest. Thirdly, Labour has a choice in its long-term strategy which is not open to its opponents. The Labour Party could, if it chose, direct its policies and propaganda to the end of securing the support of the overwhelming majority of working-class voters. If Labour were supported by 80 per cent of manual workers it could, on these figures, win elections without getting support from any other groups. The Conservatives, in contrast, can only hope to win if they get support from all the main social groups. In well over 500 of the 623 British constituencies the majority of the electors are manual workers or their dependants, so that the Conservatives would be doomed to perpetual opposition if they were not able to retain the support of a substantial proportion of voters in this occupational category.

The characteristics and motives of working-class Conservatives have long been subjects of speculation. One widely canvassed argument is that many of them are deferential in their social and political attitudes, thinking it desirable that the government of the country should be in the hands of members of the traditional ruling classes. But, while there are undoubtedly some voters of this kind, it is clear that this argument has been greatly exaggerated. 'Deference' is not easy to define or measure, and empirical studies suggest that (in so far as it exists) it is to be found among middle-class people as well as among workers, among Labour voters as well as among Conservatives. In a survey of two Yorkshire constituencies in 1964, for instance, the author and three colleagues asked voters whether they 'looked up to' the respective leaders of the parties. The responses showed that the proportion of Labour voters who looked up to Harold Wilson was not significantly different from the proportion of Conservative voters who looked up to Sir Alec Douglas-Home. The surveys conducted by Butler and Stokes also led them to play down the argument about deference,[10] while the whole notion that British politics can be interpreted in these terms has been the object of a devastating attack by Dennis Kavanagh.[11]

A second line of argument is that some working-class Conservatives are people who upgrade themselves socially, so that voting Conservative can be interpreted as one aspect of their middle-class aspirations. It is certainly true that manual workers who describe themselves as middle-class are more likely to vote Conservative than those who see themselves as working-class.[12] However, only a small minority of manual-worker Conservatives upgrade themselves in this way, and in any case it is impossible to know whether their social aspirations influenced their vote or, conversely, their political allegiance led them to identify with the middle classes. It has always to be remembered that a statistical correlation is not in itself an explanation.

A third explanation of working-class Conservatism lies in the fact that Labour is a relatively young party. In 1950 nearly half the electors had reached voting age before Labour had become one of the main parties, while over 80 per cent of them had been brought up by parents who were in that position. Given the tendency for British people to accept their parents' political views and to be loyal to their party over long periods, it follows that non-Labour voters in the 1950 and 1951 elections should be thought of not as people who had somehow been seduced away from their natural allegiance to Labour but as people whom Labour had failed to convert from their inherited allegiance to the Conservative or Liberal Parties. This interpretation, first put forward in relation to the behaviour of voters in Glossop at the 1951 election,[13] has now received powerful support from the analysis of the relationship between age and party preference made by Butler and Stokes.[14] It follows from this that Labour has gained and is to some extent still gaining simply from the passage of time, though this is of course only one among many factors, not all of which point in the same direction.

A good deal of intellectual energy has been devoted to the explanation of working-class Conservatism, and the three arguments outlined above are not the only ones that have been canvassed. However, electors are individuals with opinions and wills of their own, and there are strict limits to the power of sociological explanations of their behaviour. When all the social factors have been accounted for, there remain several million working-class people who habitually vote Conservative for no reason that the social determinist can pinpoint, but simply because they prefer the Conservative Party. Equally there are many professional and business people who vote Labour, less numerous than the working-class Conservatives but particularly significant because they provide the Labour Party with most of its parliamentary leaders.

One measure of the limited extent to which social factors influence voting behaviour has been provided by Richard Rose,[15] who has shown that in the 1964 election only 38 per cent of the variance between Conservative and Labour voters could be explained by social factors of the types mentioned above. The remaining 62 per cent of the variance has to be explained in terms of the political perceptions and judgements of the voters about the issues and the parties.

Opinions about issues and policies

The numerous analyses that have been made of the role of issues in British elections show surprisingly little correlation between issue preferences and voting behaviour. The 1950 survey in Greenwich showed that, on average, only 61 per cent of Labour supporters approved of the various Labour policies, compared with 41 per cent of Labour supporters who approved of Conservative policies and 31 per cent of Conservative supporters who approved of Labour policies.[16] A 1955 study in Bristol yielded similar results, and an index of political opinion constructed on this occasion showed that 39 per cent of Labour voters favoured Conservative policies while only 34 per cent favoured Labour policies and 27 per cent were more or less neutral.[17] In the 1959 election it was shown that a majority of Labour supporters were opposed to the renationalisation of steel, which was one of the more important planks in Labour's platform. In short, in these elections many millions of electors voted for the party of their choice in spite of its policies, not because of them.

This conclusion is reinforced by the analysis Jean Blondel has made

of opinions on twenty-two issues tested by the British Institute of
Public Opinion. He shows that on questions of foreign affairs and on
non-economic domestic issues there was little or no relationship
between opinions and party preference. On some issues the great
majority of electors were in agreement. On other issues opinion was
more evenly divided, but not on party lines. On most questions relating
to the economy and the social services there was some relationship
between opinions and party preference, but not a very close relationship. On all issues there were divisions of opinion amongst supporters
of the same party.[18]

All these studies suggest that specific party policies have only a
limited influence on the decisions of voters. There are numerous
cross-currents of opinion among the electorate, and the division
between left and right on issues, in so far as it exists, does not
correspond at all closely to the division between party supporters. It is
fair to conclude that when people think about how they will vote only a
minority do so in terms of party policies.

The evidence suggests that a far more important factor is the
experience that electors gain of various governments. By and large,
when things go well for the nation the government tends to get the
credit for this, and when things go badly it tends to get the blame.
Movements of opinion between one election and the next are most
easily explained in these terms.

British electoral history since 1959 provides ample evidence for this
proposition. In 1959, after a decade of continuous economic growth,
the Conservative Government was re-elected with a larger majority
than ever, and became the first Government since 1832 to improve its
position in three successive general elections. However, after 1960
things began to go badly. The balance of payments became adverse, so
that it was necessary to impose credit restrictions in 1961 and continue
them into the following year. The Prime Minister's decision to dismiss
a third of his Cabinet in 1962 did nothing to revive confidence, and in
1963 the Government's prestige suffered from the trivial but protracted scandals of the Profumo affair. In October bad health forced
Macmillan to retire while the Party Conference was in session, a
singularly unfortunate piece of timing which led to an undignified
public contest for the succession. In 1964 there were ominous warnings of a further economic crisis.

Any party which experienced such misfortunes could be expected to
lose support, and clear evidence of the loss was provided by a survey in
which 400 electors in Yorkshire who had been interviewed at the time
of the 1959 election were re-interviewed at the time of the 1964
election. In 1959 the respondents had been asked a battery of questions to test their opinions on the competence and leadership of the

two main parties, and their judgements were graded on a nineteen-point scale. When these gradings were compared with ones derived from similar questions which were asked in 1964, it was found that all groups in the electorate showed a loss of confidence in the Conservative Party and an increase of confidence in the Labour Party. This was just as true of consistent Conservatives and of consistent Labour supporters as it was of the fairly small proportion of people who had actually changed their vote, so that in their movement of opinion over this period the floating voters were typical of the electorate as a whole.[19] If these findings are put alongside the statistics showing how little the swing of votes varies from one area to another, it seems reasonable to conclude that movements of public opinion about the merits of the two main parties in Britain are pretty coherent and homogeneous, with the floating voters serving as an accurate guide to their nature.

Although no similar survey was conducted in 1970, the result of that election is entirely compatible with this view of British voting behaviour. The Labour Government, so full of ideas in 1964, had run into heavy weather by 1967. The economic situation had deteriorated, the attempt to draw up a national economic plan had proved to be a fiasco, and the public had had to accept higher taxes, severe credit restrictions, higher unemployment, a devaluation of the pound, higher prices and complete government control over wages and salaries. When this dismal record was combined with failure to secure entrance to the Common Market, failure to deal with the Rhodesian problem, and failure to carry through a reform of industrial relations which the Prime Minister had declared to be vital, it is hardly surprising that Labour suffered a withdrawal of public confidence between 1966 and 1970. Indeed, if the performances of British governments in the 1960s are scrutinised with a cold eye, what is remarkable is not that the Conservatives lost the 1964 election and Labour lost in 1970, but the narrowness of the margin in each case.

The election of February 1974 was exceptional in that it was provoked by a confrontation between the miners' union and the Government, and the result might have been different had the election been held a few weeks earlier or a few months later. However, the result reflected the doubts of many voters about the wisdom of the Government's actions in the field of industrial relations, and it therefore supports the general proposition under discussion. The transfers of power in 1964, 1970 and February 1974 owed much more to the perceived shortcomings of the Government of the day than to the policies or propaganda of the Opposition. Labour had little of special attraction to offer floating voters in 1964 or 1974, and the Conservatives had little special to offer in 1970. In each case what was offered, essentially, was a change from an administration that was not thought to be doing very well. The overall conclusion must be that the swing of opinion between one general election and the next is a verdict on the performance (helped or hindered by fortune) of the Government in power, though the magnitude of the swing is kept within bounds by the strength of party loyalties and the influence of social factors on political allegiance.

The final question to be dealt with in this section is that of changes in the pattern of voting behaviour in recent years. These can be summarised briefly under four headings.

First, with the passage of time the Labour Party has lost the disadvantage of being a relatively young party. To put it very bluntly, there were more working-class Conservatives among the generation who died in the 1960s and 1970s than there are among the younger working-class voters who have taken their place. The factor of traditional allegiance is no longer of much help to the Conservative Party.

Secondly, and working in the opposite direction, class consciousness is less marked than used to be the case. The general rise in the standard of living between 1945 and 1970 eased feelings of class rivalry; social mobility increased; and the class system became more complex (and thus less divisive) as a consequence of technological progress and the growth of service industries. Butler and Stokes report that 'In 1970 more than half of our respondents said that class differences had decreased, whereas only slightly more than a tenth thought that they had increased. Indeed, 44 per cent described such differences as "not very wide" or non-existent.'[20] The overall relationship between occupation and voting became less significant because of this. However, during the 1970s there were signs of a resurgence of class rivalries, and it is difficult to make predictions about the 1980s.

Thirdly, voters have become more volatile. Gallup polls show a greater variation in party support from month to month than was recorded in the 1950s and early 1960s. Governments lose support in by-elections to a greater extent than in the past.[21] Party loyalties are not as durable or reliable as they were.

Fourthly, the two main parties have both lost support. As they have taken turns since 1960 in a failure to solve Britain's economic problems, this is not at all surprising. Since many voters form their judgements of the parties on the basis of the prosperity of the nation under successive governments, it would be surprising if both parties had not suffered in public esteem. Nevertheless, the trend is highly significant. Both parties have experienced a loss of membership, very seriously in the case of Labour. The proportion of voters who said they identified very strongly with either the Labour or the Conservative Party fell from 40 per cent in 1964 to 24 per cent in October 1974 and

17 per cent in 1975. The proportion of the electors who voted for the two main parties fell from 80 per cent in 1951 to 56 per cent in October 1974. In this last election Labour was returned to power with the support of only 29 per cent of the electorate, which was a slender basis for governmental authority. The whole pattern of voting behaviour has become more fluid, with consequences for the future that are not easy to predict.

ELECTORAL SUPPORT FOR THE SMALLER PARTIES

Most of the analysis in this chapter has focused on the two main parties, because since 1924 they have taken turns in controlling the government. However, the 1974 Parliament contained representatives of seven political parties, none of which seems likely to fade away during the 1980s. The electoral support given to these smaller parties cannot be ignored.

 Of the five smaller parties currently represented in Parliament, only the Liberal Party has a country-wide basis of support. Its organisation has survived more or less intact from its years of glory before 1918, and it has enough money to be able to contest elections in most British constituencies. In the two 1974 elections it won nearly 20 per cent of the popular vote, with 6·1 million supporters in February and 5·3 million in October. In 1979 it won nearly 14 per cent of the vote.

Who are the Liberal voters? They comprise a fairly small core of faithful party supporters together with a much larger number of floating voters, many of whom vote Liberal only two or three times in their lives. Because the Liberal Party occupies the centre of the ideological spectrum, it attracts the support of floating voters who are in transition between the two larger parties. Former Conservatives moving to the left and former Labour supporters moving to the right often find a temporary resting-place with the Liberals before going over to their traditional opponents. The Liberals also attract protest votes from supporters of the governing party who are disappointed with its performance, but do not wish to go right over to the main opposition party.

The faithful Liberal supporters, though to be found in small numbers all over the country, are thickest on the ground in peripheral areas where the nonconformist churches are strong: in rural Wales, in the Scottish Highlands, in Cornwall, and in parts of East Anglia. They tend to be a cross-section of the electorate in social terms. The volatility of the temporary Liberals is remarkable. Only just over half of the six million Liberal voters in February 1974 repeated their vote in

October. About two and three-quarter million of them deserted the Liberal fold, and the Liberal vote only held up in the October election because about two million new converts joined the ranks.[22]

It follows that the Liberal Party could have a determining influence on a general election even though, because of the electoral system, very few Liberal candidates actually get into Parliament. In practice this has not so far happened. When the Liberal Party gains support it tends to draw converts from the Labour and Conservative Parties in fairly equal proportions. Statistical analyses of the results in 1974 confirm what was found in 1964 (when the Liberals also gained votes): namely that the overall impact of the Liberal gains was minimal except in those few seats which Liberal candidates actually won.

The other four parliamentary parties are confined to Scotland, Wales and Northern Ireland, and the overwhelming concern of all four is with the status of their countries within the United Kingdom. The Scottish National Party and Plaid Cymru stand for the autonomy of Scotland and Wales. The Social Democratic and Labour Party wants Northern Ireland to be detached from the United Kingdom to become part of the Irish Republic. The Ulster Unionist Party stands for the maintenance of the union between Northern Ireland and Great Britain.

In ideological terms the SNP is a middle-of-the-road party which has attracted support from former Conservative, Labour and Liberal voters. The SNP has grown very rapidly, winning 11 per cent of Scottish votes in the 1970 election, 22 per cent in February 1974, and 30 per cent in October 1974. In 1979 the proportion fell to 17 per cent. The Party won seven seats in February 1974 and eleven in October, but 1979 was an unlucky year for them and they succeeded in holding only two seats.

Plaid Cymru has until recently drawn most of its support from the rural areas of Wales, particularly those where the Welsh language is still spoken. In the 1970s it extended its appeal to the industrial areas and is now well organised throughout Wales. It won three parliamentary seats in October 1974, with 10 per cent of the Welsh vote, and held two of them in 1979, with 8 per cent of the vote. Its ideological position is slightly to the left of the Labour Party and it therefore draws most of its support from former Labour voters. However, the voters who deserted Labour in 1979 appear to have gone over to the Conservatives rather than to Plaid Cymru, and the fact that Welsh voters defeated the proposal for a Welsh Assembly in March 1979 by a majority of four to one suggests that the nationalist cause is unlikely to thrive in Wales in the foreseeable future.

In Northern Ireland the British parties do not compete in elections, and voting follows sectarian lines to a very large extent. About two-thirds of the voters have supported Ulster Unionist candidates, whose main policy has been to maintain the constitutional status of the Province as part of the United Kingdom. From 1922 until 1972 the Ulster Unionist Party had a working alliance with the Conservative Party at Westminster, and Unionist votes and MPs were often included in the Conservative figures (as they have been in Table 5.1). This alliance was abruptly terminated in 1972 when the Heath Government suspended the Northern Ireland Parliament and proceeded to rule the Province directly from London. The Unionist Party subsequently split, and three rival Unionist groups contested the Westminster elections of 1974 and 1979. However, the groups share a basic similarity of political outlook, and between them they won ten of the twelve Ulster seats on each occasion.

The Roman Catholic electors of Northern Ireland are in a permanent minority. Since 1970 their main support has gone to the Social Democratic and Labour Party, which has held one parliamentary seat at each election. Over the years, they have also supported a variety of small parties and independent candidates. The most recent of these is Frank Maguire, who has held Fermanagh and South Tyrone as an Independent since October 1974. Being opposed in principle to the inclusion of Northern Ireland within the United Kingdom, he has normally boycotted parliamentary debates, but was persuaded to attend for the crucial vote of confidence which defeated the Labour Government in March 1979. Government Whips had calculated that they would lose by one vote unless they could induce Maguire to turn up and save the day, but when the count was taken he stood behind the Speaker's chair while Labour MPs filed into the division lobbies and went down to the predicted one-vote defeat. When asked why he had made the long journey to London if he were not going to vote, he earned a place in this book by replying: 'They told me it was a very important vote, so I thought I had better abstain in person.'

It follows that the smaller parties are a mixed bag, having little in common except an interest in the decentralisation of government. However, they won 25 per cent of the total vote in October 1974 and their thirty-nine MPs held the balance of power in the House of Commons during most of the life of the 1974–9 Parliament.

In addition to these parties, there are several fringe groups which contest elections without winning seats. One is the Communist Party, which was represented in Parliament between 1922 and 1929 and between 1935 and 1950, but has come nowhere near winning a seat in recent years. There is also a Trotskyite group called the Workers' Revolutionary Party, which polls a derisory number of votes, and an extreme right-wing group called the National Front. The Front has only one real issue, namely opposition to coloured immigrants, and its main activity is the organisation of public demonstrations. However, since 1968 it has also fought a number of parliamentary elections. Between 1968 and 1978 the Front entered a candidate in 179 contests, 154 in the three general elections and 25 in by-elections. In the 1970 general election its candidates secured an average of 3·6 per cent of the votes in their constituencies; in February 1974 the average was 3·3 per cent; and in October 1974 it was 3·1 per cent. In the 1979 election the Front put up 301 candidates, but they all lost their deposits and secured an average of only 1·3 per cent of the vote in the constituencies in which they stood. Their vote dropped in nearly all the constituencies that they had also contested in the previous election. As the immigration issue is of declining importance it is unlikely that the Front will ever win a parliamentary seat.

THE ELECTORAL MANDATE

It is frequently suggested that a general election provides not only a verdict on the policies of the government before the election but also a mandate for the policies of the government that takes office (or remains in office) after the election. This doctrine has a weak form which has been endorsed from time to time by leaders of all parties and a strong form which is accepted only by some left-wing writers and some spokesmen for the Labour Party.

In its weak form the concept of the mandate is extremely vague and seems to be comprised of two rather different ideas. The first is the idea that the party which wins an election has 'a mandate to govern', it being understood that unless the election happens to have been dominated by a single issue (which is exceptional) the government should be free to pursue whatever policies it thinks appropriate. This usage of the term amounts to little more than an acknowledgement of the fact that, since the reform of Parliament, the government's political and moral authority has rested upon its popularity with the voters at the previous election. The second idea is that a general election dominated by one specific issue may be desirable as a way of gaining the authority of a popular vote for a controversial reform. Thus, in 1831 a special election was held in connection with the Reform Bill, and in 1910 and 1911 special elections were held in connection with the Finance Bill and the Parliament Bill. Each of those elections was caused by the opposition of the House of Lords to an important measure proposed by the Government and in each case the election resulted in a victory for the Government and the subsequent passage of the disputed Bill. Other examples are the elections of 1906 and 1923, each of which was fought on the issue of free trade versus protection because Balfour and

Baldwin, the respective Prime Ministers, felt that they could not introduce a protective tariff without first getting a mandate from the people (which in the subsequent elections the people refused to give).

However, in 1846 Peel ignored the idea of the mandate when he repealed the Corn Laws, and in 1886 Gladstone did the same when he introduced his first Home Rule Bill. In 1925 the Government had no mandate for the decision to return to the Gold Standard, which was said to be justified by economic necessity, and in 1927 there was no mandate for the Trade Disputes Bill, which was said to be justified by the General Strike. In 1962 the Government did not think it necessary to go to the country before applying for British membership of the Common Market, though some Labour spokesmen suggested that this would have been appropriate, while after 1964 the Labour Government proceeded to emulate the 'stop-go' economic policies of their opponents, which they had specifically promised not to do in their election campaign. The truth is that Conservative leaders, at least, have invoked the concept of the mandate when political conditions made this tactically appropriate but have felt free to ignore it in other circumstances. Even though they have sometimes fought an election on one dominant issue, they have regarded this as an exceptional circumstance. They maintain that the Government should judge each issue on its merits and in relation to the opinions expressed in Parliament and the country, and should not feel that its hands are tied by pledges made some time previously in the possibly different circumstances of an election campaign.

The Labour Party's attitude to the concept of the mandate has been more positive than this, for two reasons. First, it has always been one of the principles of the British trade union movement that leaders and delegates should not only be elected but should be mandated to pursue policies endorsed by the members, and Labour politicians with trade union backgrounds have instinctively tended to assume that the same principle should apply to the government of the nation. Secondly, as Labour is a reforming party it has seemed appropriate to present the electorate with a manifesto setting out the reforms that the Party would introduce, if given a majority, during the life of the following Parliament. Labour spokesmen have often tended to say not only that their party should do this but also that all parties should publish clear statements of policy so that the electors would have the information necessary for them to make a rational choice between alternative programmes. The subsequent government, it is said or implied, should try to implement its stated policy unless circumstances change.

In this strong form the concept of the mandate constitutes a reasonable view of how parties, electors and politicians ought to behave, but it is a quite misleading guide to how they do behave. In the first place, party manifestos tend to outline their proposed policies in fairly vague terms. Secondly, only a very small proportion of electors decide how they will vote on the basis of the programmes published by the parties: as noted above, most electors decide how to vote on other grounds and many do so in spite of their opposition to the policies of their party. This is particularly true of Labour supporters, whose propensity to disagree with their party's policies is very high. And, finally, politicians are naturally reluctant to regard themselves as bound by promises made in the election campaign. The 1945 Labour Government kept to its plans, but the circumstances were exceptional in that the Government came to power armed with a set of intended reforms which had been worked out over a period of many years. The 1970 Conservative Government kept its promises to take Britain into the Common Market, to provide a new legal framework for the conduct of industrial relations, and to simplify and reform the taxation system. But few governments are as determined as these two, and the more general tendency is for governments to feel that their main duty is to pursue the policy that seems most likely to advance the national interest at the time that the decision is made. Because of this, politicians are usually cautious about committing themselves in advance to specific proposals, though an opposition party seeking election normally has to go farther in this direction than a government party seeking re-election.

It may be concluded that in its weak form the doctrine of the mandate exists but is not of great importance, particularly since the Parliament Acts of 1911 and 1949 make it highly unlikely that there will again be a crisis caused by conflict between the two Houses which will need to be resolved by a general election. In its strong form the doctrine of the mandate would be an important principle of the constitution if it were accepted by all parties and if it corresponded to the facts of political life. But it does not meet these tests and is in reality little more than an idealistic view of how things ought to work.

NOTES

1 D. E. Butler and M. Pinto-Duschinsky, *The British General Election of 1970* (Macmillan, 1971), p. 332.
2 See the essays in S. E. Finer (ed.), *Adversary Politics and Electoral Reform* (Anthony Wigram, 1975).
3 J. Trenaman and D. McQuail, *Television and the Political Image* (Methuen, 1961), pp. 207–8.
4 See R. S. Milne and H. C. Mackenzie, *Marginal Seat, 1955* (Hansard Society, 1958), p. 161.
5 Trenaman and McQuail, *Television and the Political Image*, p. 192.
6 Richard Rose (ed.), *Studies in British Politics*, 3rd edn (Macmillan, 1976), p. 227.

7   Source: David Butler and Donald Stokes, *Political Change in Britain*, 2nd edn (1974), p. 52.
8   Rose, *Studies in British Politics*, p. 227.
9   Source: John Bonham, *The Middle Class Vote* (Faber, 1954).
10   Butler and Stokes, *Political Change in Britain*, pp. 113–15.
11   See Dennis Kavanagh, 'The deferential English: a comparative critique', in *Government and Opposition*, vol. 6 (1971).
12   See Butler and Stokes, *Political Change in Britain*, p. 78.
13   See A. H. Birch, *Small-Town Politics* (Oxford University Press, 1959), pp. 110–11.
14   Butler and Stokes, *Political Change in Britain*, pp. 104–12.
15   Rose, *Studies in British Politics*, p. 227.
16   See Mark Benney, A. P. Gray and R. H. Pear, *How People Vote* (Routledge & Kegan Paul, 1956), pp. 140–1.
17   Milne and Mackenzie, *Marginal Seat, 1955*, p. 119.
18   See Jean Blondel, *Voters, Parties and Leaders* (Penguin, 1963), pp. 75–81.
19   See R. J. Benewick, A. H. Birch, J. G. Blumler and Alison Ewbank, 'The floating voter and the liberal view of representation', in *Political Studies*, vol. XVII (1969).
20   Butler and Stokes, *Political Change in Britain*, p. 194.
21   ibid., pp. 206–7.
22   James Alt, Ivor Crewe, and Bo Sarlvik, 'Angels in plastic: the Liberal surge in 1974', *Political Studies*, vol. XXV (1977).

FURTHER READING

P. G. Pulzer, *Political Representation and Elections in Britain* (Allen & Unwin, 1972), is a useful general guide to the system; after each election there is published a Nuffield College study of the campaign and the results, written by David Butler and a series of co-authors, of which the most recent is David Butler and Dennis Kavanagh, *The British General Election of October 1979* (Macmillan, 1980); David Butler and Donald Stokes, *Political Change in Britain* (Macmillan, 1969, 1974), provides a comprehensive analysis of voting behaviour in the period 1964–70; voting behaviour since 1974 has been analysed by James Alt, Ivor Crewe and Bo Sarlvik in articles in *Political Studies* and the *British Journal of Political Science;* the influence of the mass media on elections is analysed in Jay Blumler and Denis McQuail, *Television in Politics* (Faber, 1968). A valuable set of articles on the 1979 election will be found in Howard Penniman (ed.), *Britain at the Polls, 1979* (American Enterprise Institute, 1981).

Chapter 6

Group Spokesmen

INTEREST AND PROMOTIONAL GROUPS

Seen in the light of democratic theory, the citizen is first and foremost
an elector, having general views about government and expressing
preferences between one political party and another. Seen in another
light, the citizen is not so much a whole man as a bundle of interests,
having views about particular matters which reflect his interests in
these matters. If he has children, he will have an interest in the
maintenance of child allowances; if his mother is widowed, he will be
concerned about widows' pensions; if he is buying a house, he will be
worried about mortgage rates and therefore about the general level of
interest rates; if he is a trade unionist, he will be concerned about the
legal privileges of trade unions and about the conditions of industrial
negotiation; if he likes to bet on horses, he will be in favour of betting
shops and alarmed at the prospect of a general tax on gambling; if he is
a weekend fisherman, he will be concerned about access to rivers and
their pollution by industrial effluents. The list could be extended
indefinitely.

It is clear that many people are more active in defence of their
various interests than they are in their role as electors. What the
Government does about pensions or interest rates or taxation affects
people directly and immediately. Many of those likely to be affected
naturally take advantage of their right to organise societies to defend
and advance their interests. In modern Britain there are innumerable
societies of this kind, best described by the general title of interest
groups. They range from trade associations and trade unions to
motoring organisations, sporting organisations, and the Bookmakers'
Protection Association. Nobody has ever taken a census of interest
groups, and their multiplicity and variety are perhaps best illustrated
by a random selection of titles, as follows:

The Small Pig Keepers' Council
The Television Programme Contractors' Association
The National Federation of Wholesale Poultry Merchants
The National Union of Railwaymen
The Society of Authors

The Royal Yachting Association
The National Union of Students
The British Limbless Ex-Service Men's Association
The National Cyclists' Union
The Free Church Federal Council
The Royal Automobile Club
The Society of Civil Servants

Very few of these organisations are concerned exclusively with political action. The majority of them provide services of various kinds for their members and many of them regard this as their main function, turning to politics only on those perhaps rare occasions when the interests of their members are threatened by government action or by the activities of other groups in a way that can only be prevented by government action. But the range of government activities is now so great that most interest groups take on a political role from time to time. When they do so they act through spokesmen of various kinds. The chairman or secretary of the group may write to the press or to the ministry involved. MPs who share the interests of the group, or who are paid to act on its behalf, may take up the matter in Parliament. If the group has extensive dealings with Whitehall the full-time officials of the group will probably cultivate close personal relations with the civil servants with whom they negotiate. Group spokesmen of these various kinds play a vital role in British national politics.

While all citizens have interests to defend, many citizens also have causes which they wish to advance. Some people are interested in religious causes; others in the improvement of educational and social services; others in political causes of various kinds; and others again in the welfare of animals. Such people naturally join groups for the promotion of these causes, and the list of promotional groups which play a role in the British political process is as varied, though not so long, as the list of interest groups. Some examples are as follows:

The National Society for the Prevention of Cruelty to Children
The League Against Cruel Sports
The National Council of Physical Recreation
The Anti-Vivisection Society
The Third Programme Defence Society
The Lord's Day Observance Society
The Howard League for Penal Reform
The Child Poverty Action Group
The Council for the Preservation of Rural England
The Family Planning Association

The Simplified Spelling Society
The Abortion Law Reform Association

Promotional groups tend to have smaller memberships than interest groups and, unlike the latter, to draw their members very largely from the upper and middle classes. Some promotional groups are quite well off – there really are people who leave their money to animal welfare societies – while others have to spend much of their energy trying to raise funds. But the success of promotional groups in their political activities does not depend either on their ability to claim a mass membership or on their ability to mount an expensive campaign; it depends rather on the quality of their arguments, the prestige of their leading members, and the existence or otherwise of a group opposed to the cause which they are supporting.

GROUP SPOKESMEN AND GOVERNMENT

Group spokesmen engage in politics in various ways. They write to newspapers; they organise public demonstrations; they speak in Parliament; they sit on government advisory committees; they negotiate directly with government departments. As a broad generalisation it is probably true that the more conspicuous their activities are, the less influence they are likely to exert. Public demonstrations are rarely effective; speeches in Parliament are only occasionally effective; while representation on official committees is always helpful, and informal negotiations with government departments pay more dividends than any other form of activity. It is a generalisation to which exceptions can be found, such as the marked success of the National Campaign for the Abolition of Capital Punishment, which proceeded first by a public campaign and then by the conversion of backbench MPs. But the generalisation is true enough for it to be sensible to pay most attention in this chapter to the relations of group spokesmen to government departments.

It would be a complete mistake to assume that there is anything sinister about the influence of group spokesmen in Whitehall or to imagine that they usually have difficulty in gaining a hearing. On the contrary, government departments think it both proper and necessary to consult the 'affected interests' in the normal process of administration. They think it proper because the affected interests, broadly defined, will include nearly all those likely to have an informed opinion on any issue that may be in question. They will know best how the existing arrangements work and what their shortcomings are; they are in the best position to judge how effective any proposed changes are likely to be; they can draw attention to the particular difficulties involved in the introduction of reforms. Of course, the responsibility for government policy rests with the minister, and he should not allow himself to be 'captured' by the affected interests, but in the British political tradition it is thought entirely proper that he and his permanent staff should consult fully with these interests before notifying Parliament of any modifications in policy that he proposes to introduce.

The tradition of constant consultation with the affected interests is strengthened by two further considerations. One is that, as will emerge in Chapter 10, British civil servants are not specialists. They are intelligent people with a good education who acquire a facility for familiarising themselves with specific problems, but they need advice on technical matters and they often find that they can get it most conveniently by consulting the spokesman for the industry or activity with which they are concerned. The other consideration is that government departments need the co-operation of the relevant sections of the public if administration is to be efficient and government policies are to be successful. No government could be happy with a situation in which it had constantly to rely on its powers of coercion. Economic policies need the co-operation of both sides of industry if they are to succeed; educational policies need the co-operation of teachers and local authorities; health policies need the co-operation of the medical profession. Consultation does not guarantee co-operation but its absence would almost certainly cause resentment; it is a necessary even though not a sufficient condition of successful administration.

Of course, not all group spokesmen are consulted by government departments because not all groups are recognised as having a legitimate interest in the matters at stake. The Ministry of Defence does not consult pacifist groups, who have to resort to other means of bringing their views to the attention of those in authority. But government departments are generally liberal in their attitudes to this matter, and many promotional groups enjoy fairly close contacts with the relevant departments. Certainly this is true of the groups concerned with social welfare and with penal reform.

At the other end of the spectrum, there are some groups who owe their existence to government initiative or whose position has been deliberately strengthened by government support. In 1924 the University Grants Committee, consisting largely of academics, was established to take charge of the distribution of government grants to universities, thus enabling these institutions to draw about 80 per cent of their income from public funds without becoming subject to direct political control. In the 1930s government action led to the establishment of the Milk Marketing Board, the Potato Marketing Board, the

British Iron and Steel Federation and similar organisations, whose function was to represent the views of their industry about the measures the Government should take to help the industry recover from the Depression. In 1946 the Cotton Board was set up by statute to act as an intermediary (and buffer) between the Government and the various branches of the cotton industry, all firms in the industry being compelled to subscribe to the Board. These and other examples indicate that the practice of consultation between government departments and interest groups is as valuable to the Government as it is to the interests involved.

The complexity of the consultative process varies from one field of activity to another and depends largely on the number of interest groups involved. In most aspects of economic and industrial policy, the government department concerned will have to balance conflicting pressures from the trade associations on one hand and the trade unions on the other. In regard to agricultural policy, the situation was for many years more straightforward because the National Farmers' Union was the only group involved. From 1947 until 1972, the level of government support for agriculture was determined by lengthy negotiations between officials of the NFU and officials of the Ministry of Agriculture, which resulted in a 'global award' for the industry. Although the NFU was not always happy with the size of the award, it was rarely willing to jeopardise its good relations with the civil servants involved by attacking the Ministry in public. A somewhat cosy relationship therefore developed, which was transformed in January 1973 by Britain's membership of the European Economic Community. Since then, the most important decisions regarding British agriculture have been taken in Brussels, and the relationship between group spokesmen and decision-makers has become more complex.

For some years, the British Medical Association enjoyed a relationship with the Ministry of Health which was rather similar to that between the NFU and the Ministry of Agriculture. However, this relationship also has become more complex recently, primarily because other spokesmen for groups within the Health Service have challenged the virtual monopoly of the BMA. Some of the general practitioners are now represented by another organisation and some of the junior hospital doctors have formed a third organised group. Moreover, the nursing profession has become unionised and hospital porters have attempted to influence government policy through the National Union of Public Employees.

The situation regarding universities has always been rather complex. In Britain higher education is largely financed by the Government but, as noted above, university grants are distributed by the University Grants Committee, a body whose members (all part-time except the chairman) are drawn largely from the academic profession. The network of organisations dealing with the government of universities is illustrated in Figure 6.1, in which the writer's former university is taken as an example.

Messages, inquiries and proposals flow constantly in all directions along the lines of communication indicated in this diagram. The universities are engaged in what seems to be an almost continuous process of framing and revising plans for future expansion, plans for new buildings, and plans for modifying the methods of admitting or teaching students. Nearly all changes affect the size of the grants that will be needed and the plans therefore have to be communicated to the Grants Committee, which in its turn constantly bombards the universities with requests for information about their activities.

The Association of University Teachers, while out of the mainstream, is not without influence. It speaks for an extremely articulate group of men who also speak for themselves, though without much consistency, in a never-ending flow of letters, articles and talks in the mass media of communication. Governments are apt to ignore academic opinions about foreign policy but they cannot afford to ignore academic views about higher education. The National Union of Students also enjoys a fair degree of influence. Its representations about student grants are listened to and sometimes heeded. When its dissatisfaction with the quality of university teaching was impressed on the ministry, this resulted in a request to universities from the Grants Committee for information about any steps they might be taking to train junior lecturers in the art of lecturing. When the Department of Education and Science proposed in 1971 to abolish the system whereby student unions enjoy a large measure of autonomy in their expenditure of the public funds given to them, the opposition of both the NUS and the Vice-Chancellors' Committee induced the Department to drop the proposal.

This network of institutions and channels of communication is paralleled by similar networks for polytechnics, for colleges of education, for technical colleges, and for the world of adult education. In the case of training colleges and technical colleges the local authorities are also involved, and they have their own influential spokesmen in bodies like the County Councils' Association. Those responsible for higher education in the ministry have to deal with all these numerous spokesmen, on whom, indeed, they rely for information and for guidance about what is feasible. Since higher education cannot be entirely separated from secondary education, they have also to consider the views of the various and influential spokesmen for both state and private schools.

It follows that civil servants in the ministry dealing with education

Figure 6.1 *The University Network*

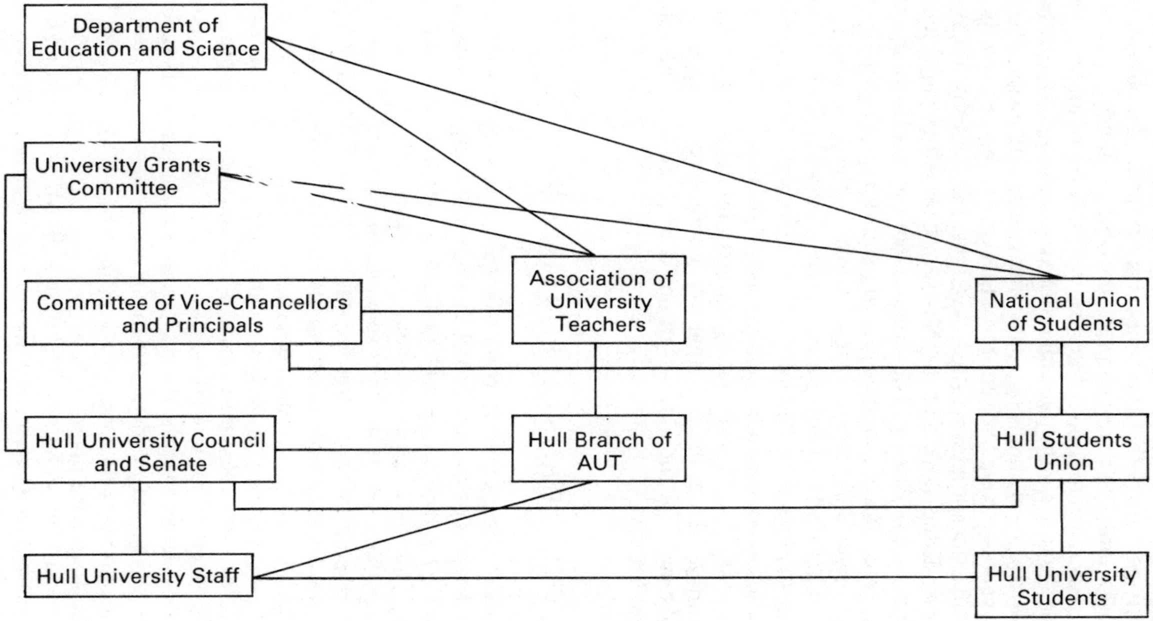

have to deal with a variety of spokesmen for the various sections of the educational world, who are usually in disagreement with one another. Partly because of this, the ministers responsible for education are given to appointing advisory committees which will hear evidence from all interested groups and contain representatives of many of them, in the hope that the committee will relieve the minister of the difficult task of balancing rival claims and assessing conflicting proposals. In the past few years we have had reports of this kind from the Crowther Committee on Education from Fifteen to Eighteen, the Robbins Committee on Higher Education, and the Newsom Committee on Education from Thirteen to Sixteen. The composition of the Robbins Committee illustrates one of the roles played by group spokesmen. It contained a vice-chancellor, three university teachers, the directors of two colleges of science and technology, the director of an institute of education, a headmaster and a headmistress, a member of the London County Council who was also vice-president of the Workers' Educational Association, and two leading industrialists. This was a not untypical example of an official advisory committee composed largely of spokesmen for the various groups concerned with the activity under consideration.

ACTION THROUGH PARLIAMENT

Because the great majority of British legislation is sponsored by the government of the day, which can normally rely on party discipline to ensure its passage, Parliament is somewhat less important than Whitehall as a focus of group pressures. Most important interest-groups have parliamentary spokesmen who act on their behalf, particularly during the committee stage of public Bills, and these activities result in numerous detailed amendments. However, it is rare for group spokesmen to secure the adoption of a major amendment to government legislation through parliamentary action, and Parliament is therefore much less influential as a channel of group pressures than is the United States Congress.

It is also noteworthy that in Parliament there is nothing like the level of lobbying on foreign affairs that is accepted as normal in Congress. In 1974, for instance, the Greek American lobby, representing only a very small proportion of the population, was powerful enough to secure an arms embargo on Turkey following the fighting in Cyprus – a decision which weakened the entire Western alliance and caused anxiety in the State Department, the Pentagon and the White House. It is inconceivable that any pressure-group could have this kind of impact on defence or foreign policy in Britain.

However, there are some fields of activity in which group spokesmen have achieved considerable influence through parliamentary action. One is the whole field of animal welfare, in which the Royal Society for the Prevention of Cruelty to Animals has acquired a position of dominance because there are no countervailing groups arguing the opposite case. Group spokesmen have also acquired considerable influence in regard to various types of moral issue, because governments are often reluctant to insist on party discipline in such matters.

One example of group activity on a moral issue was the work of the National Campaign for the Abolition of Capital Punishment, which succeeded in getting enough backbench support for its cause in 1956 to induce the Government to introduce the Homicide Act of 1957, which abolished the death penalty for all but a few special categories of murder. In 1965 the abolitionists got a Private Member's Bill through Parliament which ended the death penalty completely. Another legislative reform was the legalisation of homosexual acts between consenting adults, sponsored by a group of backbenchers in 1967. A third example was the liberalisation of the abortion laws, promoted by the Abortion Law Reform Association and also accepted in 1967. These reforms show that in some areas of legislation Parliament is still very amenable to influence by a well-organised and determined group of reformers.

PUBLIC CAMPAIGNS

Sometimes group spokesmen organise a public campaign to support their viewpoint. Usually this is a sign that the group has failed to secure acceptance by the appropriate government department as an affected interest (or a body with useful information), and cannot achieve its aims by a Private Member's Bill. Because of this, a public campaign is often a sign of weakness rather than strength, and if this is so its chances of success are not high.

Thus the Campaign for Nuclear Disarmament was not regarded by the Government as representing an affected interest; it had no specialised information not possessed by the Government; and it was not accepted as a responsible body whose views should be heard and taken into account, as is the position of organisations like the Royal Society for the Prevention of Cruelty to Animals. In these circumstances the CND had no direct access to government departments and had little choice, given that it wanted to make a rapid impact, but to resort to a public campaign. While this brought it a great deal of free publicity, there is no evidence that it advanced its cause. Certainly it increased awareness of nuclear disarmament as an issue, but the public-opinion polls suggest that the number of converts made by the CND was less than the number of previously apathetic citizens who were activated into opposition to the aims of the movement. Its campaign within the Labour Party appears to have had similar consequences: it made nuclear disarmament a central issue for a time, but at the 1961 annual conference of the Party the CND was decisively defeated.

Two other public campaigns since the war have been equally unsuccessful. One was the campaign launched by the Road Haulage Association in 1945–7 against the Government's proposal to nationalise the road haulage industry. The country was saturated by posters and sticky labels; two propaganda films were shown to large audiences; hundreds of speeches were made and thousands of leaflets were distributed; nearly a million people were induced to sign a petition; and 2,500 telegrams were sent to MPS. The whole campaign cost £100,000, and it had no influence whatever on the Government or on the treatment by Parliament of the nationalisation Bill, which was passed without any substantial concessions to the hauliers.

In 1949–50 a similar campaign was launched against the proposal to nationalise the sugar-refining industry. This campaign was backed by even more money and was conducted in a much more professional way. But there is no evidence that it had any impact: the plan to nationalise sugar was abandoned only because the Labour Party had such a small majority after the 1950 election; and the public opinion polls suggest that, if the campaign had any effect on public attitudes, it may have had the opposite effect to that intended.[1]

Public campaigns are not always a failure. One notable success was the campaign launched by the National Union of Teachers in 1956 in opposition to a government Bill which would have had the effect of increasing teachers' superannuation payments. The NUT approached MPS, spent £100,000 in a very short period on advertising and publicity, and persuaded its members to refuse to perform ancillary tasks like collecting savings and supervising school meals. These threats of 'direct action' attracted nationwide attention and the campaign as a whole led a number of Conservative backbench MPS to waver in their support of the minister. The result was that the Government conceded the main points made by the teachers.

Another success was the campaign launched in 1964 to prevent Stansted being adopted as the site of London's third airport. This was fought against heavy odds, for the departments concerned had committed themselves to Stansted before the public had appreciated what was happening and certain other decisions had been made in the light of this commitment. However, the choice of an inland site in attractive and well-populated countryside, but with poor transport facilities, made no sense to anyone outside government circles and the airlines. The issue of airport noise became front-page news and it was suggested that a better solution would be to build the airport on reclaimed land on the Essex coast at Foulness. A body called the North-West Essex Preservation Association was established to fight the Stansted decision and its campaign was supported by the entire national press. The Government fought a determined rearguard action but eventually, after nearly four years of public agitation, it was decided to find another site for the airport. After a period in which another official committee recommended another inland site, which led to a further though much shorter campaign of protest, the Conservative Government eventually decided in 1971 to build the airport at Foulness. Ironically, the Labour Government which achieved power in 1974 decided that the country could not afford a new airport at all, and the entire scheme was abandoned after ten years of argument.

Further campaigns of a similar kind, though smaller in scale, have been fought up and down the country to persuade planners to abandon or amend proposed highway developments. It has been found that, if the government department concerned can be pushed into ordering a public inquiry, the opponents of the plan can frustrate the whole enterprise by creating so much noise at the inquiry that the inspector is unable to hear the witnesses. In Britain's tolerant political atmosphere, the authorities have as yet found no answer to this kind of tactic. Other groups, by appealing to public opinion, have prevented the demolition of condemned housing, prevented the construction of a reservoir in south Devon, and prevented the imposition of a speed limit which would have made water-skiing impossible on the estuary of the River Exe. All these successful campaigns have been waged by 'fire-brigade groups' (to use Finer's term); that is, by groups of citizens, not normally active in politics, who spring into activity to oppose some particular policy. They normally have very little money and no professional staff, but they can wield a decisive influence if their campaign is skilfully managed. However, it remains true that campaigns of this kind are a poor substitute for the continuous influence that groups can have if their spokesmen are consulted and respected by government departments, as a great many of them are.

GROUP SPOKESMEN AND DEMOCRACY

The activities of group spokesmen, important though they are, have no place in most liberal and democratic theories about political organisation. It is open to question whether the influence of sectional pressures in the process of government is entirely compatible with the view that policy ought to reflect the wishes of the public, as expressed through their elected representatives in Parliament. It is certainly arguable that group spokesmen, whose influence tends to be greatest when it is least conspicuous, enjoy more power than the general public realise and more power than they would think proper if they fully understood its dimensions.

The answer to this kind of charge involves a number of considerations which, taken together, suggest that the role of group spokesmen is more compatible with democratic ideals than might at first be supposed.

First, there is as much freedom to organise sectional groups as there is to contest elections or form political parties. The world of political pressure is open to all. And, lest it be said that in this respect it is like the Ritz Hotel, it should be added that wealth is not necessary to success and can never guarantee it. Money is always useful, but as a resource for a pressure-group it appears to be less valuable than specialised information, good contacts, the absence of organised opposition, favourable publicity, or the power to hinder the administrative process by withholding co-operation. The expensive campaigns against the nationalisation of road haulage and sugar appear to have achieved nothing. The free publicity the teachers got from their threat of direct action was much more extensive and helpful than the publicity they paid for. There is no money in penal reform, but the Howard League has exercised a good deal of influence over the years. The weekend walkers who formed the Friends of the Lake District have fought successful battles against industrial firms and the Central Electricity Generating Board. The spokesmen for Welsh dinghy sailors and yachtsmen took on the Standard Oil Company with the result that the Company modified its plans to build a harbour and oil refinery at Milford Haven so as to preserve the facilities for sailing in the estuary.

Secondly, one of the most familiar justifications for democratic government is that only the wearer knows where the shoe pinches. When citizens vote at a general election they express their feelings about the impact of government policy only in the most general and undifferentiated fashion. A much more specific, and therefore more valuable, reaction from the 'consumers' is obtained when trade unionists demand improvements in working conditions and safety regulations, when industrialists suggest ways in which government policy can help them to compete in export markets, or when motorists and road hauliers draw attention to the need for new roads. Information, and therefore pressure, of these kinds is essential if government is to adapt itself to meet the varying needs of society, and this is as true in a democracy as in any other kind of political system.

Of course, these pressures are sectional pressures and other consid-erations must also be borne in mind by policy-makers. Group spokes-men commonly believe that what they are advocating is in the interest of the whole community as well as that of their group, but their view of the public interest tends to be rather one-sided. Often their claims will be checked by the demands of rival groups, but this does not always happen: for instance, no organised group has opposed the claims of British farmers. However, it is the essential task of policy-makers, with which all senior civil servants and ministers are familiar, to balance the claims of rival groups and to consider them all in the context of wider considerations such as the level of government expenditure and the accepted aims of social policy. If policy-makers fail in this task, it is they who are to be blamed (as it is they who must face the conse-quences of their decisions), not the spokesmen who put forward the views of groups of citizens.

In practice, of course, policy-makers often do fail in this task, either because their predictions and judgement are faulty, or because they try to please too many groups for electoral reasons, or simply because some groups enjoy so much influence that they distort the balance of the system. Which groups enjoy 'too much power' is a contentious question, for the answer inevitably involves value judgements. How-ever, there are some groups in some periods that are widely agreed to be in this position. In the United States in the 1960s and 1970s, for instance, the success of the National Rifle Association in blocking effective gun-control laws was clearly contrary to the interests of American society, and polls show that a majority of American citizens recognise this to be the case. In Britain in the same period, the trade unions were the groups that enjoyed too much influence, in the view of the majority. In national surveys conducted in 1966, 1969 and 1970, between 64 and 66 per cent of respondents agreed that 'trade unions have too much power'.[2] In a survey conducted in nine urban areas in 1979, 80 per cent of respondents agreed with this proposition, includ-ing 70 per cent of Labour Party supporters.[3] The argument that pressure-groups are a desirable and necessary feature of British demo-cracy should not be thought to imply that the pressure-group system is free of problems.

NOTES

1   See S. E. Finer, *Anonymous Empire*, 2nd edn (Pall Mall Press, 1966), pp. 94–5.
2   David Butler and Donald Stokes, *Political Change in Britain*, 2nd edn (Macmillan, 1974), p. 198.
3   *New Statesman*, 11 May, 1979.

FURTHER READING

The best introduction to the role of the group spokesmen is S. E. Finer, *Anonymous Empire,* 2nd edn (Pall Mall Press, 1966); a discussion of channels for the communication of pressures will be found in A. H. Birch, *Representative and Responsible Government* (Allen & Unwin, 1964), chs 15 and 16; and there are numerous case-studies, of which the following deserve mention because they illustrate the activities of different types of pressure group: Harry Eckstein, *Pressure Group Politics* (Allen & Unwin, 1960); P. G. Richards, *Parliament and Conscience* (Allen & Unwin, 1970); Maurice Kogan, *Educational Policy-Making* (Allen & Unwin, 1975); and Denis Barnes and Eileen Reid, *Governments and Trade Unions: The British Experience 1964–79* (Heinemann, 1980).

Chapter 7

Political Parties

THE NATURE OF BRITISH PARTIES

In all democratic countries the development of liberal institutions has been accompanied by the growth of organised political parties, who act as essential intermediaries between the public and the Government. Their functions are numerous and vital. They encourage popular interest and participation in politics; they select candidates for political office and campaign on their behalf; they reflect and moderate the interests and views of diverse groups within society; they discuss issues and formulate policies; and they provide both organised support for the Government of the day and organised opposition to it.

Although all democratic countries have party systems, the differences between countries and between parties are very great. In some countries there is normally a multi-party system in which several parties jostle for influence and no one has a majority. In other countries the political scene is normally dominated by the conflict between two large parties which dwarf their minor rivals. Some parties have mass memberships with branches in every area, while others are organisations of politicians who do not try to recruit members on a large scale. Some parties are highly centralised, while others are loose alliances of local groups. Some parties are committed to a specific ideology, while others are almost entirely pragmatic in their approach to questions of policy. It is therefore appropriate to begin this chapter by outlining the salient characteristics of the British party system.

The first point to note is that in the modern era the British political scene has normally been dominated by two parties. From 1832 to 1918 the dominant parties were the Conservatives on one hand and the Whigs or Liberals on the other. There followed a transitional period of six years during which the Labour Party replaced the Liberals as the main party of reform, and since 1924 Parliament has been dominated by the Conservative and Labour Parties, with the leader of one as Prime Minister and the leader of the other occupying the salaried office of Leader of the Opposition.

The decline of the Liberals after 1918 surprised many because at that time they could look back on a period of great achievement. They had been largely responsible for a series of reforms which had democratised the representative system and transformed the administrative system; they had deprived the House of Lords of its power to veto legislation passed by the Commons; and they had laid the foundations of the modern Welfare State with the introduction of health insurance, unemployment insurance, and old-age pensions. They had every reason to claim that they were the party of progress and reform, and their spectacular decline after the war shocked impartial observers as well as the Liberals themselves.

The main reasons for the decline, however, are now fairly clear. First, the Liberals fell between two stools in their reactions to the new political situation created by the enfranchisement of the majority of working-class men in 1867 and 1884. They were sufficiently radical in their speeches and some of their social policies to frighten away most of the business groups who had previously supported them, who one by one switched their allegiance to the Conservative Party. On the other hand, they remained too much of a middle-class party to prevent the establishment in 1900 of the Labour Representation Committee, which became the Labour Party six years later. Secondly, the Liberals were seriously divided by Gladstone's policy of Home Rule for Ireland, which alienated many of their supporters and drove some of their leaders to cross the floor and join the Conservative ranks. Thirdly, the Liberals lost the three main issues which had rallied their supporters in the second half of the nineteenth century. Parliamentary reform ceased to be an issue after 1918 because all the main objectives of the reform movement were achieved; free trade ceased to be a helpful issue since its economic advantages for Britain were a matter of serious controversy after 1918; and economy and the limitation of government activities ceased to be Liberal policies altogether. Finally, the split between Lloyd George and Asquith during the war had a fatal effect on the Party's subsequent fortunes: after the war Asquith lost his seat in the 1918 election, while Lloyd George compromised the radical reputation he had gained through his pre-war social policies by presiding over a coalition Government dominated by the Conservatives.

Weakened in all these ways, the Liberal Party was in no condition to withstand the challenge of the Labour Party, backed by the trade unions and claiming to be the only true defender of working-class interests. But what is interesting is the rapidity of Labour's success. While at the end of the war the Liberals held 260 seats to Labour's 39, only four years later they were overtaken by Labour, and in the election of October 1924 Labour won 151 seats to the Liberal Party's 40. It is clear that the British electoral system did not act as a serious obstacle to the realignment of parties in this period. On the contrary, the system shortened the process of transition: under a system of proportional representation the Liberal Party would have retained far more seats than it did in 1924 and would still be a force to be reckoned with.

The second point to note about the British party system is that the main parties are parties of mass membership, having branches in every part of the country and collecting monthly or annual subscriptions from their millions of members. The Conservative Party has between 1·5 and 2 million members, paying annual subscriptions which vary widely according to the inclinations and income of the member. The Labour Party has less than half a million individual members but it has also over 5 million affiliated members, who subscribe through their trade unions. The subscriptions of affiliated members are small, but they add up to an appreciable sum. Labour Party accounts show that over 80 per cent of its income comes from the trade unions.

These membership figures are extremely high by international standards. The total of over 7 million subscribers in England and Wales amounts to nearly a quarter of the electorate, and this does not include members of the smaller parties. There is probably no other country in which as large a proportion of the electors subscribe regularly to political parties.

Of course these figures give a somewhat exaggerated impression of the degree of political interest and activity in the country. Trade unionists belonging to unions which are affiliated to the Labour Party pay the political levy unless they 'contract out' of doing so; and surveys suggest that at least half of the present affiliated members subscribe more because of inertia than because of deliberate choice. If allowance is made for this, the proportion of the electors who subscribe to one or other of the two main parties by deliberate choice is reduced to about 15 per cent of the electorate. Many of these do nothing apart from subscribe; many others take part only in social and fund-raising activities like whist drives, dances, garden parties, and drinking in the political clubs that flourish in industrial areas; and only a minority are active in party organisation or in electoral campaigning. The size of this minority varies from area to area and party to party. In the Labour Party very few of the affiliated members do any political work, but the proportion of individual members who do is considerably greater than in the Conservative associations, so that over the whole country the number of voluntary workers available to each party at election time is not so different as the membership figures would suggest. The studies of Greenwich and Glossop suggest that about 1 per cent of the electorate are willing to do voluntary work during the elections, which would produce an average of about 500 workers per constituency if this were the general pattern. The number who actually turn out is probably a little less than this, but as paid canvassers are not permitted in British elections these party workers fulfil an important function during the campaign.

The parties are very different in social composition. Labour Party members are overwhelmingly working-class, though the officers of the local branches are often drawn from the ranks of white-collar workers whose skills equip them for organisational work. Labour Party members are thus similar in social background and type of occupation to Labour voters but different from Labour MPs and national leaders, the majority of whom are drawn from the white-collar and professional classes. Conservative members, on the other hand, are like Conservative MPs and leaders in being overwhelmingly middle-class or (to a much smaller extent) upper-class. The Conservative working men who provide almost half of the Party's votes rarely join Conservative associations, not because they are deliberately excluded but because, by and large, they would not feel at home there. The composition of the parties therefore provides some basis for the common stereotype of British politics as being dominated by class rivalries.

A third characteristic of the British party system is that the parties are highly centralised. In the United States the real party managers operate at state and local level, and the national parties are no more than loose alliances formed for electoral purposes. But in Britain the local party branches have little real power except over the nomination of candidates, and even in this they are subject to the veto of head office. Local branches are encouraged to discuss questions of policy and to send in resolutions for debate at the annual conference, but in practice their influence on national party policy is slight.

Finally, it may be asked how far the British parties are committed to ideological objectives. Clearly there are wide variations between parties in this respect. The Communist Party in any country is an example of a party based on an ideology, which means that the party's policies are shaped by a distinctive set of beliefs and are justified in terms of the ideology which embodies these beliefs. The main American parties, on the other hand, are almost entirely pragmatic, each claiming to be in pursuit of ideals which are shared by American society as a whole and neither having a set of policies or beliefs which clearly distinguishes it from the other.

The British parties have names which indicate a degree of ideological commitment. Equally, it is possible to make some generalisations about the beliefs which their leading members hold, so that if it is known that a man is a leading member of a certain party it can be predicted with some chance of success that he will adopt this kind of view about that kind of issue. On the other hand, the policies pursued by the parties when in power are not strikingly different from one another, and research suggests that a party's supporters in the country are apt to disagree among themselves almost as much as they disagree with the supporters of the other party. It would seem therefore that

British parties can best be characterised as 'semi-ideological', but the whole question of party doctrines and policies will be explored later in this chapter.

THE ORGANISATION OF THE CONSERVATIVE AND LABOUR PARTIES

The two parties which now dominate British political life are very different in their origins and their social bases, and their organisational structures reflect these differences. The Conservative Party existed as a group of MPs and peers for many years before national party organisations developed, and when Conservative associations were formed in the country to work for Conservative candidates these had some of the characteristics of 'supporters' clubs', being primarily concerned with raising money and getting out the vote. To this day only MPs and peers are members of the Conservative Party, properly so-called, while the two million or more subscribers belong to local Conservative associations which are affiliated to a body known as the National Union of Conservative and Unionist Associations. The National Union discusses questions of party policy at its annual conference and elsewhere but it does not have any formal power to make decisions or even recommendations about policy, since in the Conservative Party policy decisions are entirely the prerogative of the Party Leader. The function of the National Union is to support the Party, not to control it, although Conservative politicians will naturally be aware of views current among Party supporters and will sometimes be influenced by them. Two other national organisations are the Conservative Central Office, which is responsible for national publicity and for arranging speakers' tours, and the Conservative Research Department. Each of these is directed by a Chairman who is appointed by and responsible to the Party Leader.

The Labour Party was formed as the political wing of the trade union movement with the object of securing working-class representation in Parliament. In a sense the formal relationship between the Labour MPs and the mass movement is the opposite of that which prevails among Conservatives: the Conservative mass movement exists to serve the interests of the Parliamentarians, whereas the function of Labour MPs is to serve the interests of the Labour movement. The democratic principles of organisation which characterise the trade union movement are extended to the Labour Party: the Annual Conference has (in principle) supreme authority to decide Party policy, while the National Executive Committee takes policy decisions between conferences and Labour MPs are charged with the duty of advancing Party policy in

Parliament. The entire organisation is known as the Labour Party, and the parliamentary group is called the Parliamentary Labour Party. The leader is officially only the Leader of the Parliamentary Labour Party, he holds his position subject to annual election, and – in complete contrast to the position of the Conservative Leader – his formal powers are very slight.

Until 1965 there was a substantial difference between the methods by which the parties selected their leaders. The Labour Party, believing in open decisions openly arrived at, has always regarded the counting of heads as the only proper way to choose a leader. He is elected by a simple majority of Labour MPs, it being provided that if nobody gets a majority of votes the candidate with the fewest votes will be eliminated and a further ballot held, and so on until one candidate gets an absolute majority. In the Conservative Party, on the other hand, it was felt that an open contest for the leadership was inappropriate. There was formal provision for election by a body consisting of Conservative MPs and peers, prospective Conservative candidates and the Executive Committee of the National Union of Conservative Associations, but in practice this large body simply elected by acclamation the single candidate who was presented to it. This candidate was selected by a process of private consultation among the elder statesmen of the Party, and normally he did not appear before the Party Meeting until after he had taken office as Prime Minister. If the change occurred while the Conservatives were in power, the new Prime Minister would be appointed by the monarch either on the advice of the retiring Prime Minister or on the advice of senior Conservative Privy Councillors. If the Conservative Leader resigned or died while the Party was in opposition, the practice was for the Party simply to appoint a parliamentary leader in the Commons and another in the Lords, deferring the selection of Party Leader until victory at the polls had brought the Party back to power, when the man appointed as Prime Minister would also be appointed to the leadership.

This system of selection was changed as a consequence of the events of 1963. From about 1960 onwards it had been expected that Macmillan's successor would be one of three much younger men: Edward Heath, Iain MacLeod and Reginald Maudling. Unfortunately for the Party, Macmillan's retirement was precipitated by his illness so that the contest was thrown open before any of the three had the standing and seniority within the Party that was expected of a new Leader. Equally unfortunately, the retirement was announced while the Annual Conference of the Party was in session in Blackpool, and the result was an undignified public contest between three older men, which was eventually resolved in favour of Lord Home (who renounced his peerage and became Sir Alec Douglas-Home). This unseemly spectacle damaged the public image of the Party and led the Party's leaders to decide that it was time to revise the selection procedure.

The new procedure was introduced in March 1965, and is remarkably similar to that used by the Labour Party. The leader is now elected at a meeting of Conservative MPS, provision being made for more than one ballot. To be elected on the first ballot a candidate has to receive both an overall majority and 15 per cent more of the votes cast than any other candidate. Thus, if 300 MPS voted and there were only two candidates, one of them would have to get 173 votes to win. If no candidate does as well as this, a second ballot is held between two and four days later. New nominations are required for this, a provision which encourages consultation and negotiation. In the second ballot an overall majority is sufficient for election. If no candidate were to get an overall majority, the three leading candidates would be entered for a third ballot, in which MPS would record their first and second preferences. The normal system of transferring the second preferences of the least-popular candidate would then produce an overall majority for one man, who would be elected. The chosen leader has to be endorsed by the full Party Meeting, constituted as it always has been, but this is simply a matter of acclamation.

This new procedure was used for the first time in July 1965, when Douglas-Home retired. Three candidates were nominated, and Edward Heath was elected on the second ballot. The procedure was used again in February 1975, when Heath was forced by internal party pressures to put himself up for re-election and was defeated by Margaret Thatcher.

This new procedure brings the parties very close to one another in their means of selecting a leader, but they differ in the degree of security which leaders enjoy once they are chosen. In view of the greater importance that the Labour Party has always attached to the principle of intra-party democracy, it is somewhat paradoxical to note that in practice the Labour leader is much more secure than his Conservative opponent. Of the six Labour leaders before James Callaghan only George Lansbury was forced out of office by criticisms within the party. Of the others, MacDonald effectively excluded himself by forming a coalition government with the Conservatives and Liberals against the opposition of most Labour MPS; Henderson lost his seat in an election; Attlee and Wilson resigned at times of their own choice; and Gaitskell died in office. Of the ten Conservative leaders before Margaret Thatcher, no fewer than five were forced out of office by party pressures, namely, Balfour, Austen Chamberlain, Neville Chamberlain, Douglas-Home and Heath. In view of this record it would seem that the recent democratisation of the Conservative Party (whose leader now has to stand for re-election every year) is unlikely to have made the leader any less secure than he was under the old system. As is so often the case in politics, institutional arrangements are a poor guide to practice.

In the sphere of policy-making the constitutions of the parties suggest a sharp contrast between Conservative and Labour arrangements. In the Conservative Party policy-making is officially the prerogative of the Party Leader, who does not have to report either to an executive committee or to the annual conference of the National Union. The stated function of the National Union is to support the Leader and his parliamentary colleagues, not to engage in argument with them about matters of policy.

In the Labour Party, in the words of an official statement: 'The Parliamentary Party is one centre of decision-making, the National Executive Committee another and the Annual Conference a third. Policy therefore cannot be laid down: it must be agreed.[1] In this process the official powers of the Parliamentary Leader are not great. He does not take the chair at either the Executive Committee or the Annual Conference, and he has very little influence over the composition of the Executive Committee, whose members are elected at the Conference.

These formal differences are reinforced by ideological differences. The true Conservative believes that politics is an art rather than a science, that the function of the Government is to adjust its measures to changing circumstances and needs, and that since each issue must be judged on its merits when it arises the best course is to give the leader authority to do what is thought necessary. The helmsman must have full control over his crew; if he frequently misjudges the wind or the tide it may be necessary to replace him; but, good or poor, he is more likely to keep the ship on an even keel if he has the power to adjust its course to the weather than he would be if his actions were supervised by a committee or mass meeting.

The true socialist, on the other hand, believes both that policies should be planned in advance and that leaders should be controlled by the mass movement. The principle is that policy questions should be discussed at length within the movement; that a properly constituted conference should take decisions by open vote after a free discussion; and that the Party leaders should then regard themselves as mandated to pursue the policies argued upon. This principle is accepted in the British trade union movement, and it is thought appropriate that the Labour Party should act in the same way.

In practice, as R. T. McKenzie has pointed out, neither party conforms to these canons. No matter what party he leads, a party leader is at the centre of an intricate network of communication channels, through each one of which pressures are applied which bear upon his actions. If he is Prime Minister, the most influential pressures will come from within the administration and the most important policy decisions will be taken by the Cabinet. Whether he is in power or in opposition, he is subject to pressures from backbenchers, from his party organisation, from group spokesmen, and from the annual conference which reflects the views of voluntary workers on whom his party depends for success at the next election. The differences between the positions of Conservative and Labour Prime Ministers cannot be adequately summarised by suggesting that one can dictate to his party on policy questions while the other is a servant of his party.

On the other hand, as Richard Rose has stressed, the differences cannot be ignored.[2] The Conservative leader can be checked by his Cabinet and, in the last resort, can be deposed by a revolt of backbench MPs. But he does not have to face any rival centre of power within his party. The party organisation is firmly under his control, and resolutions passed by the conference of the National Union can be ignored if they are inconvenient. Labour's parliamentary leader, in contrast, does not control either the National Executive Committee or the Annual Conference, both of which are dominated by trade union representatives. The Parliamentary Party does not have to obey resolutions passed by the extra-parliamentary bodies, but it cannot ignore them. Thus, when the 1960 Annual Conference passed a motion in favour of nuclear disarmament and the rejection of NATO defence policy, Hugh Gaitskell declared that he had no intention of changing the policies of the Parliamentary Party to conform to the wishes of Conference; but he also spent much of his time during the following year persuading the trade unions to rescind the motion at the 1961 Conference.

The Labour leader tends to have more power in relation to the NEC and the Annual Conference when Labour is in power than when it is in opposition, because he can claim that a rejection of a Labour government's policies by its own supporters would have an adverse effect on the Party's image. However, between 1974 and 1979 this appeal was rejected on several occasions, and the Government's authority was weakened in consequence. Whether this intra-party conflict will continue in the future depends on whether union representatives continue to be markedly more militant and more left-wing than the parliamentary leadership.

PARTY DOCTRINES AND POLICIES

Being semi-ideological, the British parties aim not only at putting their own leaders into power but also at shaping government policy in ways which accord with their own beliefs and attitudes. There are three ways of discovering the nature of the differences between the doctrines and policies of the two main parties, each of which will be pursued below. One way is to study the manifestoes and other publicity put out by the parties so as to get an impression of how they see themselves. Another way is to analyse the opinions of voters so as to get an idea of what the ordinary citizen thinks the parties stand for. A third way is to study the policies pursued by the leaders of the parties in Parliament.

If we consult party propaganda and essays written by party publicists, we find that both parties regard themselves as standing for particular principles of political action that have been defined and interpreted over the years by political thinkers and leaders whose writings form part of the heritage of the party. Since Labour principles are easier to grasp than Conservative principles, it will be convenient to discuss them in that order.

The Labour Party's picture of itself is of a party of idealists, dedicated to the brotherhood of man, to the pursuit of world peace, and to the principles of democratic socialism. The socialist objective is to use the power of the State to reconstruct society in such a way that class differences will be abolished, the national income will be distributed more equally among citizens, and the injustice and exploitation which socialists associate with the capitalist system will be replaced by a happier and more just set of social relationships. In the formative period of the Labour Party its leaders accepted the Marxist belief that the root of most social evils was the private ownership of the means of production, and public ownership was therefore written into the constitution as one of the objects of the Party.

Recent developments have led the Party to retreat from a policy of full public ownership, but the spirit of the original programme remains intact in Labour propaganda. 'Our claim to the office', states a 1961 pamphlet, 'is not just that we can manage things better than the Conservatives; we aim to create a different and better society.' The principles to which the Party pays homage today can be gauged from the following selection of extracts from a statement on 'Labour's Aims' approved by the National Executive Committee in March 1960.

> The British Labour Party is a democratic socialist party. Its central idea is the brotherhood of man. Its purpose is to make this ideal a reality everywhere. Accordingly –
>
> a. It rejects discrimination on grounds of race, colour, or creed. . . .
> b. . . . it stands for the right of all peoples to freedom, independence and self-government.

c.   . . . it seeks to build a world order within which all live in peace. . . .

d.   . . . it affirms the duty of richer nations to assist poorer nations. . . .

e.   It stands for social justice, for a society in which the claims of those in hardship or distress come first. . . .

f.   . . . it rejects the selfish, acquisitive doctrines of capitalism, and strives to create instead a socialist community based on fellowship, co-operation and service. . . .

g.   Its aim is a classless society from which all class barriers and false social values have been eliminated.

h.   It holds that . . . the nation's economy should be planned. . . .

i.   It stands for democracy in industry. . . .

j.   It is convinced that these social and economic objectives can be achieved only through an expansion of common ownership substantial enough to give the community power over the commanding heights of the economy. . . .

Conservative ideas are very different from these and rather more subtle. The following outline does not do them justice but will serve as a brief guide. First, Conservatives do not believe that politics is the most important of human activities or that political action is the best way to improve society. Government is recognised to be necessary to maintain a framework of order, but because governments impose their will by the threat and sometimes the application of force an extension of their activities is not thought to be the most promising way of improving the quality of life. In Conservative eyes the onus of proof rests with those who wish to extend the powers of government, not with those who wish to restrict them. Regulations and controls and even public ownership may be needed to meet particular problems, but Conservatives believe citizens should be left in freedom to do as they please whenever possible. This belief was reflected in slogans like 'Trust the people' and 'Set the people free' which were used when the 1945 Labour Government was in office. 'If people want a sense of purpose,' Harold Macmillan once said, 'they should get it from their archbishops. They should certainly not get it from their politicians.'

Secondly, Conservatives do not think that abstract principles can ever be a good guide to political action. The variety of human ambitions and the diversity of human talents are such, they believe, that the proper function of political leaders is not to induce citizens to conform to a blueprint worked out in advance but to adjust the policies of the Government to meet the changing needs and demands of the citizens. A pattern of government activities may emerge, but the approach should be 'from the particular to the general, from the view that such and such an arrangement, having proved appropriate to the catering industry, may be applied in a modified form to the grocery trade, not . . . from the general to the particular, e.g. from the view that property should be public to the view that ICI should be nationalised'.[3]

Third, Conservatives support the free-enterprise system and believe that a certain degree of social and economic inequality is inevitable. Their economic policy is to improve the efficiency of private enterprise while shielding the less-privileged sections of the community from exploitation. Their social policy is summarised in the phrase 'the ladder and the safety net': they want to give opportunities to all, while maintaining a safety net of social services for those who are less successful.

THE PARTIES AS SEEN BY ELECTORS

If we turn from the doctrines and propaganda of the parties to the views of the electors about the parties, we enter a different world. Only a minority of electors perceive the parties in the terms that the parties see themselves. The approach of the average British voter to politics is not ideological and the fact that he supports a party does not mean either that he agrees with all that party's policies or even that he conceives of the parties primarily in terms of the policies for which they stand.

If voters are asked what the parties stand for, the answers are confused and contradictory on most particular issues but show a broad measure of agreement on one general issue. This is, to put it crudely, that the Labour Party stands for the working classes and the Conservative Party for the middle and upper classes. In 1959 and 1960 two surveys were conducted in which fairly large samples of electors were shown various statements and asked to which party or parties the statements applied. In each case the statements which produced the clearest differentiation between the parties were 'stands mainly for the working class' and 'stands mainly for the middle [or, in one survey, upper] classes'. The other statements which most Labour supporters thought applied to their party only were:

Is out to help the underdog.
Is out to raise the standard of living of ordinary people.
Would try to abolish class differences.
Would extend the welfare services.

The other statements which most Conservative supporters thought applied to their party only were:

Would make the country more prosperous.
Out for the nation as a whole.
Really respects British traditions.
Is most satisfying for the man with ideals.[4]

That is, supporters of both parties agreed that the main conflict between the parties was in their sympathy with the interests of different social classes. Labour supporters saw party politics almost entirely in these terms, feeling that all the distinctive merits of their party were related to the advancement of working-class interests (which included the extension of welfare services designed to help poorer people). Conservative supporters, on the other hand, saw no conflict between the interests of the middle and upper classes and the interests of the nation as a whole, and consequently saw their party as the best defender of national interests.

It has been argued by some critics that, as the salience of class conflict has declined since the 1950s, this difference between the public image of the two parties is bound to be to the long-term disadvantage of the Labour Party. However, while the logic of this argument is clear, there are several complicating factors which may invalidate the prediction.

The first complicating factor is that the statistics showing an overall decline in public perception of the significance of class conflict, already mentioned in Chapter 5, are aggregate statistics which conceal sharp differences between different sections of the community. In 1970 a survey revealed that, while only 25 per cent of middle-class Conservative voters believed that politics was about the representation of class interests, no fewer than 84 per cent of working-class Labour voters held this belief.[5] Secondly, although the real income of the British people increased fairly steadily from 1845 to 1973, it declined slightly between 1973 and 1979. A decline in living standards necessarily sharpens group and class rivalries, particularly when it shatters the expectations created by three decades of increasing prosperity. The increased militancy of British trade unions in the 1970s is a symptom of these sharpened rivalries. And while they do not necessarily follow the traditional lines of class conflict, for many of them are between groups of workers, they are likely to prevent class loyalties and resentments from fading away.

A third factor is that voters are only influenced to a limited degree by the images they hold of what the parties stand for. Repeated surveys of voting behaviour suggest that, on the whole, floating voters are more likely to be influenced by their impressions of the competence of the parties when in power – i.e. by their ability to deliver the goods in terms of attractive policy outcomes. Statistics show that public perceptions of the competence of the parties fluctuate widely and rapidly. The Conservatives are consistently thought to be better than the Labour Party in their handling of foreign policy and national defence. But the volatility of public opinion in regard to domestic issues is indicated by Table 7.1, summarising the answer to the same question in three successive nationwide surveys.

Table 7.1   *The Attribution of Blame for Britain's Economic Difficulties*

Government mostly at fault	1966	1969	1970
	%	%	%
Labour Government	13	29	25
Last Conservative Government	43	21	33
Both equally	30	38	29
Do not know	14	12	13

Source: David Butler and Donald Stokes, *Political Change in Britain,* 2nd edn (Macmillan, 1974), p. 456.

PARTY POLICIES IN PRACTICE

The policies actually pursued by the parties when in government have shown less difference than might be expected from reading their propaganda, but the extent of the difference has fluctuated over the years. It was considerable between 1945 and 1950; was very small between 1950 and 1964; grew a little sharper between 1964 and 1970; and has again become considerable since 1970.

During the thirteen years of Conservative rule from 1951 onwards there were remarkably few areas of major disagreement between the parties. There was no real disagreement on foreign affairs except in relation to the Suez crisis, and in 1964 Harold Wilson went out of his way to emphasise Labour's support for the Government's policies in Malaysia and southern Arabia, both of which were involving British troops in dangerous hostilities for causes which the ordinary British citizen was bound to find somewhat obscure. There was no major disagreement on defence policy until 1964, when the Labour Party announced that it would abandon the independent nuclear deterrent if it were returned to power, but when it won the 1964 election it made no attempt to honour this pledge. There was very little disagreement about the dramatic developments in colonial policy which resulted in the achievement of independence by almost all Britain's former colonies.

Turning to domestic affairs, there was general accord on the Health Service and the other social services, with some competition between the parties in promising more generous schemes of pensions and superannuation. There was disagreement about housing when the Government passed legislation in 1957 freeing a small proportion of houses from rent restriction and allowing rent increases in others, but the heat was taken out of the argument when the Conservatives gave an undertaking just before the 1959 election that they would make no further moves to decontrol rented property. There was a lively but short dispute about the control of immigration from Commonwealth countries which died a rapid death when the Labour Government appointed in 1964 decided not only to continue but to tighten the restrictions imposed by the Conservatives. There was a difference of view about the merits of comprehensive schools, but until 1964 there was no conflict at the national level since both parties agreed that local authorities should have freedom to experiment with comprehensive and other types of school. There was very little difference in economic policy.

This lack of contrast between the policies of the parties led many observers to suggest that the country had entered a period of consensus, in which elections simply decide which team of politicians would administer the policies on which everyone was substantially agreed. However, this conclusion was premature. Harold Wilson, who became leader of the Parliamentary Labour Party when Gaitskell died in 1963, was determined to give the Party a more radical image. From 1964 to 1970 his government launched a succession of experiments and reforms. A National Economic Plan was commissioned; industrial mergers were promoted by the Government; there was compulsory control of prices and incomes; the civil service was reformed; government departments were restructured and retitled; the transformation of the system of secondary education was begun. The impact of these changes on parliamentary and public opinion was heightened by the personal style of the Prime Minister – restless, voluble, abrasive and well calculated to secure maximum publicity.

It should be noted, however, that only a few of this Government's reforms were distinctively socialist in character. The steel industry was renationalised and government ownership of bus companies was extended. Rent control was extended to all property and rent tribunals were established which had power to lower rents if they were deemed to be too high. Local authorities were instructed to develop a system of comprehensive schools, whether they wanted to or not. The other reforms were made in the interest of efficiency rather than socialism, and were not very successful. The National Economic Plan was outdated by the time it was published and was never implemented. The restructuring of government departments made little difference. The restructuring of the motor industry produced British Leyland, which collapsed in 1975. The compulsory control of incomes proved highly unpopular, and Wilson vowed publicly never to repeat it; commenting (in characteristic style) that 'you only lose your virginity once'. The final year of this Government was dominated by two ambitious but abortive attempts to modernise British institutions. One was the attempt to modernise the House of Lords, which has been described in Chapter 4. The other was an attempt to create a new legal framework for the conduct of industrial relations, which was abandoned in face of protests from within the Labour Movement.

The Conservative Government elected in 1970 came to power with a team of new leaders and a determination to change things. Edward Heath said: 'We were returned to office to change the course and the history of this nation, nothing else.' This did not mean that the Conservatives intended to put the clock back by repealing reforms introduced by Labour. On the contrary, the new Government accepted the nationalisation of steel and bus transport, accepted the reform of secondary education, and nationalised Rolls-Royce when that company faced bankruptcy in early 1971. The object of the Conservatives was reform, not reaction or conservation, and the most sweeping of the reforms they introduced were Britain's entry to the European Economic Community, the transformation of the whole system of subsidies for rented dwellings, and the establishment of an entirely new legal framework for the conduct of industrial relations.

These reforms were not specifically right-wing in character. The application to join the EEC was a renewal of the application that had been made unsuccessfully by the Labour Government. The Housing Finance Act transferred the subsidy from the house to the tenant. By imposing a means test it removed subsidies from the wealthier tenants of municipal dwellings, but it also gave subsidies for the first time to the poorer tenants of privately owned dwellings. It could thus be regarded as a reform in the interest of social justice. The 1971 Industrial Relations Act was similar in its objects and principles to the measure which the Labour Government had drafted in 1969. However, in the political atmosphere of the 1970s all these changes were passionately denounced by the trade unions and the Labour Party, Harold Wilson being compelled to turn a somersault on the question of the EEC by the strength of opinion within the Labour Movement. The refusal of trade unions to comply with the provisions of the Industrial Relations Act played a major part in the eventual downfall of the Conservative Government, and the Labour Government elected in 1974 repealed nearly all the Acts that had been passed in the previous four years, with the significant exception of British membership of the EEC.

During the 1970s the two main parties have therefore been at loggerheads. However, the differences between them do not correspond to the ideological differences expounded in their propaganda and in the writings of their theorists. Labour policies since 1964 cannot be distinguished from Conservative policies in terms of the statement on 'Labour's Aims' quoted above. Labour leaders have not shown any greater concern than Conservative leaders to promote the brotherhood of man, to safeguard peace, to help poorer nations, or to create 'a socialist community based on fellowship, co-operation and service'. They have been more concerned to promote economic efficiency, restrain wage claims, and tax the middle classes. Equally, Conservative policies under Heath did not have the somewhat passive quality suggested by Conservative philosophers. They were more concerned to use the power of the State to promote efficiency, restrain wage claims, and lead the British people towards European integration. They did not succeed, but these were their intentions.

It can therefore be argued that the parties have moved closer together in their objectives. Equally, they have been somewhat similar in both their efforts and their failures to improve economic efficiency. In view of this partial convergence, it may seem surprising that relations between them have become more abrasive and hostile. To explain this, three other factors (plus the personalities of their leaders) have to be invoked.

One factor was the fury of the trade unions at having their activities regulated by the Industrial Relations Act. Having defeated the Labour Government's attempt to introduce such legislation, the unions were in no mood to accept the Conservative version, and they deliberately defied the law to make the Act unworkable. For the first time since the war (and arguably for the first time ever) Labour's parliamentary leaders found that union leaders and committees of shop stewards had completely pre-empted the right to make policy for the Labour Movement.

A second new factor was the use of the budget and the social insurance system to effect the distribution of after-tax incomes in a period of economic decline. When Denis Healey became Chancellor of the Exchequer in 1974 he announced that one of his objects was to squeeze the middle classes until they howled with anguish. He achieved this object with complete success, and his policies also upset some of the higher-paid industrial workers. In a period of economic growth redistributive fiscal policies mean that the better paid gain less than other groups, but in a period of no growth (such as 1974–9) such policies can only mean that some groups suffer an actual reduction in real income, which inevitably causes resentment.

The other new factor is that since the oil crisis of 1973 British affairs

have been dominated by the triple economic problems of rapid inflation, high unemployment and low productivity. By general agreement,
there has been little the Government could do to reduce unemployment or raise productivity in the short run. Public attention has
therefore been concentrated on the struggle to reduce inflation, which
both main parties have claimed to be within their power. Without
economic growth, inflation can only be contained if wage rises are kept
to a minimum, so the government of the day (of whatever party) finds
its economic strategy dependent on union restraint or co-operation.
The absence of restraint in 1975 resulted in inflation of over 25 per
cent in one year; the breakdown of co-operation in the winter of
1978–9 resulted in a series of bitter strikes as various unions struggled
to grab a larger slice of a non-expanding cake for their own members.

The combined consequence of these three factors is that the conflict
between the two main parties in the 1970s was essentially a reflection
of class conflict and sectional conflicts between different groups of
workers. The somewhat simplistic views of electors about the parties
reported a few pages earlier are a better guide to recent practice than
the images the parties have of themselves, not because party leaders
are particularly cynical but because economic developments and trade
union policies have had this impact on the political scene.

THE SMALLER PARTIES

The most important of the smaller parties is the Liberal Party. It has
existed for well over a century, has constituency branches in all areas of
the country, and has something like a quarter of a million members. It
also has some wealthy supporters whose contributions have enabled it
to contest hundreds of seats, at election after election, which it had no
real chance of winning.

As in the two main parties, the Liberal leader is elected at a meeting
of Liberal MPs. However, he has to report to the Annual Conference,
and in practice the views of the mass organisation probably carry more
weight with the Liberal leadership than is the case in either of the two
main parties. If a party's leaders are in the Cabinet, or expect to be in
the next Cabinet, there is a tendency for the rank-and-file members to
defer to their views except on issues where passions run high. The
Liberal leaders lack this advantage.

In its economic and social policies the Liberal Party lies, as could be
expected, somewhere between the two main parties. It does not believe in the nationalisation of industry but it is committed to industrial
co-partnership, whereby workers could acquire shares and be represented on boards of management. It supports the policies of the

Welfare State and can indeed claim more credit for them than any other party: the original system of social insurance was introduced by the Liberal Government of 1906–14, while the post-1945 reforms and developments were mainly based on the report written in 1943 by Sir William Beveridge, Director of the London School of Economics and a leading Liberal. Equally, the techniques of monetary management which dominated the economic policies of successive governments between 1945 and 1973 were based on the economic theories of John Maynard Keynes, who was a lifelong Liberal. In the election of 1974 the Liberals were the only party to produce a new idea for coping with wage demands, in the form of an ingenious proposal for a tax surcharge to be levied on firms which raised wages and prices.

In other spheres of policy the Liberal Party is distinguished by its consistent idealism and breadth of vision. It gives active support to the United Nations and similar agencies. It campaigns in favour of human rights and civil liberties. It supported British entry to the EEC several years before any other party came round to this view. It has campaigned for the establishment of Scottish and Welsh Assemblies since 1918.

With all these ideas, and the evidence that millions of electors are favourably disposed towards the Liberals, it has to be asked why the Party has been unsuccessful since 1924 and has had only a handful of MPs since 1945. Part of the answer lies in the nature of the British electoral system, which has been discussed in Chapter 5. Another part of the answer is that Liberals tend to be more concerned with their political principles than with the struggle for political power. Their professional staff are rarely given the freedom necessary to function efficiently, for fear that they might become too powerful. An American scholar has said that the Liberals think it 'better to remain in the wilderness and be democratic than to run the risk of giving the professional staff the power requisite to building an effective machine'.[6] The same author reports that:

> In an effort to obtain only those people who are so committed to Liberal principles as to be willing to sacrifice and fight for them, the secretary of the Liberal Central Association discourages any potential candidate who indicates he is interested in standing because he hopes to get into Parliament.[7]

Nor does Liberal strategy seem to be primarily directed towards securing power. As the Liberals see themselves as a radical party their long-term aim must presumably be to replace the Labour Party. This could come about only if the Labour Party were to split or if it were to spend a long period in opposition, during which time a new generation of voters might be won over to the Liberal cause. It follows that the one thing the Liberals should never do is to sustain or strengthen the Labour Party. However, the Liberals refuse to accept the logic of this argument. Their instinctive sympathies lead them to prefer Labour to the Conservatives. When Heath asked the Liberals to join a coalition with the Conservatives in February 1974, the Liberals turned the offer down. Butler and Kavanagh report that 'the mass of the Liberal activists and a majority of the MPs would have recoiled from such a deal'.[8] Three years later, in the summer of 1977, the Liberal MPs agreed to support a minority Labour Government which was highly unpopular in the country and would probably have been forced to call an election without this pledge of assistance. The Liberals did not get any seats in the Cabinet, or any other significant concessions, in return for this crucial support. And by giving it they greatly strengthened the opposition of most Conservative MPs to the pressure group within the Conservative Party which was then advocating the adoption of proportional representation.

It therefore seems evident that the Liberal Party is not willing to adopt the strategy and tactics that are necessary if it is to have any chance of becoming a major party once again. Unless it changes its outlook it is likely to remain with a very small number of MPs, producing ideas which are adopted by one or both of the two main parties.

The other small parties can be dealt with more briefly. The Communist Party, while always contesting a few seats at elections, devotes most of its energy to activities in the trade unions and on the shop floor. The Workers' Revolutionary Party is a Trotskyite organisation which may or may not survive for long. The National Front is an extreme right-wing party whose only significant policy is hostility to Commonwealth immigrants. At the time of writing none of these parties seems likely to win a seat in the House of Commons.

The Scottish National Party (henceforth SNP) and Plaid Cymru (the Welsh equivalent) got their first MPs elected in by-elections in 1967 and 1966 respectively (with the exception of a three-month tenure by an SNP Member in 1945). In 1970 and 1974 they made an impact on general election results for the first time. The SNP won 11 per cent of the Scottish vote and 1 seat in 1970, 22 per cent of the vote and 7 seats in February 1974, 30 per cent of the vote and 11 seats in October 1974. Plaid Cymru, polling between 10 and 11 per cent of the Welsh vote, won 2 seats in February and 3 in October. As already noted, they did less well in 1979.

The aim of both parties is to secure national independence for their countries. They welcome measures of governmental decentralisation, but only as a step on the road towards independence and not as a solution in their own right. The SNP leaders believe that independence would bring not only political benefits to Scotland but also important economic benefits. They think that a Scottish government could regenerate Scottish industry and they know that Scottish control of the North Sea oilfield would bring the country considerable wealth. As the annual production from the oilfield is about ten times as great as Scotland's annual consumption of oil, an independent Scotland could expect to have a healthy surplus on its balance of payments.

The Welsh nationalists are not so concerned about economic issues as their Scottish counterparts. They lay more stress on the cultural advantages that would follow independence, notably a revival of the Welsh language (now spoken by only one-fifth of the Welsh people) and the preservation of a traditional way of life in rural Wales.

In addition to these parties, there are also the Northern Irish parties mentioned in Chapter 5. Until 1972 the Ulster Unionist Party was a firm ally of the British Conservative Party, and supported the Conservative leaders on almost all issues. However, the Ulster Unionists felt betrayed by the 1972 decision of the Conservative Government to suspend the Northern Irish Parliament for an indefinite period, and since then they have acted as an independent group (indeed, sometimes as three independent groups) instead of as Conservative supporters. In 1978 Margaret Thatcher made overtures designed to win back their support, but this may not be easy.

CONCLUSION

Between 1965 and 1975 the British party system changed from being one of three parties to being one of seven parties. A parliamentary system operating with seven parties could normally be expected to produce coalition governments, as happens in several other European democracies. An oddity of the British system, however, is that none of the parties wishes to join in coalition with the others, except that the Conservatives would probably welcome the Ulster Unionists back into the fold so long as they did not insist on unacceptable concessions in regard to Northern Ireland. It therefore seems likely that in the foreseeable future the powers of government will continue to be monopolised by the Conservative and Labour Parties, with the smaller parties using such leverage as they possess to extract piecemeal concessions for the interests they hold dear.

NOTES

1   *Labour in the Sixties* (Labour Party, 1960), p. 19.
2   Richard Rose, *The Problem of Party Government* (Penguin, 1976), pp. 334–7.

3   T. E. Utley, 'The principles of state intervention: a Conservative view', in *Public Law* (Autumn, 1957), p. 206.
4   Mark Abrams and Richard Rose, *Must Labour Lose?* (Penguin, 1960), pp. 12–18, and J. Trenaman and D. McQuail, *Television and the Political Image* (Methuen, 1961), pp. 274–7.
5   David Butler and Donald Stokes, *Political Change in Britain*, 2nd edn (Macmillan, 1974), p. 91.
6   J. S. Rasmussen, *Retrenchment and Revival* (Arizona University Press, 1964), p. 92.
7   ibid., p. 212.
8   *The British General Election of February 1974* (Macmillan, 1975), pp. 257–8.

FURTHER READING

The best general book on British parties is Richard Rose, *The Problem of Party Government* (Penguin, 1976); there are some valuable readings in J. D. Lees and Richard Kimber (eds), *Political Parties in Modern Britain: An Organisational and Functional Guide* (Routledge, 1972); H. M. Drucker, *Doctrine and Ethos in the Labour Party* (Allen & Unwin, 1979), is very helpful; Neill Nugent and Roger King (eds), *The British Right* (Saxon House, 1977), contains useful articles on the Conservative Party; J. S. Rasmussen, *Retrenchment and Revival* (Arizona University Press, 1964), provides a valuable analysis of the Liberal Party; the doctrines and policy statements of the major parties are best studied in books of documents and readings, of which the most useful are probably R. J. White (ed.), *The Conservative Tradition* (A. & C. Black, 1964); Frank Bealey (ed.), *The Social and Political Thought of the British Labour Party* (Weidenfeld, 1970); Alan Beattie (ed.), *English Party Politics*, Vol. II (Weidenfeld, 1970); and F. W. Craig (ed.), *British General Election Manifestos, 1918–74* (Political Reference Publications, 1975). The best single book on the minor parties is George Thayer, *The British Political Fringe* (Blond, 1965), still valuable for its general approach and insights, even though its facts need to be updated. Useful new studies include S. E. Finer, *The Changing British Party System: 1945–79* (American Enterprise Institute, 1980); and David Howell, *British Social Democracy: A Study in Development and Decay* (Croom Helm, 1980).

Chapter 8

Politicians and Leaders

The process of government is a complex activity in which the participants fill a variety of roles, including those of elector, party worker,
group spokesman, legislator, administrator, and minister of the
Crown. All are engaged in political activity, but in a democratic system
the term 'politician' is normally reserved for those who compete for
public office: councillors and aldermen in local government and MPs
and ministers in national government. This book is concerned mainly
with national government, and the purpose of this chapter is to
examine the recruitment and characteristics of Members of Parliament, their role in parliamentary politics, and the way in which some of
them emerge as ministers and national leaders.

GEOGRAPHY AND THE RECRUITMENT OF
POLITICIANS

One of the features of British politics that often surprises foreign
observers is the absence of what Americans call the locality rule. In the
United States there is a firm convention (to some extent backed by
law) that candidates for political office should be residents – and
usually long-standing residents – of the area in which they are nominated. The rare man who tries to ignore this rule is known as a
carpet-bagger, and his chances of electoral success are much less than
they would be if he were a local man. Partly because of this,
the aspiring politician normally has to work his way up a well-established ladder in which he is first active in the local political clubs, then
runs as a candidate for some local office, then often becomes a member of the state legislature, and only after success in these endeav-
ours is able to secure his party's nomination for a Congressional
election. It follows that the great majority of members of the United
States Congress serve a long apprenticeship in local and state
politics before going to Washington. In most European countries
– and indeed most countries of the world – there is also a strong
tendency for representatives to have roots in their constituencies,
even though there may not be such a strict locality rule as obtains in
America.

In Britain, on the other hand, most MPs have only rather tenuous connections with their constituencies when they are first elected, and more than half of them have no experience whatever of local government. In American terms, most British MPs are carpet-baggers. Equally, most MPs are amateurs when first elected, in the sense that they have no experience of work in a representative assembly: they serve their apprenticeship after they get to Parliament, not as a condition of being nominated.

This state of affairs is a reflection in political life of the fact that English society is rather homogeneous. Candidates for parliamentary elections are selected by the local political parties, who in this matter are virtually (though not quite) autonomous. But, except in a few areas, local parties do not have any particular preference for local men. Local selection committees want the best candidate they can get, and by and large they do not mind much where he comes from. Most candidates have weak points as well as strong ones, and a local man labours under the disadvantage that his weaknesses may be known to the committee, if not to the voters. Moreover, if there are two local contenders it may be difficult for the committee to choose between them and easier, and perhaps more tactful, to pass over both in favour of an outsider.[1] Nor (as a general rule) does place of origin have any perceptible effect on the support given to candidates by voters: as we have seen, they vote for the party, not for the man, and are quite uninterested in the accent and personal characteristics of the person nominated by the party they support. In the 1959 general election only about 12 per cent of the candidates made any claims to local residence in their election addresses.[2]

Persons seeking nomination may either approach the head office of their party or apply to a local party branch. If they approach head office they will be interviewed and, if thought satisfactory, their names will be put on the list of approved persons which head office will make available, on request, to any local party. The other method (and most would-be candidates try both) is to make direct application to local parties known to be looking for a candidate. Between general elections there is a constant search for seats, much discreet canvassing and an endless stream of gossip along the political grapevine. If a death or resignation leads to a by-election this may produce a flood of applications from people in all parts of the country. Thus, when the Member for the fairly safe Conservative seat of Hall Green (in Birmingham) announced his resignation from Parliament on being appointed Chairman of the National Board for Prices and Incomes, the chairman of the Hall Green Conservative Association received over 150 applications within a week. *The Times* reported that 'the applications comprise well-known figures in the Party as well as people who are not on the official candidates' list. Many of them have never been heard of in Hall Green.'[3]

Of course there are exceptions to these generalisations. Most candidates in Scotland are Scots, most candidates in Wales are Welsh, and most candidates in Northern Ireland are Irish. But candidates are not tied to any particular area within these countries, except perhaps on Clydeside, where something like a locality rule seems to prevail. For instance, eleven of the fifteen Glasgow Members elected in 1964 had served on the Glasgow City Council, as had eight of the thirteen elected in 1974. In England the parties in the nine or ten biggest cities have shown a slight preference for local candidates, but no more than that. The one area in England that seems to have something approaching a locality rule is the London area. Of the forty-two MPs elected for London constituencies in 1964, twenty-one had served in local government in the London area and a further fifteen had been active in other spheres of political life in the metropolis. By 1974 the boundaries of London had been extended to include ninety-two constituencies. Of these Members, forty-two had served in local government in the London area and a further ten had been active in other spheres of London political life. Paradoxically, however, these MPs have not acted as a regional pressure group to the extent that MPs from Scotland, Yorkshire or Lancashire have done, and the special interests of the London area have been given an exceptionally low priority by successive governments since 1945.

SOURCES OF RECRUITS

How are people recruited to a career in national politics in Britain? What are the sources of applicants for nomination in national elections? Over the country as a whole local government provides the largest identifiable group of parliamentary candidates. In the election of 1951, 36 per cent of all successful candidates had at some time in their careers been elected to a local council, though not always to a council in their parliamentary constituency. In the 1964 election, the proportion was 40 per cent and in 1974 it was 37 per cent.

It should not be thought that all these candidates had fixed their eyes on a parliamentary career and had become active in local government as a step towards this goal. Doubtless this happens in some cases, but for most people in this group recruitment to national politics is a discontinuous three-stage process. First they become active in a local party; then they volunteer or are persuaded to stand for the local council; and later they decide or are persuaded to seek a parliamentary nomination.

Why do people become active in local parties? In one study more than half the people interviewed gave as a reason the fact that they had been brought up in a politically active family, which is an interesting sidelight on the way in which political élites, at all levels, are recruited and sustained. The other main reason quoted was commitment to a certain set of political principles, often stimulated or precipitated by particular events like the General Strike or the war.[4] Why do some party workers go on to stand for the local council? In the two areas where this step has been systematically studied the general answer is that they are persuaded to do so by local party leaders. Pressed men are far more common than volunteers: few people want to serve in local government, and the party leaders often have difficulty recruiting candidates. The authors of the study of Barking (Essex) endorsed the conclusion of the earlier study of Glossop (Derbyshire): namely, that 'membership of the Council is maintained not by the enthusiasm or ambitions of the potential candidates but by the perseverance of the party leaders in seeking candidates'.[5] However, once a man is elected he usually finds satisfaction in council work, and a small proportion of councillors go on to seek selection as parliamentary candidates. Of thirty councillors and aldermen interviewed in Barking, twenty-two had no wish to stand for Parliament and had not seriously considered it, four had been approached but had declined, and the other four had at one time or another been included in the parliamentary panel of their party or union, though none of them had ever been selected.

Another established ladder to a career in national politics is through the trade unions, which sponsor and finance many Labour candidates. These candidates, like the local government men, are usually recruited by a three-stage process. First, they are active in union affairs in their place of work; then they often become branch officers or full-time union organisers; later they are chosen by the union as prospective parliamentary candidates. One or two unions, notably the AEU, choose people when they are fairly young and consciously attempt to prepare them for political work, either by asking them to study the social sciences or by first putting them up for election in hopeless seats, or by a combination of these methods. But most sponsored candidates are middle-aged when they first stand, and the union concerned normally finds them a safe seat. A union like the National Union of Mineworkers is able to do this because it controls constituency branches of the Labour Party in many mining areas. Other unions get safe seats for their nominees by offering a substantial contribution to campaign expenses and local party funds. Since 1945 about two-fifths of the Labour Members in each Parliament have been sponsored in this way. Many of them have served in local government, so there is a considerable overlap between this group and the group described above.

The only other source of parliamentary candidates that can be readily identified is the small group of political families whose sons are brought up to think in terms of a political career. The Churchills and the Cecils have played leading roles in British politics for several generations. Other families that have contributed politicians over at least two generations in this century include the Chamberlains, the Hoggs and the Woods (the family name of Lord Halifax) on the Conservative side, the Bonham Carters and the Lloyd George family among Liberals, the Greenwoods and the Wedgwood Benns on the Labour side. The actual number of MPs recruited from this source is very small, but they are important because they have so often achieved positions of leadership.

Taken together, local government, the trade unions and the political families produce between 45 and 55 per cent of British MPs. The remainder cannot easily be 'typed'. They first make their appearance on the political scene when they apply for inclusion in the parliamentary panel of one of the three main parties, or when they apply directly for selection in a constituency. It may be appropriate to describe them as 'self-starters', since they embark on a political career without the pressures that impel members of the other three groups towards this objective.

The self-starters are on average younger than the local government men and the trade unionists when they first enter national politics, though older than the 'political heirs'. As a group they are better educated than the local government men and the trade unionists, though not so well educated as the political heirs. They are more likely than recruits from any of the other three sources to give up after an unsuccessful election campaign, or to withdraw from Parliament after only a few years. But if they stay on they are sometimes very successful: most of the country's top political leaders are drawn from the self-starters, not from the other three groups.

THE SELECTION OF CANDIDATES

In all three parties the main responsibility for selecting candidates rests with the local party branches. When a branch decides to adopt a prospective candidate a selection committee is appointed and applications are invited. Usually at least one person will have had his eye on the constituency and will have tried to cultivate good relations with the branch chairman. Sometimes members of the selection committee invite people to apply. If the seat is safe for the party, a fair number of applications are likely to be received, many of them from people who have no connections with the constituency and may never have been near it. If the seat is hopeless, on the other hand, the committee may have to search around for suitable applicants.

After the last date for applications the committee prepare a short list, usually of between two and six persons. These applicants are then interviewed, the common procedure being for each to be asked to address the committee for twenty minutes or so, after which he is questioned for a rather longer period. At the end of the interviews the members of the committee are usually able to agree on a candidate.

The head offices of the parties are involved in this process in two ways. First, each has a panel of approved applicants and on request head office will suggest names from this panel to local parties. Sometimes head office has favoured applicants for whom it wishes to find safe seats, and the names of these applicants may be suggested time and time again. But the choice rests with the local parties and they cannot be forced to accept someone they do not like. This was made abundantly clear between 1948 and 1950, when the Colonial Secretary (A. Creech Jones) and the Minister of Town and Country Planning (Lewis Silkin) both had to search for new constituencies because their own were abolished by boundary changes. Though Transport House naturally suggested their names to large numbers of local parties, neither man was able to find a local party that was willing to adopt him. In consequence both their political careers were effectively ended when Parliament was dissolved. Another clear example occurred in 1959, when the General Secretary of the Labour Party was rejected by more than one local committee and subsequently abandoned his search for a seat.

Head office is also involved in that in each party it reserves the right to veto the selection of applicants whom it considers undesirable. This right is rarely used but when it is the local party has no effective choice but to accept the decision and choose another candidate. If the local party should refuse to toe the line, the normal practice would be for head office to sponsor its own candidate, who would be advertised as the official party candidate. Since British voters are loyal to the national party, not to the local party, the chances are strong that the head office candidate would get the great majority of the votes cast by party supporters. An example of this occurred in 1950, when the MP for Gateshead (K. Zilliacus) had been expelled from the Labour Party for breaches of party discipline in Parliament. The Gateshead Labour Party supported Zilliacus and insisted on renominating him in the general election. To counter this Transport House nominated their own candidate, and though this man was a newcomer to national politics who came from a distant part of the country he received over 75 per cent of Labour votes and won the election.

A slightly different case occurred in 1951, when the Conservative

Central Office objected to the adoption proposal made by the Newcastle North Conservative Association, not because the prospective candidate was unacceptable but because Central Office wished to support the choice of the Liberal Party and of some Newcastle Conservatives, Major G. Lloyd George. In this case a minority of local Conservatives formed a rival association which nominated Major Lloyd George, who then stood as Liberal and Conservative candidate with the support of a letter from Winston Churchill encouraging Conservative electors to vote for him. In the election he had an easy victory and the breakaway group subsequently became the official Conservative Association in the area.

Another variation on the same theme (that local parties cannot successfully defy their headquarters) occurred in 1955 in the Exchange division of Liverpool. The local Labour Party there, which had become dominated by left-wing elements, decided not to renominate the sitting Member (Mrs E. M. Braddock), largely because she had supported the parliamentary leaders in several policy decisions which were anathema to the extreme left. Unwilling to see an MP punished for conformity, the National Executive Council insisted on the reversal of this decision and made it known that any Party member in the constituency who voted against the renomination of Mrs Braddock would promptly be expelled from the Party. Most local members thereupon fell into line, though not without issuing a public statement saying that they supported Mrs Braddock 'with a gun at their head'.[6] Other members resigned and gave their support to one of their number who stood as an Independent Labour candidate. In the election Mrs Braddock was returned with 19,457 votes, while the Independent Labour candidate got only 2,928 and lost his deposit.

Cases of this kind are rare but important. They provide dramatic evidence of the weakness of local parties in a showdown with party headquarters. This weakness is of course a consequence of the national orientation of the great majority of voters. By and large, voters are no more concerned about the views and policies of the local political parties than they are about the personalities and place of residence of the candidates: the loyalties of the voters are to the national parties and their support goes to the candidates endorsed by the national leaders.

It cannot be stressed too often that these national loyalties are the foundations on which party discipline is built. In the last resort an MP who persistently opposes the policy of his party may be expelled, and if this happens his political career will almost certainly be terminated. Thus, four Labour MPs were expelled between 1945 and 1950: three of them stood as Labour Independent candidates in the 1950 election but each of them was defeated by the official Labour candidate. Things rarely come to this pass, and it would be a mistake to think that this kind of consideration is constantly in the minds of MPs. Most of them are loyal to their party by conviction and by a sense of comradeship, strengthened in many cases by the desire for ministerial appointment. But, just as a house would have to be built differently if its foundations were different, even though those living in the house rarely think about the foundations, so British political parties would be different in structure and operation if the loyalties of British voters were more local and personal than they are.

In the great majority of cases, of course, the kind of problem discussed in the preceding paragraphs does not arise, because the local party either renominates the sitting Member or else finds that all the applicants it wishes to put on the short list are acceptable to head office. It is a normal convention of the system that a sitting Member should be renominated, though in exceptional circumstances this convention is broken. There have been occasional cases of personal disagreement between a Member and his local party. There have also been one or two cases of disagreement on policy, and these follow a pattern. Broadly speaking, local Conservative associations either agree with or are to the right of the parliamentary leadership, while local Labour parties either agree with or are to the left of their parliamentary leaders.[7] Because of this, Conservative MPs who deviate to the right can usually retain the confidence of their local associations, as can Labour MPs who deviate to the left. The Zilliacus case has already been mentioned, and on the Conservative side it is worth noting that when eight right-wing Members openly opposed their leaders in 1957 their constituency parties apparently made no objection.[8] On the other hand, a Conservative MP who deviates to the left may be in trouble with his constituency, as may a Labour MP who deviates to the right. At the time of the Suez crisis three Conservatives were disowned by their local associations for opposing the Government, while one Labour Member lost his seat for refusing to oppose the Government.

Recently there has been a new development in the Labour Party which has caused controversy. Small groups of young left-wing extremists have taken to joining local branches where the active membership is small, with a view to securing the rejection of a moderate sitting Member so as to open the way for the nomination of a left-winger. Between 1976 and 1979 three Members were rejected in this way, one of them a fairly senior minister. The National Executive Committee of the Party had the power to prevent this and discussed the possibility of doing so, but the NEC itself had a left-wing majority at the time and decided to take no action. However, in January 1978 the NEC upheld an appeal by a woman MP whose constituency party had decided not to renominate her after she had declared herself to be a lesbian. The NEC found that there had been some technical irregularities in the procedures adopted by the local party which amounted to 'a breach of natural justice'.

If a local party has to choose a candidate, either because the sitting Member is not standing again or because the party lost the last election in the area, what sort of consideration is likely to influence the selection committee?

It is not easy to give any general answer to this question. The policy preference of applicants occasionally influences the selectors but this appears to be the exception rather than the rule.[9] Local government service may be a help, but it is not an important factor except in the London area and in a handful of other cities. Religion is hardly considered except in one or two constituencies with a high proportion of Roman Catholic electors. Local residence is only an advantage in a minority of areas, as noted. Some selection committees are influenced by financial considerations, and this must be explained.

The question of finance used to loom large in Conservative associations, for until 1948 the majority of them expected their candidates to pay part or most of the campaign expenses and also to make an annual contribution to association funds. As a result most Conservative MPs were fairly wealthy. But after their crushing defeat in 1945 the Party, guided by their new Chairman, Lord Woolton, made a number of organisational changes. One of these was the adoption of a rule that candidates should not contribute to election expenses, that their maximum contribution to party funds should be £25 a year until they were elected, when it could rise to £50 a year, and that in any case the selection committee should make no inquiry about possible contributions before reaching a decision. This rule removed the financial hurdle which prospective Conservative candidates formerly had to clear. Needless to say, it has not resulted in the nomination of a flood of manual workers, largely because manual workers rarely think of standing for Parliament as Conservatives, partly because local selection committees are reluctant to adopt those who do put themselves forward. In 1959 only fourteen manual workers stood as Conservative candidates, of whom only one was elected. The importance of the reform is that it has enabled young professional and business people without private means to stand in the Conservative cause, which they have done in large numbers.

Since 1948 financial considerations have been more influential in the Labour Party than in the Conservative Party. Individual contributions by Labour candidates, though rarely as large as those previously made by Conservatives, continued until 1957, when a rule was introduced providing that no candidate should give more than £50 a year, and that selection committees should in no circumstances seek a promise of a contribution. But the really significant factor on the Labour side is the practice whereby trade unions sponsor candidates. The Party's rules permit a sponsoring organisation to pay up to 80 per cent of the election expenses and to contribute up to £350 a year to local party funds (more in rural areas or where a full-time agent is employed). The willingness of trade unions to do this is known in advance and often determines the choice made by selection committees. As noted, about two-fifths of Labour MPs are sponsored in this way, most of them having fairly safe seats.

The other factors that influence selection committees are personal factors: whether an applicant can speak well, whether he has been to the right kind of school, what occupation he follows, whether he makes a good impression at the interview, whether he has any experience of electioneering. As little information is available about the applicants who are not selected, it is impossible to produce any statistical generalisations about the preferences of selectors. But in the long run these preferences are reflected in the composition of the House of Commons, and it will be helpful at this stage in the argument to look briefly at the characteristics of MPs.

CHARACTERISTICS OF MPS

It would be absurd to expect the House of Commons to contain a cross-section of the British population. One never gets a representative sample by calling for volunteers, and in the world of politics there are special barriers to representativeness in this sense. One is the fact that very few people have either the aptitude or the desire for a political career, involving as it does insecurity, anxiety, relatively low material rewards, irregular hours of work, lack of privacy, and the need for frequent public appearances. Some people are temperamentally inclined towards this kind of career while others take it up out of a strong sense of public duty, but the two groups together will never comprise more than a small minority of the population.

Another barrier that existed until very recently in Britain was that many people who might have liked to go into politics could not afford to do so. Until 1964 the salaries paid to MPs were insufficient to meet their heavy expenses and provide them with anything like a decent standard of living. This meant that MPs were drawn almost entirely from three groups: the diminishing class of those who had substantial private means; trade unionists whose unions were willing to supplement their parliamentary salaries; and people engaged in occupations which they could combine with their political careers on a part-time basis. The last of these categories includes lawyers, company directors and journalists. Parliamentary salaries were almost doubled in 1964 but they are still low by international standards. In 1979 a British MP earned about the same as an assistant professor in a North American university. However, in April 1979 the official committee responsible for making recommendations on this question proposed that salaries should again be doubled, to bring them into line with salaries in other European democracies. If this proposal is adopted, MPs will for the first time be relatively affluent.

Tables 8.1 and 8.2 indicate the educational and occupation background of MPs elected in February 1974, the most recent election in which the main parties were evenly balanced. If these figures are compared with those for earlier elections, a very clear trend is discernible, namely that the House of Commons is becoming more and more middle-class in composition. It contains fewer landowners, men of independent means, and retired officers of the armed services, while it also contains fewer representatives of the working class. The proportion of lawyers, already low in comparison with the United States Congress and some European parliaments, has diminished slightly since the 1950s. But there has been an increase in the proportion of teachers, lecturers, accountants, and members of other professions. A consequence of this trend is that the Conservative and Labour Parties in Parliament are not quite so different in their social composition as they used to be, though there is still an appreciable difference between them.

Table 8.1   *Educational Background of MPs Elected in February 1974*

Education	Con-servative	Labour	Liberal	Others	Total
Eton	54	1	2	–	57
Other public schools	166	48	8	3	225
All public schools	220	49	10	3	282
State secondary schools	77	214	4	20	315
Elementary schools	–	38	–	–	38
Total	297	301	14	23	635
Oxford or Cambridge	159	59	6	1	225
Other universities	41	102	4	12	159
All universities	200	161	10	13	384

Table 8.2   *Occupational Background of MPs Elected in February*
1974

Occupation	Con- servative	Labour	Liberal	Others	Total
Lawyer	72	40	4	5	121
Company director	39	3	0	1	43
Business management	56	26	2	5	89
Farmer	26	–	1	3	30
Publisher or journalist	32	23	1	1	57
Teacher or lecturer	10	65	2	3	80
Armed services	9	–	–	–	9
Other professions	42	33	4	3	82
White-collar workers	–	16	–	1	17
Manual workers	1	84	–	–	85
Other (or no) occupation	10	11	–	1	22
Total number of Members	297	301	14	23	635

The figures on educational background show a marked contrast between the two main parties. Three-quarters of Conservative MPS were educated at public schools compared with only one-sixth of Labour MPS. The contrast is even more marked among Cabinet ministers. Eighteen of the twenty-one members of the Conservative Cabinet that resigned in February 1974 were public-school products, compared with only three of the twenty-one members of the Labour Cabinet that succeeded it. Moreover, the three Labour ministers all attended public schools in Inner London, where pupils are more affected by the pressures of modern life than in the typical British public school located in the countryside. Only two of the eighteen public-school products in the Conservative Cabinet had been educated in Inner London. Although less than half of the ministers in Mrs Thatcher's Cabinet were also in Heath's Cabinet, the educational background of the two Cabinets is remarkably similar. The 1979 Conservative Cabinet contained two grammar-school products, two from public schools in Inner London, and sixteen from traditional public schools, mostly situated in rural areas.

The statistics on higher education show a continuing and stable tendency for about two-thirds of Conservative MPS to have university degrees and for the great majority of these to have attended Oxford or Cambridge. All seventeen university graduates in the Heath Cabinet came from these universities and so did all but one of the sixteen graduates in Mrs Thatcher's Cabinet.

Among Labour MPS, there has been a consistent tendency for the proportion of university graduates to increase over the years. The proportion has risen from 19 per cent in 1935 to 32 per cent in 1945, 40 per cent in 1955, 51 per cent in 1966, and 56 per cent in 1974. The proportion has therefore almost caught up with the proportion on the Conservative side of the House, but only a minority of Labour graduates went to Oxford or Cambridge.

It follows that the social and educational background of Conservative MPS is considerably more homogeneous than that of Labour MPS, and it has been said that this may be a considerable advantage to the Conservative Party.[10] The argument is that Labour MPS are united only by their political beliefs, so that when these diverge there is rarely a social bond to moderate the ideological conflict. Among Conservative MPS, on the other hand, the impact of disagreement over policy matters tends to be moderated by the feeling that they are all good chaps who must stand together so as not to let the side down. The logic of this argument has been reinforced (even though its practical significance has been somewhat diminished) by the tense relations that have developed in recent years between Edward Heath and Enoch Powell, and subsequently between Heath and Margaret Thatcher, for none of these leaders attended a public school.

MPS AS GROUP SPOKESMEN

In constitutional theory MPS represent their constituencies: in practice most of them also represent interest and promotional groups of one kind or another. In some legislatures, notably the United States Congress, members are forbidden to act as the paid representatives of pressure groups, for fear that their judgement might be distorted thereby. In Britain, on the contrary, it has always been regarded as healthy for all the interests and views that exist within society to have their spokesmen in the national Parliament. Winston Churchill expressed this view in the following terms:

> Everybody here has private interests, some are directors of companies, some own property which may be affected by legislation which is passing and so forth. . . . Then there are those people who come to represent public bodies, particular groups of non-political character in the general sense, and there again we must recognise that as one of the conditions of our varied life. . . . We are not supposed to be an assembly of gentlemen who have no interests of any kind and no associations of any kind. That is ridiculous. That might apply in Heaven, but not, happily, here.[11]

The relations between MPS and pressure groups take various forms: a

Member may be sponsored by a trade union which pays a proportion (sometimes a high proportion) of his expenses; he may be paid an honorarium by a group for which he acts; he may act regularly without fee for groups with which he has something in common; and he may take up a particular cause which appeals to him. These roles are not mutually exclusive. As has been remarked: 'Increasingly Parliamentary spokesmanship is thought of as a role all private Members may undertake more or less regularly on behalf of the interests and causes to which they are attached. No MP or peer is so characterless as to fail to have a few such attachments.'[12]

The ways in which an MP can help a group are many and varied. He may ask questions in Parliament on the group's behalf. He may take up particular matters with the minister concerned. He may speak on behalf of the group at party meetings, particularly at meetings of specialised groups of backbenchers, such as the Conservative Agricultural Committee or the Labour Committee on Foreign Affairs. He may move amendments to government Bills and introduce motions calling upon the Government to modify its policy in this way or that: for instance, in 1956 over half the Members of Parliament were persuaded to sign a motion asking the Government to abolish entertainments tax on the theatre. He may introduce a Private Member's Bill, which will normally have been drafted in consultation with the group concerned. The RSPCA appears to be the group which enjoys most success in promoting legislation, partly because it is very well organised and partly because, although not all MPs care much about animal welfare, hardly any MPs are actually opposed to it. The Association has a Parliamentary Department which advises friendly MPs and provides them with draft legislation, and between 1949 and 1954 eight Bills sponsored by the RSPCA were passed into law.[13]

There can be no doubt that Parliament's effectiveness is increased by the fact that most Members act as spokesmen for interest or promotional groups as well as for their constituencies and their parties. MPs are even more dependent on groups than are government departments for specialised information about the activities with which the Government is concerned. Some of the most effective contributions to parliamentary debate are based on information supplied by groups, as is most of the useful work done by backbenchers in the committee stage of legislation (when details rather than principles are considered). If backbenchers were not briefed by the 'affected interests', the administration would have a near-monopoly of technical information, and the role of the ordinary MP would be much less useful than it now is. It is largely for reasons of this kind that the tradition of group representation is widely accepted and rarely challenged.

Of course, sometimes an MP's role as group spokesman is in conflict with his role as party member. In these cases 'MPS usually give their voices to the groups and their votes to the parties'.[14] Party discipline is normally too strong for MPS to withhold their votes from their party because of their attachment to particular interests. If an MP is spokesman for a cause, he may perhaps abstain from voting on grounds of conscience, but even this is the exception rather than the rule.

It is also true, in principle if not in practice, that the role of an MP as group spokesman may conflict with his assumed role as a legislator exercising independent judgement about the nature of the public interest. To protect the independence of Members the House of Commons has rules of 'parliamentary privilege' under which it is an offence to exert undue pressure on a Member. These rules were invoked in 1947 by W. J. Brown, Independent MP for Rugby. Brown, who had previously been General Secretary of the Civil Service Clerical Association, was appointed Parliamentary Secretary on his election, in which post he received a substantial salary. His political views subsequently diverged from those of the leaders of the Association, who (it was alleged) threatened to discontinue his appointment unless he advanced the views of the Association in certain parliamentary debates. Brown thereupon asked that the matter should be referred to the Committee of Privileges of the House, on the ground that members of the Association were attempting to curtail his independence of action. The Speaker ruled that there was a *prima facie* case to investigate, but the Committee subsequently found that no breach of privilege had been committed, as Brown had voluntarily placed himself in a contractual relationship which, in its nature, might one day be terminated. In its report the Committee observed that it was perhaps unwise of MPS to accept the formal status of parliamentary representative of an outside body, which would appear to put their independence in jeopardy.

It might also be a breach of privilege to allege that a Member was putting a sectional interest before the public interest. In 1965 the Speaker ruled that it raised a *prima facie* matter of privilege for the Chancellor of the Exchequer (James Callaghan) to have made the following remark in a weekend speech:

> When I look at some Members discussing the Finance Bill I do not think of them as the Hon. Member for X, Y or Z. I look at them and say 'investment trusts', 'capital speculators' or 'that is the fellow who is the Stock Exchange man who makes a profit on gilt edged'. I have almost forgotten their constituencies, but I shall never forget their interests. I wonder sometimes whom they represent, the constituents' or their own or their friends' particular interests.[15]

The Committee of Privileges decided that the remark did not constitute a breach of privilege and this decision was widely welcomed. Commentators observed that the House had always accepted the right of Members to represent interests as well as constituencies and that it would be as unrealistic to try to conceal the fact that many Conservatives represented business and financial interests as it would be to deny that Labour members represented trade unions. The general effect of this case was therefore to reassert Parliament's acceptance of the traditional view that there is no harm and some advantage in MPs acting as group spokesmen.

THE CONDITIONS OF PARLIAMENTARY LIFE

The facilities available to Members have improved markedly during the 1970s. They all now have a desk and a telephone, which was not the case in the 1960s. However, they do not get the help that members of some legislative assemblies take for granted. They are not generally given a room of their own. They are not provided with secretarial assistance, which they have to organise for themselves and pay for out of their own pockets. They have no access to official papers unless these are published and they have no general right to question civil servants.

The poverty of these facilities could not be defended if the British political system required the ordinary MP to play an active and expert role in the drafting of legislation and the control of administration. If this were expected of him, as it is (to some extent) of Congressmen and Senators in the United States, he would clearly need an office of his own, secretarial help, the advice of legal draftsmen, and the right to question officials on the work of their departments. But the British political system allots a far more humble role to the backbench MP. His task is to support the government of the day or to criticise it, but not to take part in it. In the drama of politics he is certainly on the stage rather than in the audience, but until he is appointed to some kind of office his role is more like that of a chorus-boy than that of a leading actor.

The duties of a backbench MP are easily enumerated. First, he is expected to look after the interests of his constituents, taking up their grievances with the relevant minister when he thinks this appropriate. It has been said that if he wants to get results he should write to the minister but if he wants to make a row he should raise the matter in Parliament.[16] It is only in exceptional cases that an MP can get concessions that would not have been granted in any case, but he can sometimes hasten the process, and even when the answer is still in the negative it may be a consolation to the constituent to know that the problem has been raised and considered at the highest level, and not brushed aside by a junior official. Work of this kind takes up a good deal of time, and the majority of Members not only correspond with constituents but also make themselves available for consultation at regular 'surgeries'.[17]

Secondly, the backbench MP is expected to support his party in the division lobbies. Each party has a Chief Whip and a number of assistant Whips who are responsible for what they call party management and other people usually call party discipline. The Whips' Office in each party draw the attention of their Members to forthcoming debates by circulating notes, also known as Whips, which indicate the importance of the occasion by variations in the degree of underlining. A debate underlined once is one in which no division is expected; one underlined twice is one on which there will be a division, and which MPS are expected to attend unless they have arranged to 'pair' with a Member of the other main party or unless they have some good excuse for absence; a three-line whip means that the division is of vital importance and all Members are required to attend unless the Whips' Office have arranged a pair for them, which they will do only in cases of serious illness.

Thirdly, MPS are expected to attend parliamentary party meetings and to take part, if they have time, in the work of one of the specialised party committees of backbenchers, such as the Labour Committee on Foreign Affairs or the Conservative Committee on Agriculture. In these committees MPS can question party leaders more freely than they can in the presence of the Opposition and the press, and it is here that backbenchers may have their greatest influence on party policy in the House.

Beyond these duties, the MP can choose what role he will play. Most Members want to take part in debates, and while a few can make a reputation for themselves by wit and oratory the great majority do better if they become specialists in one or two fields. When Lord Woolton was Chairman of the Conservative Party his advice to new MPS was always that they should specialise, preferably in a field that was not already overcrowded. Most MPS come to the House with a prior interest in one or more activities or causes, and may develop their interests in these fields, often acting as group spokesmen in the ways described. Other Members deliberately inform themselves about a particular area of administration or policy and intervene regularly in debates on problems arising in these areas. A few Members with a taste for detailed work get themselves appointed to one of the select committees of the House and make a valuable contribution there which gets little publicity.

PARTY DISCIPLINE IN PARLIAMENT

In their attitudes to party discipline Members on each side of the House can be divided into three broad groups. First, there is a large group who have serious hopes of achieving ministerial office. They will usually be assiduous in attendance and careful not to give any sign of disloyalty which may be noticed by the Chief Whip or the party leaders. Some of the country's most notable leaders have had periods as rebels before reaching the top, including Churchill, Macmillan and Wilson, but to pursue this course requires courage and an unusual degree of self-confidence. Secondly, there is a large group who may have no serious hopes of achieving office but who fall into line by both instinct and conviction. Many trade union Members fall into this category, and their Conservative counterparts are generally from safe rural seats. These Members may be described without disrespect as the ballast of their respective parties, essential if the ship is to be kept on an even keel when it is beset by ideological storms or lashed by gales of moral indignation. Thirdly, there is in each main party a small group of independently minded Members who are willing to challenge the views of their leaders and colleagues in public, not minding that such action will probably reduce their chances of office. When crucial divisions are held such men will normally be found voting for their party, but their willingness to voice unorthodox opinions contributes much to the vitality and range of parliamentary debate.

The above paragraph applies to party discipline as it has normally operated since the beginning of the twentieth century. Between 1969 and 1972, however, three important issues arose on which large numbers of backbenchers asserted their independence. The first was the attempt to transform the composition of the House of Lords, promoted by the Labour Government with the tacit acquiescence of most members of the Conservative front bench, which had to be abandoned as the consequence of determined opposition by backbenchers of both parties. The second was the Labour Government's Bill to reform industrial relations, which had to be abandoned because of opposition from the trade union movement, supported by many Labour backbenchers and more than one minister. The third issue was the Conservative Government's proposal that Britain should accept the terms for membership of the EEC that had been negotiated in Brussels. This was opposed by the Parliamentary Labour Party, but there was a sizeable and passionate group of dissidents on each side of the House. In the crucial division on the issue in October 1971, thirty-nine Conservatives voted against entry while sixty-eight Labour Members voted in favour of entry.

Each of these three incidents constituted a considerable reversal for party leaders and managers which was surprising in view of the effectiveness of party management during the previous fifty years. It would be rash to assume that they will lead to any permanent change in parliamentary practice. On the other hand, they cannot be written off as three isolated incidents. On the Labour side there are deep ideological divisions between moderates and radicals which may lead to further splits. In the Conservative Party there are conflicts about the Rhodesian question which have led MPs to take different sides in parliamentary divisions and may possibly do so again. In both parties there are basic differences of attitude to the EEC and also to the arguments about the devolution of authority to Scotland and Wales. A Scottish National Assembly would have been established in 1979 had Labour backbenchers not ignored pressure from party leaders and supported the amendment which required 40 per cent of the electors (as well as 50 per cent of the voters) to vote 'yes' in a referendum on the subject as a condition of establishing the Assembly. Independence breeds independence, and the effectiveness of party management on issues of fundamental importance can no longer be taken for granted.

THE WAY TO THE TOP

It was noted earlier that the majority of Members reach Parliament without having served in any other representative assembly or political post. Once there, however, they normally have to serve a long apprenticeship before reaching high office. With only a few exceptions, the way to the top in British politics is through a successful performance in Parliament, first as a backbencher attracting favourable comment by his speeches and questions, then as a junior minister and finally as a minister. It is a hard struggle, with insecurity at every stage, in which only a minority succeed. Of over two thousand MPs who served in Parliament between 1918 and 1955, 74 per cent failed to get any kind of ministerial appointment. A further 10 per cent achieved only the comparatively humble office of Parliamentary Private Secretary, 9 per cent became junior ministers, and only 7 per cent became full ministers (most of whom remained outside the Cabinet).[18]

A study has been made of the careers of the 282 ministers first appointed to Cabinet posts in the ninety years following 1868, the best date to mark the beginning of the modern system of disciplined parties.[19] This shows that 214 were drawn from the House of Commons, twenty four were former MPs who had gone to the Lords, fifteen had acquired their parliamentary experience entirely in the Lords, and the other twenty-nine were unorthodox appointments in the sense that they could not be described as career politicians (even though most of them had had some brief membership of the Lords or experience as non-Cabinet ministers before being appointed). Although all but one of these unorthodox appointments were made since 1916, it cannot be said that they indicate a trend, since most of them were made as a direct result of one or other of the two world wars. The 238 who had come up in the normal way through the House of Commons had on average spent fourteen years in that House before reaching the Cabinet. Seventy-five per cent of them had served in the Commons for between six and twenty years, 17 per cent had served for twenty-one years or more, and only 8 per cent had had less than six years' service. They were experienced Parliamentarians, and in considering the view that the Cabinet has 'usurped' Parliament's position as the centre of political power it should be remembered that Cabinet ministers are themselves Parliament men, whose careers have been established over many years of activity in the Commons.

A small minority of ministers reach one of the top posts, to become Foreign Secretary, Chancellor of the Exchequer, or Prime Minister. Since the last war thirty politicians have filled these posts, fifteen from each main party. An examination of the careers of these top leaders reveals two ways (apart from their success) in which they are not representative of the Commons as a whole. One is that 77 per cent of them are university graduates compared with 60 per cent of the total body of MPs, a difference which is of marginal significance. The other is that more of them are 'self-starters' (as defined above): 80 per cent compared with about 50 per cent of all MPs. Of the others, Churchill came from a political family, Bevin and Brown were trade unionists, Attlee, Morrison and Amory reached Parliament after serving in local government. All but one of the eleven leaders who have held these top posts since 1970 have been self-starters, and it may be expected that this will be a continuing tendency in view of the increased professionalisation of politics as a career.

NOTES

1   See Austin Ranney, *Pathways to Parliament* (Macmillan, 1965), p. 110.
2   D. E. Butler and Richard Rose, *The British General Election of 1959* (Macmillan, 1960), p. 132.
3   *The Times*, 27 March 1965.
4   See A. M. Rees and T. A. Smith, *Town Councillors* (Acton Society Trust, 1964), ch. vii.
5   ibid., p. 76, and A. H. Birch, *Small-Town Politics* (Oxford University Press, 1959), p. 123.
6   *Daily Telegraph*, 29 April 1954. See P. G. Richards, *Honourable Members*, 2nd edn (Faber, 1964), pp. 20–3, for a discussion of this and some other cases.
7   See A. H. Birch, *Representative and Responsible Government* (Allen & Unwin, 1964), p. 125, for some statistics on this point.

8 See Richards, *Honourable Members*, p. 165.
9 ibid., p. 23.
10 See Jean Blondel, *Voters, Parties and Leaders* (Penguin, 1963), pp. 144–5.
11 Quoted in S. E. Finer, *Anonymous Empire,* 2nd edn (Pall Mall Press, 1966), pp. 46–7.
12 Allen Potter, *Organized Groups in British National Politics* (Faber, 1961), p. 276.
13 ibid., pp. 285–6.
14 ibid.
15 Reported in *The Times,* 7 July 1965.
16 See Richards, *Honourable Members*, p. 178.
17 See R. E. Dowse, 'The MP and his surgery', in *Political Studies,* vol. XI (1963).
18 P. W. Buck, *Amateurs and Professionals in British Politics* (Chicago University Press, 1963), p. 47.
19 F. M. G. Wilson, 'The routes of entry of new members of the British Cabinet, 1868–1958', in *Political Studies,* vol. VII (1959).

FURTHER READING

A general account of the recruitment and selection of parliamentary candidates is given in Austin Ranney, *Pathways to Parliament* (Macmillan, 1965); a short but brilliant picture of how one candidate was selected is included in J. D. Lees and Richard Kimber (eds), *Political Parties in Modern Britain* (Routledge & Kegan Paul, 1972); some valuable data about candidates and MPs are given in each of the Nuffield election studies; an interesting analysis of leadership styles by Dennis Kavanagh will be found in William Gwyn and Richard Rose (eds), *Britain: Progress and Decline* (Macmillan/Tulane University Press, 1980); an account of the position and activities of backbenchers is given in P. G. Richards, *The Backbenchers* (Faber, 1972).

Chapter 9

Government and Opposition

As we have seen, the leaders of the two main parties are now chosen by their parliamentary colleagues. Each can claim, in Disraeli's celebrated phrase, that he has 'reached the top of the greasy pole'. But which of them becomes Prime Minister depends on the electorate, and in a closely fought election it is not until nearly all the returns are in that one man knows he will spend the duration of the next Parliament in 10 Downing Street and the other knows that his role is to be Leader of the Opposition. For one, the following days will be crowded with activity as he picks the members of his Government; the other will be faced with the less rewarding task of conducting a post-mortem on his party's defeat.

THE CHOICE OF MINISTERS

Commentators have vacillated in their accounts of the relations between the Prime Minister and his senior colleagues. It used to be fashionable to describe him as 'first among equals', a description which is clearly inaccurate in view of the fact that he, and he alone, has the power to appoint them to and dismiss them from ministerial office. Recently the pendulum has swung to the other extreme and it has become fashionable to liken the powers of the Prime Minister to those of the United States President. That this is also misleading can be demonstrated by citing one simple example. When John F. Kennedy was elected to the Presidency in 1960 he did not give one of the three top posts in his Cabinet to leading members of his party: the Republican Secretary of the Treasury was kept on in that office; the chief executive of the Ford Motor Company (also a Republican) was appointed Secretary of Defence; and the post of Secretary of State went to a man active in social welfare who had not previously held political office. No British Prime Minister has anything like this degree of freedom: in peacetime his choice is almost entirely limited to leading members of his party whose parliamentary careers have put them in the running for ministerial appointments.

Some members of the party have such status that their inclusion is almost automatic: thus, Harold Macmillan had to give senior posts to

R. A. Butler and Selwyn Lloyd; Lord Home had to appoint R. A. Butler, Edward Heath and Reginald Maudling; Harold Wilson had to appoint George Brown, James Callaghan and Patrick Gordon Walker. On the other hand, even the most senior people cannot choose which posts they will have, for getting the right balance of people and posts in the Cabinet is a tricky matter which must be left to the Prime Minister. For instance, in 1945 Hugh Dalton wanted to be Foreign Secretary and was told that there was a good prospect of this; at noon on the crucial day Attlee phoned him and said he would know for certain by tea-time; but at 4 p.m. Dalton was told that he was to be Chancellor of the Exchequer instead. The apparent reason for this change of plan is also interesting. It had been thought that Ernest Bevin would be Chancellor and Herbert Morrison would be put in general charge of home affairs, but relations between the two men were so bad that at the last moment the Prime Minister decided to reduce their points of contact by asking Bevin to go to the Foreign Office. Further examples of the inability of politicians to choose their ministry are the appointment of an apparent reluctant Herbert Morrison to the Foreign Office in 1950 (after Bevin died) and, conversely, the number of years which Butler had to wait before getting to the Foreign Office in 1963.

The Prime Minister has to bear various considerations in mind when making his appointments. He must get a team who will work together in the senior posts. He must consider the balance of power in the party and appoint people who represent the various viewpoints within it. He must get a balance of ages in his administration and encourage young men of ability. He may have to consider sectional interests: these are not important at this level in the Conservative Party, but a Labour Prime Minister will have to appoint an appropriate number of trade unionists, one or two Scotsmen, and one or two Welshmen. He has a large number of posts to distribute – between ninety and a hundred in most recent governments – and he can find room to take account of all these factors, but much energy and thought must be spent in getting the right combination for effective government.

One of the problems which most Prime Ministers have to face is the existence of senior colleagues whose views on policy differ from their own. Experience shows that it is much wiser for a Prime Minister to include such critics in the Government than to leave them out, for if they are included they will be forced to support government policy in public, no matter how many private reservations they may have. In extreme cases their reservations may be obvious, as exemplified by the *Guardian*'s comment on Anthony Wedgwood Benn's position between 1974 and 1979: 'For much of the last Parliament, Mr Tony Benn occupied a position of almost total isolation within the Cabinet, acquiescing in its collective decisions while frantically signalling to the

Party outside that it hurt him grievously to do so.'¹ But, even so, it was safer for Wilson and Callaghan to have the Party's leading radical partially muzzled than to have him leading an open revolt against their policies. Heath's decision to exclude Enoch Powell from his government confirms this general rule, for although it may have been almost inevitable in the circumstances it is nevertheless the case that Powell's subsequent attacks on the Government weakened it and may have contributed to its defeat in 1974.

Normally ministers are drawn from the two Houses of Parliament, the great majority being MPs who have climbed the political ladder rung by rung in the way described in the previous chapter. As noted there, outsiders are occasionally brought in to strengthen the team, and two at least of these unorthodox appointees proved to be superb politicians who have left their mark on British history and British government. One was Ernest Bevin, who as General Secretary of the Transport and General Workers' Union was invited to become Minister of Labour and National Service in 1940, largely because it was thought desirable to have a leading trade unionist to deal with the delicate problems posed by conscription and direction of labour. He subsequently became one of the 'big three' of the 1945 Labour Government and a Foreign Secretary of great distinction. The other was Lord Woolton, who as chairman of a chain of department stores was asked to become Minister of Food during the war, who subsequently (as Minister of Reconstruction) had some responsibility for the formulation and publication of the Government's policy to maintain full employment, and who played a leading role in the reform and revitalisation of the Conservative Party after its defeat in 1945.

Unorthodox appointments of this kind are exceptions to the general rule that Prime Ministers must select their ministers from the two Houses of Parliament. But in peacetime it remains true that nine out of ten senior ministers (as well as all junior ministers) are Parliamentarians before they are appointed. It should be added that when a non-Parliamentarian is appointed he must (by convention) be either given a peerage or found a seat in the Commons within a matter of weeks, but there is rarely any problem about this as it is not difficult to persuade a backbencher of long service to retire to the Lords to make way for the new man.

THE MINISTERIAL HIERARCHY

At the beginning of this century there were no more than fifteen departments of state, each one of them headed by a minister who was automatically a member of the Cabinet. The great expansion of governmental activities since that time has changed the picture. There are more departments and since 1964 at least nine of them have had a second full minister (usually known as a Minister of State) while one or two have had three or even four full ministers. As there are also the Law Officers and the holders of non-departmental appointments like the Lord Privy Seal, the result is that in recent years there have been at least forty ministerial appointments. Not all of their holders can be in the Cabinet, since by general agreement a Cabinet of more than about twenty members would be too large for effective discussion. It follows that the ministerial hierarchy is more complex than it used to be. There are now: (*a*) Cabinet ministers; (*b*) ministers holding offices which might but do not at the moment entitle them to a place in the Cabinet; (*c*) other full ministers (e.g. Ministers of State); and (*d*) junior ministers (i.e. Under-Secretaries and Parliamentary Secretaries).

In times of peace the Cabinet normally has about twenty members: since 1946 the minimum has been sixteen and the maximum twenty-three. In this period the holders of the following ten offices have always been members of the Cabinet:

Lord President of the Council
Lord Chancellor
Lord Privy Seal
Home Secretary
Foreign Secretary
Chancellor of the Exchequer
Secretary of State for Defence
President of the Board of Trade (now Secretary of State for Trade)
Minister of Labour (now Secretary of State for Employment)
Secretary of State for Scotland

Of these the first three are included because 'they are posts of dignity given only to very senior men', the following six because the work of the departments is always of great importance, and the last because his omission would cause a political outcry in Scotland.[2] The relatively new offices of Secretary of State for Wales and Secretary of State for Industry can now be added to the list. The other departments represented in the Cabinet have varied from year to year, depending partly on the personal status of the ministers concerned and partly on which issues are thought likely to cause most controversy. Thus, in 1945 the Ministry of Fuel and Power was represented in the Cabinet partly because coal nationalisation was on the government's agenda and partly because the minister was Emmanuel Shinwell, but in the autumn of 1947 nationalisation had been achieved. Shinwell was moved to another post, and his successor was not given a Cabinet place.

RESIGNATION AND DISMISSAL OF MINISTERS

As a class, ministers have less security of tenure than members of any other profession, with the possible exception of football managers. Their appointments are the fruits of a long struggle and confer high status upon them, yet within a year or two they may be wondering how long they will survive. Junior ministers – that is, Parliamentary Secretaries and Under-Secretaries – know they are on probation and that if they are not promoted within four or five years they will soon find themselves backbenchers again. They also know that the odds are against them. The minority who are promoted can look forward to only a few years as full ministers, unless they are exceptionally talented and also blessed with a modicum of good fortune. Thus, when the Conservative Government took office in 1951 thirty-eight ministers and thirty-six junior ministers were appointed. Ten years later only ten of the ministers and six of the junior ministers were still in office.[3] Many of the others had retired or abandoned political life for a career which offered them greater security: some had been asked to resign or openly dismissed from office.

It cannot be easy for a Prime Minister to dismiss one of his colleagues but all Prime Ministers who hold office for any time find that it is an inescapable duty. Sometimes it becomes clear that a minister is unsuited to his post; sometimes there are disagreements over policy; and sometimes a Prime Minister finds it necessary to rejuvenate a government which is beginning to look (or to get) a little stale. Most Prime Ministers are quite frank about this. Churchill has said that a Prime Minister must be 'a good butcher'. Attlee has stated that a Prime Minister should always warn his ministers that 'if you don't turn out all right I shall sack you', adding that: 'It's awkward to have to sack a man and tell him he doesn't make the grade. But I always think it's best to tell him so frankly.'[4] Macmillan dismissed seven of his senior colleagues in one fell swoop in 1962. Harold Wilson announced within a few days of accepting office that he would not hesitate to reshuffle his administration when this proved necessary.

When ministers resign or are dismissed, they may be offered a seat in the House of Lords, which is a gracious way of compensating a man who has given many years of his life to public service. They may return to business or the Bar, where the financial rewards are higher than they are in politics. Or they may simply return to the back benches in the hope that hard work or good fortune will carry them into office again a year or so later. This last choice was made by Peter Thorneycroft when he resigned from the post of Chancellor of the Exchequer over a policy disagreement in 1958 and by Selwyn Lloyd when he was abruptly dismissed from the same post in 1962; each of them was back in the Cabinet after a little more than two years in the wilderness.

THE PRIME MINISTER AND THE CABINET

The Prime Minister is chairman of the Cabinet and wields a good deal of authority over it. He determines the agenda, guides discussion, and declares the sense of the meeting. He derives a great deal of power from the fact that ministers owe their appointments to him and know that he can without notice either dismiss them or promote them to posts which are higher in the ministerial hierarchy. And since the Cabinet is not only an administrative body but also a committee of party politicians, the position of the Prime Minister is further strengthened by the fact that he is the chosen leader of the governing party, bearing more responsibility than anyone else for its success in the previous election and its fortunes in the next.

This does not mean that he can act as a dictator. The tradition is that the Cabinet reaches agreement on matters of policy, not that the Cabinet acts as a rubber stamp to policies enunciated by its chairman. The convention of collective responsibility means that Cabinet members have to be prepared to defend Cabinet decisions in public once they are reached, and if a minister is not prepared to do this the alternative is for him to resign. Naturally ministers do not want to resign, and this strengthens the hand of a Prime Minister who is trying to get his colleagues to agree to his proposals. But it is equally true that a series of resignations would weaken the position of the Prime Minister, and this strengthens the hand of his critics. Moreover, politicians do not forget that at least one Prime Minister (Asquith, in 1917) was forced to resign because his Cabinet colleagues were dissatisfied with his conduct of affairs. It is the only clear example in the twentieth century, but, as was said of Admiral Byng when he was shot in front of his fellow-officers, 'it encourages the others'.

Relationships within the Cabinet depend on a variety of personal and political factors and vary from one Prime Minister to another. Churchill was a very different leader from Attlee, and Macmillan was different from both. Moreover, in all governments there is a handful of senior ministers whose support is much more crucial for the Prime Minister than that of the lesser ministers. The formal meetings of the Cabinet are supplemented by informal discussions between the Prime Minister and these senior colleagues (sometimes known as the 'inner

Cabinet') and if they all agree on a policy it is almost certain to be accepted by other ministers. As an example, the strong men of the 1945 Labour Government were Ernest Bevin, Herbert Morrison and Stafford Cripps. They often disagreed, but if they and Clement Attlee were all of one mind the combination was irresistible.

In Cabinet meetings the Prime Minister has to ensure that disagreements between ministers are resolved and to see that policies advocated by particular ministers for their departments are understood and supported by their colleagues. He also has to guide the Cabinet in its discussions of broad issues of policy and to persuade (but not coerce) them into supporting his own views on questions of political strategy. On occasions he may find that the weight of opinion is against him and yield to the majority view.[5] In exceptional circumstances he may act in a more authoritative way, the two outstanding postwar examples being the Suez crisis of 1956, when the Cabinet was not told of the ultimatum to Egypt until after it had been sent, and the decision to manufacture a British atomic bomb, which Attlee took after consulting only a small group of colleagues. In normal circumstances a Prime Minister would not act without Cabinet authorisation, but his ability to control the agenda gives him a good deal of power provided he has the support of the departmental minister or ministers most involved. Thus, the Wilson Cabinet barely considered the case for the devaluation of sterling between 1964 and 1967, although many ministers thought it should be discussed. The Prime Minister and the Chancellor of the Exchequer were well known to be against devaluation, and 'it would have cut across the normal patterns of Cabinet conduct for ministers whose departments were not concerned' to have asked for the matter to be put on the agenda.[6]

A further power that can be exercised by the Prime Minister is that of controlling the information which goes to Cabinet. During discussions on Britain's application to join the Common Market the President of the Board of Trade (Douglas Jay) produced a paper prepared by his department on the industrial and commercial consequences of entry which was much more pessimistic than the view taken by Harold Wilson and other ministers. To deal with this, 'The Prime Minister evoked the rule that the Cabinet will consider only opinions and not disagreements on matters of fact and Mr Jay's paper therefore was not circulated, though his continual efforts to reopen the issue finally led to his dismissal in August 1967.'[7] But Prime Ministers do not behave in this way unless they have very clear preferences themselves, and there are many issues on which they are open-minded and willing to let all points of view be aired in Cabinet.

Further reference to the role of the Cabinet in administration will be made in Chapter 11. But before we turn to the role of the Opposition, it is worth stressing that the Cabinet is more a political than an administrative institution. It is a committee of party leaders, and as such its concerns are to plan the strategy of the ruling party in Parliament, to keep the public image of the Government as favourable as possible, and to conduct its affairs in such a way that the party will keep or increase its majority in the next election.

THE ROLE OF THE OPPOSITION

Throughout this century Parliament has normally been dominated by the conflict between two main parties, and the smaller of these parties is officially recognised as Her Majesty's Opposition. There is no parallel to this situation in France, where two or more parties of comparable importance are normally opposed to the government of the day; nor in the United States, where party discipline is weak and the support given to the President in Congress may cut across party lines and may vary from one issue to another. In neither of these countries could any politician be given the official status and salary that is now enjoyed by the Leader of Her Majesty's Opposition.

But, though in this sense the Opposition has a privileged position in Britain, the very fact of party discipline that gives it that position also denies it much influence over the activities of the Government. In normal circumstances the Government has a clear majority, party loyalty and party discipline ensure that this is reflected in parliamentary divisions, and the Opposition has no chance at all of defeating the Government on an issue of substantial importance. This means that the Opposition has no hope of coming to power until the next general election. The Opposition is almost as impotent in respect of legislation. There is no filibuster in Britain, and the Government has complete control over the parliamentary timetable, subject to various conventions that are respected by the leaders of both parties. The result is that the Opposition cannot prevent the passage of government Bills and cannot even insist on revisions to them if the Government is determined to keep them in their original form.

The main function of the Opposition, it has often been said, is to oppose. There is a good deal of truth in this. The British devotion to parliamentary democracy is based partly on the belief that no one party or group ever has a monopoly of political wisdom. Every policy has some drawbacks, and it is thought to be a good thing that the Opposition should point them out. The need to defend their policies in Parliament may well lead ministers to think more carefully about the advantages and disadvantages of each policy before it is adopted. And, quite apart from this, the exposure of government actions and plans to continuous criticism in Parliament is a reasonably effective way of keeping the public informed about what their government is doing. Press conferences and television interviews are often more lively and searching, but ministers are under no obligation to take part if they do not wish to do so. And it should perhaps be stressed that public information about government is valuable not only in the very general sense of contributing to an education in citizenship but also in two very specific senses. First, it alerts groups within the community to the prospect of government actions that may affect their interests. Secondly, it helps electors to form some kind of judgement on the efficiency and equity of government policies.

This activity of criticism and verbal opposition is carried on within limits that are fairly well defined and understood. The parliamentary game has rules which everyone normally observes, and these rules maintain a delicate line between what is regarded as legitimate criticism and what would be regarded as obstruction. Indeed, to some extent the Opposition co-operates with the Government in arrangements which contribute to the orderly progress of parliamentary and government business. Thus, a minister going abroad for a conference may pair with an Opposition Member who is going on business in the provinces. These pairing arrangements have no official status but are always strictly observed. They are often arranged by the Whips, who in both parties are responsible for the smooth running of parliamentary business, for seeing that Members are notified of debates, and for a certain amount of 'stage-management'. Other courtesies of parliamentary life ensure that snap votes are not taken at unexpected times, that all-night sittings are rarely held, and that Members refrain from abusing one another in debate.

The weekly programme of parliamentary business is arranged by the government Chief Whip in consultation with his opposite number. By convention, the subjects of debate of twenty-six days of each session (the days allotted to Supply) are chosen by the Opposition. By convention also, the Government will allow the Opposition to interrupt the planned programme (provided a request is made through 'the usual channels') in order to move a vote of censure on the Government in connection with a new development of government policy. By convention again, the Opposition normally refrain from harassing the Government in ways that would impose a physical burden on ministers or otherwise hinder the business of governing the country. In exceptional circumstances this last convention is broken, as in March 1951 when the Conservative Opposition harassed a Labour Government that had a majority of only six, was weakened by internal divisions, and yet persisted in pressing ahead with the controversial proposal to nationalise the iron and steel industry. But the harassment lasted for less than a month, and during the rest of the session the normal conventions were observed.

In a more general sense, too, the Opposition refrains from attempts to obstruct the Government. In many democratic countries the debates on financial bills are the occasion for a vigorous attempt by the Opposition party or parties to reduce taxation or to cut the expenditures authorised for government departments. In modern Britain this does not happen. Technical revisions of bills levying taxation are often urged, but there is no general attempt by the Opposition to reduce taxes and no attempt at all to cut government expenditure. The principle adopted is that it is better to give the Government enough rope to hang itself with, and Oppositions hope that an extravagant administration will be punished by loss of popularity with the electors.

This brings us to the other main function and aim of the Opposition. Not only must it criticise the Government of the day, it must also present the image of a credible alternative government. If it is to win the next general election, it must look like a united body of men who would be competent to govern the country, and if possible it must develop a theme with which to capture the attention of electors and the support of a majority of them. Experience suggests that an Opposition does not derive much electoral benefit (though it may benefit in other ways) from working out a detailed set of policies. What the public expect is not so much a programme, more a slogan which fits the mood of the period and suggests that the Opposition party might remedy some of the defects of the existing Government. The Government of the day is in such a strong position in Britain, and has such a near-monopoly of information and initiative, that no Opposition can hope to win power by its own efforts alone. What it can do is to look like an alternative government, to exploit every weakness of the administration, and to put itself in a position to win support when the Government loses momentum or popularity.

An example of this occurred in the period 1949–51, when the public began to get tired of rationing, controls and austerity. The Conservative Opposition, which had retained its unity, captured this mood with the slogan 'Set the people free' and with promises to abolish petrol rationing and to 'get red meat back into the housewives' shopping baskets'. Another example occurred in 1962–4, when the Conservative Government showed evident signs of tiredness after many years of power and (after the failure to get Britain accepted in the Common Market) seemed to have no clear policies for improving the country's economic position. The Labour Opposition, united after many years of division, found that a claim that it would 'modernise Britain' gave it the appearance of a dynamic alternative government. In 1967–70, on the other hand, the Conservative Opposition did remarkably little to attract public opinion, the consequence of which was that they only just scraped home in 1970 in spite of the failures and unpopularity of the Labour Government. The 1970 election was marked by large-scale abstentions, the turnout of 72 per cent being lower than at any general election since 1935.

FROM GOVERNMENT TO OPPOSITION

As noted in Chapter 5, it is fairer to say that governments lose elections than that oppositions win them. The governing party suffers from the disadvantage that it will be blamed for almost everything that goes wrong with the country while it is in office, and as Britain's position is now highly vulnerable to forces which she can no longer control a government has to manage things with some dexterity if it is to secure re-election for a second term of office.

One small tactical advantage enjoyed by the Government is the right to choose the date of the election, so long as it is within the maximum period of five years. During the 1950s the Conservatives achieved a remarkable success by securing re-election twice, getting a bigger majority in 1955 than they had in 1951 and a bigger majority still in 1959. This led many critics to suggest that postwar developments had strengthened the position of the Government in relation to the Opposition and, although the electoral pendulum has swung more rapidly since 1960, it is instructive to consider the arguments that were put forward for this view.

One of them was that the Government's power to control the level of economic activity by fiscal means would enable the Government to ensure that the country enjoys a period of relative prosperity before each general election. Interest rates could be reduced, pensions and other benefits could be increased, and controls on incomes could be relaxed. A second argument was that the development of public-opinion polls has enormously enhanced the value of the Prime Minister's right to choose the date of the election by giving him a monthly index of his party's popularity. A third argument was that the advent of television put ministers constantly before the public eye: being interviewed, arriving at London Airport, talking with foreign statesmen.

During the 1960s and 1970s these arguments lost much of their force. Governments retained the ability to increase pensions during the run-up to an election and even to relax income controls, but an increasingly sophisticated electorate has come to discount the more obvious moves of this kind and governments are no longer able to reduce unemployment. Opinion polls have multiplied, and a mass of information is available about public attitudes, but political opinions have become more volatile and in both 1970 and February 1974 most polls made misleading predictions about the outcome of the election. Television journalists have become much more enterprising, and it is no longer necessarily true that ministers benefit more from television exposure than Opposition leaders do.

In the 1980s these tactical points, though not without interest, seem unlikely to have any appreciable bearing on the outcome of elections. Politics in Britain is now so dominated by the country's economic problems that a government's prospect of securing re-election seems likely to depend almost entirely on its success in dealing with unemployment and inflation and in securing some increase in industrial productivity.

NOTES

1   *Manchester Guardian Weekly,* 20 May 1979.
2   See W. J. M. Mackenzie and J. W. Grove, *Central Administration in Britain* (Longman, Green, 1957), p. 338.
3   See Jean Blondel, *Voters, Parties and Leaders* (Penguin, 1963), pp. 156–7.
4   See Francis Williams, *A Prime Minister Remembers* (Heinemann, 1961), pp. 84–6.
5   Some examples are quoted in J. P. Mackintosh, *The British Cabinet* (Stevens, 1962), p. 488.
6   J. P. Mackintosh, *The Government and Politics of Britain,* 4th edn (Hutchinson, 1977), p. 69.
7   ibid., p. 70.

FURTHER READING

The standard account of the Cabinet system is that given in J. P. Mackintosh, *The British Cabinet,* 3rd edn (Stevens, 1977); a valuable discussion of the relations between the Prime Minister and his colleagues is given in J. P. Mackintosh, *The Government and Politics of Britain,* 4th edn (Hutchinson, 1977); a useful collection of articles will be found in Anthony King (ed.), *The British Prime Minister* (Macmillan, 1969); and readers interested in a day-by-day commentary on a minister's work will find it in R. H. S. Crossman, *The Diaries of a Cabinet Minister,* Vols I–III (Hamish Hamilton/Jonathan Cape, 1975–7). A shorter set of comments by a former minister is given in Gerald Kaufman, *How To Be a Minister* (Sidgwick & Jackson, 1980).

Chapter 10

Civil Servants

Over five million people, which means one in five of the working population, are now employed by public authorities in Britain. They are engaged in all kinds of activities which range from coalmining to diplomacy and include teaching, scientific research and printing. They are employed by government departments, by local authorities, by the boards of nationalised industries, and by a variety of other agencies. In view of this, it may seem a little arbitrary to concentrate all our attention in this chapter on the half-million people who staff the central departments of Whitehall.

There are two justifications for doing so. One is that the Whitehall departments control finance and therefore, in the last resort, determine what all the other public authorities can do. The other is that the civil servants in Whitehall provide the link with the minister and with Parliament: if this vast system of public administration and public enterprise is democratically controlled, it is done through Whitehall. In this chapter, therefore, we are concerned not with all those who are engaged in public administration, but simply with those who staff the central departments of state.

THE ROLE OF CIVIL SERVANTS

There are four aspects of the role of British civil servants which deserve brief comment: the tradition that they should be anonymous; the principle that they should be impartial; the principle that the task of the civil servant is to carry out the policies decided upon by ministers; and the traditional assumption that it is not the task of the civil service to initiate change or to take responsibility for planning future lines of social or economic development.

The tradition of anonymity follows from the convention that the minister and the minister alone is responsible for the work of his department. He gets the credit for all that goes well and the censure for all that is criticised. He answers to Parliament for the activities of the department and is not expected to evade this responsibility by naming or blaming his permanent officials. The principle is that they are his servants, carrying out his instructions.

There is of course a certain element of unreality about this principle. Ministers cannot have direct knowledge of all the multifarious activities of their departments and often find themselves defending actions taken by civil servants in terms drafted by civil servants, the minister's role being that of spokesman. A new minister in a department may have to accept responsibility for decisions taken before he assumed the appointment, and is expected to defend them even if they do not have his entire approval.

Nevertheless, the principle is operative. The tradition of civil service anonymity is deeply rooted and is generally respected by ministers, by backbenchers, and by others concerned with government. Many journalists, for instance, know the names of leading officials but they rarely publish them. Group spokesmen are in a similar position: when they are disappointed with the outcome of negotiations, they can easily identify the responsible officials, but they do not criticise them in public, they criticise the minister. If things go conspicuously wrong civil servants may be criticised publicly by a special inquiry or by the minister concerned, but this is by no means a common occurrence. It should be noted, however, that since about 1962 there has been less reluctance than before to breach the principle of anonymity, and some commentators have predicted that this will wither away in the next decade or so.

The principle of civil service impartiality is bound up with the tradition of anonymity: the idea is that civil servants are servants of the Crown, serving with complete impartiality whichever ministers happen to be in office. This principle was questioned between the wars by a number of left-wing writers, who argued that the middle-class backgrounds of senior officials would make it difficult for them to sympathise with Labour aims and to co-operate fully with Labour ministers. But the Labour Government of 1945–51 carried through a series of reforms with complete co-operation from the civil service, and after that no more was heard of these criticisms; as Lord Attlee said: 'all doubts disappeared with experience.[1] In point of fact, there is no evidence that civil servants are right of centre in their sympathies, let alone in their actions: the two studies made of the higher civil service both reached the tentative conclusion that higher civil servants as a group are somewhat to the left of centre in their political sympathies.[2]

The principle of impartiality carries with it certain restrictions on the political activities of civil servants. The present position is that staff in the higher grades of the service may not take any part in national politics apart from voting and may take part in local politics only if prior personal permission to do so is given by their department.

Staff in the various clerical grades may not stand for Parliament but may engage in other political activities in so far as the regulations of their department permit this. Departments were advised by the Treasury to 'grant permission or refuse it mainly according to the degree and nature of the contact with the public involved by the duties of the officer concerned, and the extent to which his political activities are likely to be known . . . as those of a civil servant whose official duties involve his taking decisions . . . affecting the personal well-being of the department's clients'.[3] This means, for example, that clerks in local employment offices may be excluded from participation in national politics and clerks in departments dealing with local authorities may not be able to take part in local politics.

The view that ministers make policy and officials carry it out is of course a very simple statement about a very complex situation. Most questions of policy emerge from the normal process of administration and are brought up from within the department for the attention of the leading officials and, if they are important enough, for the decision of the minister. When the file is given to the minister it does not end with a question mark, it ends with a recommendation, supported by reasons. The minister may accept this recommendation or he may query it. In the latter case he will normally discuss the matter with the permanent secretary and may suggest that an alternative policy would be preferable. If he does this, it would be the duty of the permanent secretary to draw the minister's attention to difficulties that might be created, and other officials might be asked to join in a frank discussion of the merits and problems of the alternative courses of action. In the end it is the minister's responsibility to reach a decision, knowing that if things go wrong he will have to justify it to his colleagues in the Government and to defend it in Parliament.

Civil servants do not obstruct their ministers, and it is often said that the duty of the most senior officials is to 'know the minister's mind', so that they give him the kind of information he needs and make recommendations which accord with the general line of policy he wishes to pursue. But of course ministers vary greatly in their personalities, their experience, and the extent of their knowledge about the work of the department. Some ministers move quickly from one department to another and in a short stay they may find it difficult not to accept the recommendations that are made to them, particularly when the problems are technical or involved. In these circumstances there may develop a 'departmental policy' which is made by civil servants and accepted by successive ministers. An apparent example of this was the Home Office view for many years that it would be wrong to abolish capital punishment, which was put to successive ministers with such persuasive arguments that at least two men who were in favour of abolition before they became Home Secretary changed their minds on assuming that office, though they later changed back again. In cases like this it appears that civil servants are making policy, not ministers. It must be added that if the ministers concerned had insisted on reform (and had the support of their colleagues in the Cabinet) the officials would certainly have had to accept this. On the other hand, a minister who spends only a short time in a department is highly dependent on his staff, and in the 1960s this led the Labour Party as well as several independent critics to propose that British ministers ought to be entitled, as French ministers are, to bring a small group of partisan advisers into the department with them, on the assumption that they will leave when the minister leaves. This proposal was adopted, and in 1978 there were about forty such advisers working in Whitehall.

A fourth aspect of the role of the civil service can be seen most clearly if a comparison is drawn with the situation in France. In that country it is taken for granted that the State, which in practice means the permanent departments of state, has a general responsibility for watching developments in the country and for providing such public services as are necessary. In recent years French ministries and commissions have compiled and published a number of reports on matters such as the expected size and location of the future population of the country, the transport needs of the country, the demand for technical and university education, and – best known of all – the five-yearly national plans for economic development. The recommendations are not always translated into practice, for they are subject to scrutiny and often to substantial revision by the National Assembly. But the ministries accept a responsibility for making recommendations and their reports provide factual information on which politicians can draw.

In Britain the departments do not normally accept this kind of responsibility. They see their role as that of dealing with routine administration, of arbitrating between conflicting interests, and of advising their ministers about matters of policy. They do not conceive it to be their duty to make predictions about the future, except in so far as these are necessary for particular decisions that have to be taken at the present time, and even when predictions are made it is not usually thought appropriate to publish them, lest they provide ammunition for critics. The 'National Plan' published by the Department of Economic Affairs in 1965 was a break with tradition, and its failure must have provided an additional argument for those who uphold the traditional approach.

A good example of the relatively modest role of the British civil service is to be found in the realm of higher education. In the years immediately after the last war there was a considerable bulge in the birth rate and it was not difficult to predict that eighteen years later this would result in a corresponding increase in the demand for higher education. However, there was no section of the central administration which accepted responsibility for making this prediction and drawing up plans accordingly. Because of this, nothing was done towards developing a national policy for the expansion of higher education until 1962, when the Robbins Committee was appointed. Like most advisory committees, this committee contained no civil servants and its members, all of whom were unpaid, were mostly drawn from the world of education. When its recommendations were published they led to comment and objections from a variety of interested parties, and though the minister accepted most of the recommendations pressure by local authorities led him to reject the proposal that control of colleges of education should be transferred from county and county borough councils to universities. In all this process the role of the civil servants was confined to giving the minister anonymous and secret advice about the extent to which he should accept the recommendations of the Committee, whether he should yield to the pressure of local authorities, and how far he should accept the universities' estimates of the cost of expansion. Civil servants had a great deal of influence in this way, but they did not exercise much initiative and they did not accept any direct responsibility for framing plans.

In 1963 the limited nature of the role of the civil service was vigorously criticised by Brian Chapman, who argued that things were done better in France and that widespread reforms were needed if the British administrative system were to cope effectively with the increased responsibilities of government in the second half of the twentieth century.[4] The merits of the French system are not our concern. The relevance of this criticism is that it draws attention to one of the most important features of British administration. In Britain, as in most advanced countries, the first half of the twentieth century was marked by a transformation in the extent of governmental activities. But, while in France and many other European countries this was paralleled by developments in the role of the civil service, in Britain this did not occur. Here the structure and the role of the civil service in 1960 were in most respects the same as they were at the end of the nineteenth century, and it is only since the mid-sixties that important reforms have been made.

This relative lack of change has been possible partly because of the habit of consultation with affected interests, partly because of the habit of appointing committees of eminent outsiders to advise on delicate problems, and partly because of the creation of a rich variety of autonomous and semi-autonomous institutions to deal with many of the responsibilities of the State. No attempt will be made in this book to delineate the powers and duties of the BBC, the Monopolies Commission, the Racecourse Betting Control Board, the National Insurance Advisory Committee, the Local Government Commission for England, the Wages Councils, the Bank of England, the Regional Hospital Boards, the British Board of Film Censors, or the numerous other bodies which are engaged in public administration but cannot be regarded as government departments. But the student should realise that it is partly because of this tendency to proliferate administrative institutions that the civil service as such, sitting at the centre of the web, has been able to retain for so long the main features which character-ised it at the end of the last century: an impartial and anonymous service, composed largely of non-specialists, enjoying remarkable freedom from public scrutiny and criticism.

RECRUITMENT AND TRAINING

The modern British civil service is essentially a career service of professional bureaucrats and there have been two marked turning-points in its development. The first of these was the publication in 1854 of the Northcote–Trevelyan Report, which outlined a set of principles about the organisation of the civil service which were adopted by the government of the day and were not seriously challenged until very recently. The second turning-point is the publication in 1968 of the Fulton Report, which consciously questioned or rejected several of these principles and set in train a number of reforms.

The changes in the size and composition of the service between these dates were very extensive and there were a number of intermediate inquiries and reports. Nevertheless the basic principles enunciated in 1854 remained virtually intact until 1968, and this gives the period a certain unity.

The first of these principles is that civil servants should be recruited immediately or very shortly after the end of their full-time education, by open competitive examinations which were directly related to the candidates' studies at school or university. The argument for this procedure was put in the following terms by Lord Macaulay (Tre-velyan's brother-in-law) in a parliamentary speech on 23 June 1853: 'It seems to me that there never was a fact proved by a larger mass of evidence, or a more unvaried experience, than this; that men who distinguish themselves in their youth above their contemporaries almost always keep to the end of their lives the start which they have gained.'

The long-standing belief in the merits of competitive examination reflects the desire to select civil servants from among the most gifted members of each age-group. The dominant official view for over a hundred years was that intelligent recruits could be trained to do whatever was required, leaving no need, save in exceptional circumstances, to recruit people of more mature years who had experience in other occupations. Of course, exceptional circumstances obtained during the Second World War, when the civil service almost doubled in size, and many of the temporary recruits were given permanent appointments after 1945. Further, administrative developments after the war created a demand for professionally qualified staff which could only be met by recruiting people of above normal entrance-age, and the 1950s and 1960s saw the appointment of a fair number of statisticians, economists and scientists who moved to Whitehall from industries or the universities. But the general principle of recruitment immediately after the completion of full-time education survived in spite of these exceptions.

Another principle of recruitment which lasted for a century from the acceptance of the Northcote–Trevelyan recommendations after 1854 was the principle that staff should be recruited for general classes of work, not for particular jobs. The three main classes, common to all departments, were the clerical class, the executive class and the administrative class. The clerical class was recruited from school-leavers at the age of 16 or 17. Its members (and those similarly recruited today) do the general clerical work of the service, including routine correspondence, filing and compiling statistics. Recruitment to the executive class was for many years by competitive examination at the age of 18 or 19 and was subsequently based on school examinations, supplemented by an interview. A fairly recent development has been the appointment of university graduates to the executive class, where they stand a good chance of earning fairly rapid promotion. Civil servants in executive posts do work which involves more discretion than that handled by the clerical grades, and executive officers could earn promotion to very well-paid posts within the class as well as to the administrative class.

It will be clear by now that the civil service has not been organised in a direct hierarchy, as many commercial firms are. Instead, its staff have been divided into categories according to the kind of work they did, so that an office might contain a senior member of the clerical class earning much more than a junior executive officer, but in some sense inferior to the latter in status. The former would characteristically be in charge of a large number of clerks doing routine work; the latter would be handling special cases arising from the routine work.

This kind of distinction has been particularly marked in the case of the administrative class, the élite of the home civil service. To get into this class at the normal point of entry it has been necessary to have a first- or second-class honours degree and to pass a highly competitive examination. (In 1964 there were eighty-eight vacancies in the administrative class for which 835 candidates applied, but only forty-eight appointments were made.) The entrance examination could be taken by either or both of two methods. In Method I candidates took a written examination of five papers which were based on university syllabuses and could be taken in any of the normal subjects read at university, from classics to chemistry. In Method II candidates were subjected to two days of interviews, psychological tests and trial problems, at first at a house party in the country, then in more prosaic surroundings in London.

Officials in administrative grades are concerned with questions of policy within departments, and their training and duties are arranged so as to give them a spread of experience and to enable the brightest among them to rise to the very top of the service. Their original qualifications bear no necessary relationship to the kind of work they do and until very recently they had no specialised training for administration. This belief that high administrators should be 'generalists' rather than specialists, though not so clearly formulated as the first two principles, is nevertheless the third main principle underlying civil service recruitment and training. It is in sharp distinction to the principles adopted in most other advanced countries. In the United States, for instance, top officials are in most cases picked for their special skills, with agricultural economists taking jobs in the Department of Agriculture and specialists in strategic studies being appointed to the Department of Defence. In France, all recruits for the equivalent of the administrative class spend three years in the Ecole Nationale d'Administration, which provides them with the specialised training that the French consider necessary for high administrative office. The British tradition has been one of slight suspicion towards the specialist and a preference for giving men of broad general education and experience the responsibility of assessing specialised advice in terms of the public interest. However, critics have dubbed this guiding principle 'the cult of the amateur'.

CRITICISMS OF THE HIGHER CIVIL SERVICE

These principles of civil service recruitment, accepted without serious question for over a hundred years, were the object of mounting criticism during the 1960s. It was in this decade that the British realised that most of the other industrial states of Western Europe had grappled with their economic problems more successfully than Britain, and to some extent the blame for this was laid at the door of the higher civil service. A series of writers alleged that higher civil servants were 'amateurs', lacking the training in the social or natural sciences that they were thought to need. It was suggested that an education in the humanities may have been appropriate when the domestic role of government was simply to hold the ring, but was inadequate in an age when the Government has direct responsibility for a public sector employing over 20 per cent of the country's workers and indirect responsibility for the level of economic activity in the private sector employing the other 80 per cent. One well-known economist who held this view described the higher civil service as 'the apotheosis of the dilettante'.[5]

In the 1960s many critics added their voices to a lively but somewhat confused debate about the higher civil service. The confusion arose partly from the fact that it is easier to suggest that an arts graduate who has had no formal post-entry training is an amateur than it is to define exactly what kind of education and training would produce professionals. Three possible propositions can be distinguished, to each of which answers could be (and were) produced by defenders of traditional Whitehall methods. The propositions were:

(1) That not enough higher civil servants had the benefit of an education in economics, law, science or technology.

(2) That senior administrative posts should be filled by specialists in the activity controlled by the department, with doctors staffing the department responsible for health, and transport engineers and economists staffing the transport section of the Department of the Environment.

(3) That all senior civil servants should be given a systematic post-entry training in the elements of such subjects as statistics, cost–benefit analysis, public finance and public law.

The answers that were given to these propositions were as follows:

(1) That the critics invariably underestimated the number of higher civil servants who had been educated in subjects other than the humanities. Figures produced in 1955 showed that about two-thirds of the members of the higher civil service at that date had been trained as lawyers, economists, scientists, doctors, engineers, architects and surveyors.[6] It is true that the proportion was lower in the very highest positions, but in 1964 about a third of the permanent and deputy secretaries in Whitehall had been trained in either science or economics.[7]

(2) That this view was based on a misunderstanding of the role of the administrator, who has to assess the advice given by various specialists and to mediate between them and the minister.

(3) That by 1962 a start had already been made on post-entry training of this kind and it was planned to extend this in the future.

During the 1960s the allegation of amateurism was supplemented by several other criticisms. One was that the whole system of division into classes produced an excessively rigid staffing structure, which inhibited good people in the lower classes from rising to senior positions. Critics who made this comment normally underestimated the extent to which promotion between classes was possible. In 1967 only 56 per cent of members of the administrative class had entered the service in that class, the other 44 per cent having reached it by promotion.[8] Nevertheless, this is not a complete answer to the criticism, which could not easily be disproved. A second line of attack was that the class system of the service made recruitment to the higher grades difficult. This could not be denied, since throughout the 1950s and early 1960s the Civil Service Commission found it impossible to fill all the vacancies for the administrative class. Large numbers of people applied, but the standards set excluded the great majority of applicants, and it could well be argued that there were many among those excluded who might have made perfectly good civil servants even though their performance in the entry competitions did not reach the standards thought necessary for a permanent position in the administrative class.

A third line of criticism was that the activities of Whitehall were surrounded by unnecessary secrecy. Complaints of this kind by scholars and journalists were supplemented by complaints by politicians who argued that Parliament could not properly perform its function of supervising the administration unless more information about the work of departments was made available to MPs. A fourth type of criticism came from Peter Shore, the Labour MP who was shortly to become a Cabinet minister. He alleged in 1966 that 'the poor quality of official advice tended to ministries over the past decade has been one of the major causes of our dismal national record.'[9] Later in his book he said:

> The power that comes from the processing and selection of information, from permanent position, from the tight hierarchical discipline within the Service, from the iron curtain of secrecy which separates the present from the past, from the inter-departmental committees that strangle Whitehall – the dimensions of this essentially political power can scarcely be disputed.[10]

If the record of British government since 1945 is scrutinised with a critical eye, it is of course easy to find instances of lack of foresight by government departments and failure to appraise proposed developments with sufficient care. To name only a few examples at random, there is the disastrous miscalculation of the number of doctors who would be needed; the continuing failure to produce a coherent plan to deal with London's worsening traffic problems, either by subsidising public transport or by building new roads; the fantastic miscalculation of the costs involved in developing the TSR2 and the Concorde; the lack of foresight shown in planning the location of London's airports; the slowness in replacing outmoded schemes of apprenticeship by modern methods of industrial training. Critics of the central administration have ample evidence at their disposal, for these and other failures cannot all be laid at the door of politicians.

It would be unfair to blame the civil service alone for these failures, and naïve to suppose that they would all have been avoided if the system of recruitment and training had been different. But by 1966 a mood of disenchantment with the civil service had set in, and it was in this atmosphere that the Fulton Committee was appointed with the obvious expectation that the Committee would propose radical changes.

THE FULTON REPORT AND ITS CONSEQUENCES

The Fulton Committee set out deliberately, and perhaps a little self-consciously, to remodel the civil service. The opening paragraph of its Report stated bluntly: 'The Home Civil Service today is still fundamentally the product of the nineteenth-century philosophy of the Northcote–Trevelyan Report. The tasks it faces are those of the second half of the twentieth century. This is,what we have found; it is what we seek to remedy.'[11]

The recommendations of the Committee were sweeping, even though somewhat predictable. The Committee did not take the line: 'These criticisms of the civil service are justified but these others are not. These suggested reforms should be adopted, and implemented in such and such a way, while these other proposals that have been put to us should be rejected as unnecessary or inappropriate.' Instead, they gave a degree of endorsement to nearly all the criticisms that were being made of the service in the mid-sixties, and recommended the adoption of nearly all the reforms that were being canvassed, including some that had already been accepted.

Because their recommendations were couched in such sweeping terms, they did not constitute a precise blueprint for a restructured service. The Fulton Report cleared the ground, but it remained for ministers and (more particularly) senior civil servants to decide which of the Report's suggestions should be adopted and how they should be put into practice.

Predictably, the changes made constitute a modification of the pre-existing arrangements and do not alter the basic character of the service. The proposal that preference should be given to social-science graduates has been rejected. The civil service continues to be staffed by generalists rather than specialists, and officials are to remain anonymous and impartial. The main reforms can be summarised as follows:

(1) The distinction between the administrative and executive classes has been blurred during the early years of service, so that university graduates can be appointed as trainees and sorted out according to their talents. This change has had a beneficial effect on recruitment and may improve the efficiency of the service as the new recruits reach senior positions.

(2) A Civil Service College has been created to provide post-entry training for senior officials, giving courses in economics, statistics, computation, and social and public administration. The courses last only four or five months, so they do not compare with the three-year courses given by the Ecole Nationale d'Administration in Paris. But they nevertheless increase the skills of senior staff.

(3) Each year a number of senior staff with particular skills and experience are recruited from outside the service, usually after eight or ten years in another occupation. In the 1970s recruits of this kind entered the higher civil service at the rate of about thirty a year compared with about 120 a year who were recruited directly after graduation.

It may therefore be concluded that the criticisms and reforms of the past two decades have had the consequence of improving and modernising the higher civil service, though it remains true that senior officials in Britain have less experience of the outside world than their equivalents in most other advanced industrial states. Some critics would say that the service remains somewhat inward-looking and old-fashioned, but they would agree that it is also notable for several old-fashioned virtues, such as courtesy, fair-mindedness and a complete absence of corruption.

NOTES

1 See W. A. Robson (ed.), *The Civil Service in Britain and France* (Hogarth Press, 1956), p. 16.

2 See H. E. Dale, *The Higher Civil Service of Great Britain* (Oxford University Press, 1941), p. 107, and R. A. Chapman, *The Higher Civil Service in Britain,* pp. 115–17.

3 Treasury Circular of 14 Aug 1953, quoted in W. J. M. Mackenzie and J. W. Grove, *Central Administration in Britain* (Longman, Green, 1957), pp. 157–8.

4 See Brian Chapman, *British Government Observed,* passim.

5 Thomas Balogh, in Hugh Thomas (ed.), *The Establishment* (Anthony Blond, 1959).

6 See Mackenzie and Grove, *Central Administration,* p. 29.

7   See Lord Bridges and others, *Whitehall and Beyond* (BBC, 1964), p. 34.
8   Chapman, *The Higher Civil Service in Britain*, p. 49.
9   Peter Shore, *Entitled to Know* (MacGibbon & Kee, 1966), p. 12.
10   ibid., p. 154.
11   *Report of the Committee on the Civil Service,* Vol. I, Cmnd 3638 of 1968, p. 9.

FURTHER READING

A penetrating critique of the civil service will be found in Brian Chapman, *British Government Observed* (Allen & Unwin, 1963); the key to recent reforms is *Report of the Committee on the Civil Service,* Vol. I, Cmnd 3638 of 1968; a useful guide to the higher civil service is provided in R. A. Chapman, *The Higher Civil Service in Britain* (Constable, 1970); a stimulating discussion of problems and developments in the 1960s will be found in Trevor Smith, *Anti-Politics: Consensus, Reform and Protest in Britain* (Charles Knight, 1972). A valuable account by insiders is given in Peter Kellner and Lord Crowther-Hunt, *The Civil Servants: An Inquiry into Britain's Ruling Class* (Raven Books, 1980).

Part IV

The Process of Government

Chapter 11

Administration and Policy

THE ADMINISTRATIVE SYSTEM

The administrator lives by the pen, and the administrative process is largely a process of communication. An administrative system is essentially a network of communication channels, and it is effective if it ensures that messages are speedily transmitted, information and advice are readily available, and the activities of those on the periphery are co-ordinated and controlled by those at the centre.

In the latter part of the last century the British system of central administration, following the Northcote–Trevelyan reforms, was both unified and simple in structure. The main functions of government were the traditional ones of defence, foreign and colonial affairs, maintaining law and order, raising revenue, and encouraging trade. The most important departments were accordingly the Admiralty and the War Office, the Foreign Office, the Colonial Office, the Home Office, the Treasury and the Board of Trade. These departments were all housed within a few hundred yards of each other in Whitehall; their staff were recruited centrally by the Civil Service Commission and were liable to be transferred from one department to another, their expenditures were closely controlled by the Treasury. Such co-ordination as was necessary between departments was facilitated by the fact that senior officials usually knew one another personally. If an issue could not be settled at this level, it would be referred to the ministers, who would either settle it between themselves or take it to the Cabinet.

In the present century this system has been immensely complicated by the vast extension of the activities of the Government. Many of the new activities differ from the old in that they involve administrators in a much greater measure of positive action on their own initiative. Partly for this reason, only some of the newer activities have been put into the hands of departments organised on traditional lines, the others being given to a variety of other institutions and agencies. The system as a whole is now untidy and cannot be said to be based on a clear set of principles. The following outline may serve as a rough guide, though exceptions can be found to every generalisation and the reader who wants specific information should consult a textbook on public administration.

The first set of environmental and social services to be provided by statute were those concerned with public health, housing and education, all of which were initiated before 1900 and have been developed since. Although departments of the central government are concerned with these services and have some control over them, their actual administration was placed in the hands of local authorities, which in a legal sense are independent bodies rather than agents of Whitehall. The administration of these services is therefore partly determined by the relations between local authorities and Whitehall, which are complex. Thus, housing policy is a hot political issue at Westminster, and the national government controls it both by detailed legislation and by a system of conditional grants to local authorities. But the national government does not build a single house or issue a single loan on mortgage, and the local authorities which do these things have their own individual policies within the national policy, for which local councillors must answer to local electors.

A second set of services are those concerned with social welfare, which were introduced by Lloyd George in 1908 and have been developed by subsequent governments. The administration of social insurance and pensions was made the responsibility of new government departments, which consequently handle large blocks of routine work which rarely raise issues of policy. (It was largely for this reason that the Government felt able to move the Ministry of National Insurance, apart from the minister's immediate advisers, out of London.) On the other hand, when the National Health Service was established in 1946 administrative control of the Service was divided between the Ministry of Health and twelve Regional Hospital Boards, each of which was based on a teaching hospital attached to a university. Since 1968 social insurance, pensions and health have all been brought under the umbrella of a giant ministry called the Department of Health and Social Security, but it is doubtful whether this amalgamation has made much practical difference to the services.

A third kind of government activity, which is not entirely new but has been greatly extended in the past fifty years, is the provision of grants, subsidies and other forms of protection for various kinds of private activity. This invariably involves co-operation between Whitehall and representatives of the activity, though the institutional arrangements for this co-operation vary. Government aid to the cotton industry is determined after discussions with the Cotton Board, which is a statutory body established by the Government to represent the industry. In the 1930s the policy of industrial protection led to the creation of a number of officially sponsored organisations like the Milk Marketing Board and the Iron and Steel Federation to act as channels of communication between Whitehall and the industries, and the direct government control of many industries during the war was carried out in part by the recruitment as temporary civil servants of members of these bodies. In the case of universities, as noted earlier, the grants are administered by a University Grants Committee of which only the chairman is a government servant.

A fourth kind of government activity is the direct management of industrial undertakings. Although the postal and telephone services were provided for many years by the GPO, it was felt inappropriate to put the industries that were nationalised after 1945 into the hands of government departments. Instead, they are managed by public corporations, semi-autonomous bodies subject to certain kinds of government control but free from the continuous control by ministers, by Parliament, and by the Treasury that characterises government departments. Various reasons were given for this decision. It was suggested that the management of the industries would lack initiative and flexibility if it were tied to civil service procedures. It was thought desirable for those in charge to have more freedom in hiring and firing staff than is enjoyed by government departments. It was felt the industries should be free from the political pressures to which ministries are subject and it was thought that they should be sheltered from the political controversy that would arise if questions in Parliament could be tabled about every aspect of their work.

The logic of these arguments has never been entirely clear. Staffing arrangements could have been varied for industrial ministries and it is not evident that British Rail has shown any more initiative than the telecommunications division of the GPO. The industries have not been at all free from political pressure and have in fact been forced to take uneconomic decisions by ministerial order. The main difference is that MPS have found it more difficult to ask questions and acquire information about the industries than they would if a minister had been in charge, though the Select Committee on Nationalised Industries has been established to bridge this gap and has enjoyed some success in doing so. However, the arguments prevailed, and the result is that most of the public sector of industry is now managed by public corporations whose activities are subject to a rather uneven form of control by the Government. If they want to buy aircraft or import fuel or close branch railway lines they are subject to direct ministerial control, as they are in planning capital developments; but in much of their day-to-day work the control is more tenuous and patchy. In 1969 the Post Office was reorganised as a public corporation, to bring it into line with other government enterprises.

Fifth, and finally, since the last war the Government has assumed overall responsibility for guiding the economy of the country. The main instrument of economic management has been fiscal policy of a

Keynesian kind, the object being to stimulate the economy in times of recession by planning for a budgetary deficit, or conversely to check inflation by increasing taxes and reducing public expenditure so as to take money out of circulation. The Treasury has responsibility for economic management of this kind, and the detailed control it exercises over all other government departments and the Bank of England enables the Treasury to make fiscal adjustments at very short notice.

During the early 1960s various critics alleged that the concern of the Treasury to protect the balance of payments and the value of sterling had led it to make frequent interventions in the economy with insufficient regard for the need to develop long-term plans for economic growth. This line of criticism led to the establishment in 1964 of the Department of Economic Affairs, the new department being made responsible for long-term economic planning while the Treasury retained control of fiscal policy. This was like a division of functions between husband and wife in which the wife did the shopping, paid the bills and managed the family bank account, while the husband compiled an elaborate dossier on the kind of mansion into which they might move if their financial situation ever permitted it. The Department of Economic Affairs was a failure, the National Plan it produced was outdated before it was published, and the Department was abolished in 1969.

Other aspects of economic management are dealt with by the Departments of Trade, Industry, and Energy, and also by a variety of semi-autonomous agencies. The most important of these is probably the National Economic Development Council, which is chaired by the Chancellor of the Exchequer and is composed mainly of representatives of industrial management and the trade unions, with a staff of professional economists. Other agencies have included the National Incomes Commission of 1961–4, the Prices and Incomes Board of 1965–70, and the Prices Commission established in 1973.

The first two reports of the Prices and Incomes Board illustrate one of the roles that this kind of quasi-autonomous body can play in the British system of government. They consisted of a criticism of the road haulage industry for an unjustifiable increase in charges and a criticism of the printing industry for inefficiency caused by restrictive practices. A government department could not easily have issued these reports, for civil servants do not think it their function to make public criticisms of private organisations, and political considerations discouraged ministers from doing so. Criticism of management by a Labour minister or of unions by a Conservative minister would immediately be discounted as prejudiced, while criticism of a minister's 'own side' would be politically dangerous. The advantages of a quasi-autonomous body are, first, that responsibility for its actions can be taken by a chairman who is not a member of the Government and, secondly, that its reports may possibly be regarded as impartial. The main disadvantages of these bodies relate to their power: if they wield executive authority, they do so without democratic control through Parliament, while if they do not have such authority their recommendations may simply be ignored when they prove inconvenient. But agencies of this kind have a specific role to fill in Britain given: (*a*) the tradition that government departments do not issue controversial publications except in justification of decisions that the minister has taken; (*b*) the evident need for authoritative reports that will cast light on industrial and social problems; and (*c*) the failure of the British Parliament to meet this need through the work of its specialised committees.

CO-ORDINATION AND CONTROL

The foregoing paragraphs give an impression of the shape of the somewhat untidy system of central administration that now exists. Co-ordination and control within this system are the responsibilities of the civil service, the Treasury and the Cabinet.

Although the civil service (excluding the semi-industrial divisions of the Ministry of Defence) employs less than a tenth of the people engaged in the public sector, it maintains fairly effective control over activities within the sector. Local authorities, public corporations and other public bodies enjoy legal and formal independence of government departments but they do not enjoy a great deal of administrative independence. Thus, education is the responsibility of local authorities and the government does not employ a single teacher or own a single school. But the administration of education is shaped by ministry circulars and teaching methods are kept in line by government inspectors who visit schools and watch teachers at work in their classrooms. Again, public corporations enjoy a good deal of independence in their day-to-day activities but they are not allowed to do anything which conflicts with government policy and are sometimes made to do things which are directly contrary to their own interests. Thus, the railways have been told to keep open a number of uneconomic branch lines; the aircraft corporations have been forced to buy British planes to help the aircraft industry instead of American planes which would make the airlines more competitive; a nationalised steel firm has been refused permission to import American coal, which was cheaper than any it could buy in Britain.

There is no question about the power of Whitehall in its relationships with these other authorities, if it chooses to use its power. A local authority which refuses to obey a ministry directive is brought to heel by the immediate suspension of its grant, without which it cannot finance its activities. A public corporation which declines to co-operate finds that its chairman is subject to abrupt dismissal, a fate which has befallen two of the chairmen of BOAC in recent years.

The Whitehall departments, staffed and organised in the way described in the previous chapter, thus sit at the centre of the administrative system. The activities of these departments are themselves co-ordinated and controlled partly by the Treasury and partly by the Cabinet. The power of the Treasury depends on its control of expenditure. Government departments cannot do much without spending money, and all expenditures are subject to the prior approval of the Treasury. Each year each department prepares detailed estimates of proposed expenditure for the following year, and these are discussed in detail with Treasury officials and are rarely approved without reductions being made. Moreover, no provision for a new service or new development may even be included in the estimates unless the department has secured the prior approval of the Treasury for it in writing.

Once the estimates are accepted the department is tied to them, and cannot transfer money saved under one sub-head for use elsewhere unless the Treasury agrees. If there is a prospect of overspending on any sub-head, the department must immediately inform the Treasury, when a decision will be taken as to whether the department should cut expenditure, should transfer money from some other sub-head, or should apply for a supplementary estimate. To emphasise its control of the purse-strings, the Treasury doles out money to each department in a monthly allowance which is carefully calculated to ensure that the departments never have very much in hand.

Of course, the departments do not always accept Treasury rulings without argument, and if officials feel that Treasury decisions are not in the interest of good government they will put the matter to their minister. He may then raise it with the Chancellor of the Exchequer, and if agreement cannot be reached between them they may take the whole problem to the Cabinet. Cabinet discussions of this kind are not uncommon, and the outcome may depend on the relative political strengths of the ministers involved as well as on the merits of the issue. But Cabinet decisions are binding and are invariably accepted by all parties. A minister has no choice but to accept or resign: civil servants have no further discretion in the matter, and stoically accept what has been decided.

The Cabinet settles differences between ministers not only over finance but also over the the application of government policy and the situations which arise when the policies of one department affect the interests of another. The Cabinet is the highest agency of co-ordination and must be prepared to discuss conflict until agreement is reached – not always unanimous agreement, but agreement that can be accepted by the minority as 'the sense of the meeting'.

The evidence suggests that this system of co-ordination and control is usually but not always effective. Occasionally mistakes are revealed, as when a new block of flats in London for which planning permission had been given had to be demolished immediately after it was built to make way for a motorway extension. The system is put to test in times of crisis. In August 1965 the Treasury announced that many public constructional projects would have to be postponed to reduce public expenditure and ease the pressure on the building industry. Within a week the Ministry of Transport sent a circular to local authorities giving details of over fifty schemes of road improvement which had been sanctioned but would now have to be put off, and in the following days various other ministries explained how the new policy would affect the building of houses, schools, hospitals, hospitals and other amenities. This suggests a fairly efficient system of co-ordination and control. It is true that spokesmen for builders, architects and surveyors complained that the effects on the industry would be confusing and wasteful, but this was probably inherent in the policy. One of the problems of hasty action of this kind is that there is not sufficient time to go through the normal process of consultation with the interests involved, and it is to this aspect of public administration that we must now turn.

CONSULTATION AND ADVICE

As explained in Chapter 6, it is the normal practice of government departments to consult representatives of affected interests before taking decisions. One reason for this is that civil servants need specialised information about the practices and problems of the group involved. A representative association is the most convenient source of such information, and even if a government department decides to collect its own data, for instance by requiring firms to make regular returns of production, the officials will need to consult the appropriate trade association about how to draw up the questionnaire. Another reason is that consultation often helps to ensure that the decisions of the department will be accepted by members of the trade or profession concerned, and that their co-operation will be forthcoming. A third point is that organised groups often act as a buffer or filter between Whitehall and the various interests, firms and individuals represented by the group, who might otherwise inundate the department concerned with letters of protest and contradictory expressions of view about what should be done. For all those reasons regular consultation with group spokesmen is now regarded as a principle of good government.

The advantages of this practice to the group spokesmen are obvious. It enables them to press the claims of their groups before decisions are taken, which is much more useful than the ability to protest after the event. It also establishes their status in the eyes of members of the group, so that their position as an organisation is made secure. Of course, the privileges such spokesmen enjoy in Whitehall imply certain unwritten obligations. They are expected to maintain the confidential nature of some discussions and to respect the anonymity of civil servants; they may feel that if they fail to gain their point they ought to accept failure gracefully rather than launch a public attack on the ministry; they often slide into the role of an intermediary between the ministry and the more demanding members of the group they represent. It is natural for an organisation which becomes an established channel of communication to transmit messages in both directions, and occasionally this leads the more impatient or radical members of a group to feel that their spokesmen have become excessively responsible and moderate. Some motorists feel that the AA and the RAC have moved in this direction; some animal-lovers feel the same about the RSPCA.

One of the features of this system of consultation is that each department has its own set of client organisations, mainly representing groups with common interests but sometimes representing groups with shared attitudes. Thus, the Departments of Trade and Industry deal mainly with trade associations; the Transport Division of the Department of the Environment deals with the Road Haulage Association, the AA and the RAC, the Traders' Road Transport Association, the Transport Workers' Union and the three unions of railway workers; the Ministry of Agriculture, Fisheries and Food deals with the National Farmers' Union, the British Trawlers' Federation, and the Country Landowners' Association; the Home Office deals with the Howard League for Penal Reform, the National Council for Civil Liberties, and organisations representing immigrants; the Department of Education and Science deals with the National Union of Teachers, the Association of Municipal Corporations, and the Association of Education Committees. If no organisation exists to represent an interest, the government department concerned may sponsor one: thus in 1956 the Forestry Commission stated that they were prepared to give a substantial sum to assist the establishment of a Woodland Owners' Association to represent the interests of private owners; in 1959 a grant of £30,000 was included in the Commission's estimates for this purpose (with the approval of the Treasury); and a few months later the new

Association was reported to be urging the Government not to accept any large increase in timber imports from the Soviet Union.[1] Equally, the Government may take action to reduce the number of organisations representing an interest if they are inconveniently numerous; in 1945 'the Ministry of Works took the initiative in setting up a National Council of Building Producers, bringing together forty-one separate trade associations for common action in dealing with the Department'.[2]

Some of the largest organisations are in frequent, perhaps daily, contact with a range of ministries. A TUC publication has explained that 'the days of lobbying are . . . past', for 'the General Council have now established their right to consult or to be consulted on all ministerial moves, bills, regulations and administrative actions which are likely to have an effect on the interests of the workers and their organisations'.[3] An equivalent statement could be made by the Confederation of British Industries.

This feature of British government is of constitutional as well as administrative importance. There is no theory or model of the constitution which takes account of the practice of consultation between government departments and the spokesmen for organised groups. Traditional theories of the constitution suggest that the influence of the citizen on the process of government is secured solely through the House of Commons, either by the general impact of elections or by the specific means of an approach to an MP, who then approaches or questions the relevant minister. In practice the citizen who wants action from the Government does not normally go to his MP. He may do this, but he is more likely to raise the matter through an organised group whose spokesmen will deal directly with Whitehall. Such groups cover all activities and all categories of the population. Newly born babies cannot organise themselves, but their mothers or prospective mothers can join the Association for the Improvement of Maternity Services; parents who are disssatisfied with the provision of playing-fields for children can approach the Central Council of Physical Recreation; students discontented with their grants can ask the National Union of Students to make further representations; workers unhappy about safety precautions at the factory can approach their trade union; shopkeepers' interests are defended by the Association of British Chambers of Commerce; consumers' interests are protected by the British Standards Association; old people, disabled people, ex-service men and other groups all have spokesmen who enjoy access to government departments. This is clearly one of the central features of the modern British constitution, and a government which failed to consult the affected interests before taking a policy decision would be open to serious criticism on this score: in 1954, for instance, the

Government was severely criticised by the Opposition for concluding the Anglo-Japanese trade agreement without adequate consultation with spokesmen for groups that would be affected by the agreement, in particular the cotton industry.[4]

Having said this, it should be added that the constitutional status of officials (i.e. their position as servants of the Crown and the minister) affects the form taken by the discussions, which are usually described as a process of consultation even when they are in reality a process of bargaining.[5] One former civil servant has written about them in the following terms:

> The conversation will preserve all proper forms. The unofficials will inquire of the official, not 'Will you agree to this?', but 'Do you think the minister will agree?' The official replies 'No, I feel sure he won't go as far as that; but I think he will probably consent to do so much, on the understanding that the rest is left over until next year'. The unofficials' answer: 'Well, we think we can persuade our people to be content with that for the present.' And they part with mutual expressions of affection and esteem, each side understanding perfectly that pledges have been given and received to the effect that the department will go some way to meet its unofficial critics, and that the critics will make no trouble in the House of Commons or elsewhere because it does not at once go the whole way.[6]

Apart from consultation with group spokesmen, government departments also rely heavily on advisory committees. At the last count there were about 900 permanent (but unpaid) committees advising the departments in London, together with an almost uncountable number of local committees. Many of the members of these committees are drawn from the ranks of group spokesmen who thus get a further opportunity to advance their views. Other members are technical experts, civil servants and independent laymen. Thus, when the Cinematograph Films Council was set up to advise the President of the Board of Trade its twenty-two members comprised four representatives of film producers, two of film renters, five of exhibitors, four of employees in the industry, and seven independent members (including the chairman) of whom some were experts and some were laymen.[7] In this case only the secretary was a civil servant, though often one or two officials are included in the committee. The reports of these advisory committees are not normally published: their function is simply to make specialised information and informed recommendations available to the departments.

In addition, special committees to inquire and to advise are frequently appointed, sometimes being known simply as committees and sometimes being given the status of Royal Commissions. These committees differ from the permanent advisory committees in that they are much more likely to contain a preponderance of independent members, who may have experience in the field of activity under consideration but are not appointed as representatives of groups. Committees of this kind hear evidence from interested parties and sometimes commission experts to conduct studies on their behalf. Thus, the Royal Commission on Population commissioned economists and demographers to make predictions about population trends and the Robbins Committee on Higher Education had studies made of several problems. The reports of committees of inquiry are normally published.

Committees of this kind are appointed for a variety of reasons. Sometimes a department realises that something has to be done and appoints a committee as the best way of getting informed advice about what is needed: an example is the Robbins Committee. Sometimes a department has a delicate problem on its hands and wants a committee, for whose work the Government takes no responsibility, to examine the alternatives and make recommendations. An example is the Committee on Homosexual Offences and Prostitution, which interviewed homosexuals and whose report caused a great deal of controversy. The Government eventually decided to accept the proposals regarding prostitution but to take no action on those regarding homosexuality, on the ground that public opinion was not yet ready for the recommended liberalisation of the law. Sometimes a department wants to prepare Parliament and public opinion for a reform which officials and the minister consider desirable and appoints a committee partly so that the evidence in'favour of the reform can be mustered and the need for the reform can be endorsed by an independent body. As has been said, a minister may feel: 'There is a big change to be made here, quite clearly, or a big advance. It will be much easier to commend it to Parliament and the country if I have set up a group of reasonable beings, well experienced and so on, and they have come to that conclusion.'[8] An example is the Royal Commission on Betting, Lotteries and Gaming, whose recommendations led to the legalisation of off-the-course betting in cash and the establishment of betting shops all over the country.

Sometimes committees of inquiry are appointed without any serious expectation that their reports will be acted upon.[9] They are appointed to pacify critics, examples being the Royal Commission on the Press of 1947 and the Royal Commission on Equal Pay for Men and Women in 1948. They are appointed to buy time, a possible example being the Royal Commission on Marriage and Divorce of 1951. Finally, they may be appointed to kill a proposal by demonstrating its disadvantages or by taking it out of the public eye; a possible example of this being the

Palestine Partition Committee of 1938, whose report helped to kill the plan of partition that a former committee had proposed. But it is probably fair to say that most committees of inquiry lead to some kind of action sooner or later, even though it is unusual for a committee's recommendations to be adopted *in toto*.

It should be clear by now that, although leading civil servants are rarely specialists, neither they nor their ministers need lack specialised advice. It is pressed on them from all sides, and the custom is for government departments to welcome this. Quite apart from their need for information, it is in accordance with the traditional role of the British civil service that other people should come forward with controversial proposals, leaving officials with the task of giving their ministers discreet and anonymous advice on the merits of the alternative courses of action that are open.

DECISION-MAKING AND POLICY

It is part of the familiar theory of British government that ministers take decisions and officials simply give advice. While this was never entirely true, it was much nearer the truth in the latter part of the nineteenth century than it is today. When departments were small ministers could be personally acquainted with all issues of any importance. But this is no longer the case: the civil service is about twenty times as big as it was a hundred years ago and there are only about three times as many ministers. Now about forty ministers, helped by about fifty junior ministers, control the work of nearly 500,000 officials. The great majority of decisions are clearly taken without reference to a minister.

Within the civil service there is a well-established hierarchy of decision-making, so that a principal knows what he can decide on his own account and what he must refer up to an assistant secretary. In Whitehall one of the basic techniques of administration is the rotating file, which is carried from out-tray to in-tray by a small army of uniformed messengers. When a file reaches the official who is empowered to decide on the case he does so unless it poses a special problem of one kind or another, which is quite rare in some kinds of department (e.g. the Department of Health and Social Security) but quite common in others (e.g. the Foreign Office). The special problems which arise out of day-to-day administration are the seeds from which many changes of policy develop.

One kind of problem is the possibility of conflict with another department. Questions about the school dental service raise the possibility of conflict, or at any rate differences of opinion, between the

Department of Health and Social Security and the Department of Education and Science. Questions about regional unemployment involve both the Department of Industry and the Department of Employment. Questions about the problems of coloured immigrants have implications for the Home Office, the Department of Employment, and the Department of the Environment. In all these and similar cases the civil servant must consult his opposite number in the other department before taking action. They may be able to settle the matter between them. But, if it is not as easy as that, each must refer the matter to his departmental superior. Sometimes issues between departments can then be settled by an informal conference or a committee; in other cases this is not possible and the files go right up the hierarchy to the Permanent Secretaries and perhaps the ministers, with each official on the way adding his comments in the form of a minute.

Another kind of problem arises where the implementation of policy gives rise to ambiguities or to developments which had not been expected. For instance, until 1962 the law provided that Commonwealth citizens, being British subjects, were allowed to migrate to Britain without special permission, without health checks, and without being counted or recorded. At some stage in the late 1950s officials in various departments realised that what had been a trickle of immigration had become a flood, that this was creating social problems, and that government action of some kind was becoming necessary. It was then their duty to bring this to the attention of senior officials and the ministers concerned, which they did. To take a more trivial example, local authorities were for years empowered to pay vacation grants to undergraduates following a course of vacation study. Some authorities interpreted this to mean a course which was physically supervised by tutors, while others paid grants for a course of home reading which was prescribed in advance. The result was that students in similar circumstances were sometimes treated differently, and in 1971 the Department of Education and Science transferred the administration of these grants from local authorities to universities.

Yet another kind of problem arises when the implementation of a routine decision seems likely to create political controversy. Thus, the decision to construct concrete lamp standards in front of a row of country houses took on a special significance when it was realised that one of the houses was owned by the President of the Royal Academy, an outspoken opponent of modern street furniture. In cases like this the department is likely to be mentioned in the press and questions may be asked in Parliament. The wise official will draw the attention of his superiors to such cases (an activity known in Whitehall as 'putting up an umbrella') so that they can be sure of their ground and be prepared to defend themselves against a possible storm of criticism.

Important questions arising from the administrative process reach the Permanent Secretary, who must decide whether or not to put them before the minister. This decision again depends on how controversial the question is, how likely it is to come up in Parliament, and how far it impinges on other questions of policy with which the minister is grappling. A Permanent Secretary will not want to worry his minister unnecessarily, but he will try to keep him in touch with the questions which may lead to criticism. The minister, unlike the officials, has to deal with questions in Parliament, in press conferences, and in public meetings, and he will not want to be caught off guard because he is ignorant of one of the problems of his department.

The minister, in his turn, has to decide whether to take matters to the Cabinet. Clearly he will have to do so if he cannot reach agreement with another minister, for the Cabinet is the only place in which differences of this kind can be solved. Apart from this, he will take matters to the Cabinet if they are intrinsically important or if they are likely to cause a major political row. All proposals for legislation are normally referred to the Cabinet, for even if they are not controversial in themselves they will take up parliamentary time and a case must be made for their priority. Developments which will affect the reputation of the Government should be brought to the attention of the Cabinet, which is a meeting of party leaders as well as a meeting of departmental heads. Thus, when a new Government takes office a minister may find that for administrative reasons it is impossible to achieve something to which his party had committed itself in the election, and this must be reported to his colleagues. Topics which arouse great public interest will tend to appear on the Cabinet agenda for a similar reason, though they may be disposed of quickly. Finally, ministers will take to the Cabinet all those knotty problems which are virtually insoluble, but which are likely to be used as a stick with which to belabour the Government. One former Cabinet minister has said that 'most of the Cabinet's time is spent in dealing with matters which are insoluble, in the sense that there are serious disadvantages attaching to any possible course of action'.[10] Obvious examples in recent years include the hostilities in Cyprus; the position of Rhodesia; and the crisis in Northern Ireland.

The agenda of Cabinet meetings is controlled by the Prime Minister. The Cabinet Secretariat is responsible for circulating papers, and when an item is reached the minister concerned speaks to it. The other members then speak and the Prime Minister eventually declares the sense of the meeting, no vote being taken. The style and character of Cabinet meetings depends partly on the personality of the Prime Minister. We learn from memoirs that Churchill was loquacious and sometimes rather arbitrary, allowing lengthy discussions on some items but dismissing others very briefly. We learn that Attlee, in contrast, was quiet, concise, methodical and sometimes extremely curt. But these are variations within limits that are set by the pressure of business, by the influence of the secretary of the Cabinet (who is a senior civil servant), and by the traditions that all Prime Ministers respect.

So far policy-making has been discussed as if all policy questions arose out of the ordinary business of administration. In fact the majority of policy questions arise in this way. Even when a team of new ministers take office after defeating the previous government, what they normally do is deal with existing departmental problems with a rather different emphasis, not come into their departments with a sheaf of new policies under their arms. Harold Laski once said that the task of a minister is to 'inject a stream of tendency' into the decisions of his department, and although the phrase is inelegant it is quite appropriate.

But of course other policy decisions have their origins in the ideas of ministers or the Cabinet. Some examples are the decisions to nationalise certain industries after 1945, to create a completely free national health service in 1946, to develop commercial television in 1954, to abolish resale price maintenance in 1963, to impose a capital gains tax in 1965, and to insist on the development of comprehensive schools instead of leaving the matter to local authorities. In cases like this the minister will get the authority of the Cabinet to draw up detailed proposals; he will discuss the idea with his senior officials, who may already have thought about alternative methods of achieving the object; and a specific set of plans will be worked out in the department. The minister will then ask· the Cabinet for approval of these plans, which he must be prepared to defend against probing questions from his colleagues, who may seek to anticipate the criticisms that will be made in Parliament and in the country. If approval is given, it is then a matter for more detailed work in the department, and for the preparation of legislation if that is required. If the Cabinet does not approve, the minister will have to think again, or may have to abandon the proposals for the time being. Occasionally a minister resigns when his proposals are rejected, as Peter Thorneycroft and his two junior ministers did from the Treasury in 1958. But politicians acquire thick skins in the course of their careers, and resignations on this ground are infrequent.

LIMITATIONS OF THE SYSTEM

The administrative system sketched in this chapter has been developing smoothly and without radical change for over one hundred years. It provides for the effective co-ordination of government policy and has other virtues that have often been described. It does not follow, however, that it is or should be the object of uncritical admiration. On the contrary, there is evidence of a lack of foresight and purposive control in central government that cannot be ascribed simply to the failings of individuals. The failure to find an answer to Britain's recurrent difficulties with the balance of payments has been mentioned before, and several other domestic examples were cited in the last chapter. There is also evidence of a certain lack of foresight in overseas policy. No satisfactory arrangement was made, while Britain had the power to enforce it, to provide for a German contribution towards the cost of keeping British troops in Germany. There was a slowness, understandable but extremely expensive, in withdrawing from overseas bases which had outlived their usefulness. British policy towards the Common Market, at the time of its inception, seems to have been based on the assumption that the venture would not be successful. Some wider British policies have suggested an exaggerated estimation of both the value to Britain of the Commonwealth connection and the reality of the so-called 'special relationship' with the United States.

This is not intended to be a radical criticism of British policies or administration. Government is an imperfect art; many difficult problems have been dealt with successfully; and the British record since the war contains nothing to compare with the appalling bloodshed in Indo-China and Algeria, the anarchy that followed the Belgian withdrawal from the Congo, or the tragedy of Vietnam. The purpose is rather to throw light on the character of British administration, which evidently leans towards caution rather than boldness and is better equipped for patient negotiation than for the prediction of trends and developments. That this should be so is not surprising in view of the traditional roles of civil servants and ministers in the British system.

On the one hand, civil servants regard it as their main task to deal with immediate problems and to give the minister such advice as he requests. Some departments are more forward-looking than others, but a common view is that it would not be appropriate for officials to take much initiative in planning future policies, for this is the function of ministers. On the other hand, ministers themselves move from post to post with considerable frequency. One former minister has said that, on average, it takes a minister about eighteen months to acquire sufficient grasp of the problems of his department to make a significant impact on its policies.[11] If this is true as a generalisation (and clearly there must be variations both between men and between departments), it throws a good deal of light on the problems of the Ministry of Defence, which had no fewer than thirteen ministers between 1945 and 1965. Moreover, the minister's role is often seen as essentially that of a politician rather than a departmental manager. Enoch Powell has said that a minister's function is 'to handle the issues, be they major or minute, that are political in character, where the management of public opinion and the interpretation of actions and events in a political sense is involved. . . . This is his business in life, and he moves from one field to another as a barrister will put down one case and take up another.'[12] It can readily be seen that if all ministers took this view of their role, and if all civil servants took the rather limited view of their own role that is hallowed by tradition, there would be nobody at all in Whitehall who would regard it as his task to prepare long-range forecasts and contingency plans and feasibility studies.

Both Harold Wilson and Edward Heath have shown their awareness of this problem. When Wilson took office he tried to bring a new look to economic policy not only by creating new institutions like the Department of Economic Affairs and the Industrial Reorganisation Corporation, but also by moving a number of academic economists (some of whom were noted for their radical ideas) into influential positions in Whitehall. They failed in their attempt to find a new strategy of overall economic management but they made a clear impact in particular fields, such as the application of cost–benefit analysis to transport policy. The reform of the higher civil service is another example of the Labour Government's view that it was necessary to modernise the administrative machine.

Edward Heath proceeded on a rather different tack when he became Prime Minister in 1970. First, he streamlined the administration at the top, reducing the overall number of ministers from a hundred to eighty-three and reducing the Cabinet to seventeen members (the smallest since the war). Secondly, he formed an exceptionally homogeneous Cabinet, most of its members being politicians who were new to Cabinet office but were dedicated supporters of Heath's own approach to political problems. Thirdly, he established an entirely new unit called the Central Policy Review Staff, which was attached to the Cabinet Office. This unit was composed in the first instance of about twenty social scientists and businessmen working under the leadership of Lord Rothschild, a scientist who previously held a senior executive position in British industry. The stated function of the unit is to help ministers evaluate 'the alternative policy options and priorities open to them' and to ensure that 'the underlying implications of alternative courses of action are fully analysed and considered'.[13]

Unfortunately these attempts to modernise the central system of administration have not resulted in the visible improvements in performance that were hoped for. However, for this the civil service cannot be blamed as the British economy and governmental system suffered in the 1970s from two developments that were completely outside the control of Whitehall. The first of these was the OPEC decisions in the autumn of 1973 which led to a fourfold increase in the price of oil, to an economic recession which has affected all industrial countries in the free world, and to the growth of unemployment in Britain to a higher level than had been seen since the 1930s. The second blow was the successful attempt by the National Union of Mineworkers to smash the Government's pay policy in February 1974, leading to a series of wage increases which gave Britain a higher rate of inflation than any other European country.

The consequence of these two developments was that economic growth in Britain came to a virtual standstill. Industrial productivity in the spring of 1979 was no higher than it had been five years previously, and only the rapid development of the North Sea oilfield prevented the economy from going into a calamitous decline. As government expenditures in the Welfare State have a built-in tendency to increase year by year, the virtual cessation of economic growth has produced a critical situation. From 1971 to 1978 the increase in public expenditure was about 30 per cent greater than the total increase in national wealth, so that people working in the private sector inevitably suffered a reduction in their disposable real income.

This development created tremendous pressure for administrative economies, which was reinforced when Britain had to give guarantees of public-expenditure cuts as a condition of getting a loan from the International Monetary Fund in 1976. Expenditure cuts are not easily seen as a form of progress, but the best judgement on the way the British administrative machine has responded to this fiscal crisis is that it has done reasonable well, in view of the political constraints within which it operated, and undoubtedly better than would have been the case had it not been modernised.

NOTES

1   See Allen Potter, *Organized Groups in British National Politics* (Faber, 1961), p. 32.
2   J. W. Grove, *Government and Industry in Britain* (Longmans, 1962), p. 146.
3   *ABC of the TUC* (TUC, 1954), p. 11, quoted in Potter, *Organized Groups,* p. 205.
4   See S. H. Beer, *Modern British Politics* (Faber, 1965), p. 78.
5   See Grove, *Government and Industry,* pp. 141–61, for a good account of this aspect of British government.
6   See H. E. Dale, *The Higher Civil Service of Great Britain* (Oxford University Press, 1941), pp. 182–3.
7   K. C. Wheare, *Government by Committee* (Clarendon Press, 1955), p. 57.
8   Enoch Powell, in Lord Bridges and others, *Whitehall and Beyond* (BBC, 1964), p. 48.
9   See Wheare, *Government by Committee,* pp. 89–91, for these and other examples.
10 Enoch Powell in Bridges, *Whitehall and Beyond,* p. 56.

11   J. Enoch Powell, *A New Look at Medicine and Politics*, p. 4.
12   ibid., pp. 4–5.
13   *The Reorganisation of Central Government*, Cmnd 4506 of 1970.

FURTHER READING

R. G. S. Brown and David Steel, *The Administrative Process in Britain*, 2nd edn (Methuen, 1979), is a good basic account of the Whitehall system; Richard Rose (ed.), *Policy-Making in Britain* (Macmillan, 1969), is an excellent collection of short discussions and case-studies; Hugh Heclo and Aaron Wildavsky, *The Private Government of Public Money* (Macmillan, 1974), gives a penetrating assessment of the crucial role played by the Treasury; a short discussion of recent developments and problems will be found in A. H. Birch, 'Westminster and Whitehall', in Gwyn and Rose, *Britain: Progress and Decline* (Macmillan/Tulane University Press, 1980). Useful case-studies of policy-making include Samuel Brittan, *The Treasury under the Tories* (Penguin, 1969); Edward Boyle and Anthony Crossland, *The Politics of Education* (Penguin, 1971); Maurice Kogan, *Educational Policy-Making* (Allen & Unwin, 1975); J. Enoch Powell, *A New Look at Medicine and Politics* (Pitman Medical, 1966); Colin Crouch, *The Politics of Industrial Relations* (Manchester University Press/Fontana, 1979); Douglas Ashford, *Policy and Politics in Britain* (Blackwell, 1981); M. Wright (ed.), *Public Spending Decisions: Growth and Restraint in the 1970s* (Allen & Unwin, 1980); and R. Williams, *The Nuclear Power Decisions: British Policies 1953–78* (Croom Helm, 1980).

Chapter 12

Parliament and the Administration

CONSTITUTIONAL THEORY

It is a basic principle of the British constitution that the function of Parliament is not to govern the country, but to control the Government. As noted in Chapter 2 of this book, the responsibility for government and administration rests with the Queen's ministers, but developments in the past three centuries have rendered them accountable to Parliament (and in particular to the House of Commons) for most, though not all, of their actions. Parliament is, in fact, the only institution which has power to control the actions of government departments, provided their officials do not break the law. There is no equivalent in Britain of the United States Supreme Court or the German Constitutional Court, both of which have power to declare executive actions contrary to constitutional principles. Nor does Britain have a system of administrative courts, like the French Conseil d'Etat or the Italian Conciglio di Stato, which can review administrative decisions and decide whether or not they were justified. In Britain government departments can do largely as they like, provided they have parliamentary approval and keep within the letter of the law. In constitutional theory there is a division, not of powers, but of functions, ministers being responsible for governing the country and Parliament being responsible for calling ministers to account as well as for legislation (which will be dealt with separately in the following chapter). The accountability of the Government is said to be ensured by two constitutional conventions: the convention that ministers are collectively responsible to Parliament for the policy of the Government as a whole and the convention that each minister is individually responsible to Parliament for the work of his department.

There is, of course, a degree of unreality about this constitutional theory, which assumes a dichotomy between the Government on one hand and Parliament on the other. In fact nearly 100 Members of Parliament at the present time are members of the Government and more than 200 other MPs are loyal supporters of the Government. The real dichotomy in British politics is between the Government and the Opposition, not between the Government and Parliament. But this is not yet reflected in constitutional theory and it will be convenient in this chapter to begin by examining the established principles and conventions.

COLLECTIVE RESPONSIBILITY

The essence of this convention is: (*a*) that members of the Government should present a united front to Parliament in defence of their policies; and (*b*) that if the House of Commons defeats the Government on a vote of confidence the Prime Minister should either ask the monarch for an immediate dissolution of Parliament or should resign, together with all his ministers. The convention was developed in the years between 1780 and 1832, and in the middle decades of the nineteenth century it led to the resignation of a series of governments. Between the first Reform Act of 1832 and the second Reform Act of 1867 no government survived for what is now regarded as a government's normal life, from a general election until the Prime Minister asks for a dissolution, at a time of his own choice, towards the end of that Parliament's allotted span. In this period the convention of collective responsibility was an effective weapon which ensured parliamentary control of the executive, and ten governments in thirty-five years were brought to an end by adverse votes in the House of Commons. It was largely on the evidence of this period that commentators and politicians based their claims, in the latter part of the last century, that the British system of government was one in which the actions of the Government were effectively controlled by Parliament.

In fact, even as these claims were gaining general acceptance, the development of party discipline was changing the situation. Between 1900 and 1979 only three governments were forced out of office as the result of parliamentary defeats. In January 1924 Liberal and Labour MPs joined forces to defeat the Conservative Government (which had lost seats in a general election a few weeks earlier). In December 1924 the Liberals combined with the Conservatives to bring down the Labour Government. In March 1979 the Labour Government was defeated by the combined votes of Conservatives, Liberals, Scottish Nationalists and Ulster Unionists.

On these three occasions no single party commanded a majority in the House of Commons, so that the government of the day was at the mercy of the smaller parties which held the balance of power. However, throughout the greater part of the present century the leading party has had an overall majority in the House of Commons, and party discipline has been so effective that no ruling party in that situation has been brought down by a vote of no confidence. This has held good even when the governing party has commanded only a tiny majority. The

Labour Government of 1950–1 survived with a majority of only six, and the Labour Government of 1964–6 got by with a majority which varied between four and one. The maintenance of a majority in the division lobbies in this kind of situation puts a severe strain on government supporters, who have to be prepared to attend no matter how inconvenient it is to them, even to the extreme of being brought into the precincts of Parliament by ambulance and being counted by the tellers while lying on a stretcher. But so far they have always measured up to these demands.

This does not mean that the convention of collective responsibility is obsolete, for clearly it still exists: a government which is defeated on a vote of confidence has no choice but to resign or to dissolve Parliament. But, as a general rule, governments in the twentieth century are defeated not by Parliament but by the electorate, and this affects the significance of the convention of collective responsibility. A Government which faced the constant possibility of defeat in Parliament would be more likely to have to resign or ask for a dissolution when things were going badly for it than when things were going well: in this sense responsibility to Parliament would provide an immediate sanction for a failure of government policy. In the modern British political system this sanction is absent. As a general rule a Government is not more likely to resign or dissolve Parliament when its policies meet with a major reversal than when it is prospering but less likely to do so. The public has a short memory, and a Government's best strategy in times of crisis is to ride the storm and hope that it will be able to recapture public support before the next general election is held. The Labour Government of 1945–50 survived through the fuel crisis of 1947, the devaluation of the pound in 1948, the collapse of its Palestine policy in the same year, and the fiasco of the groundnuts scheme in 1949. In 1950 it was returned to power, though with a reduced majority. The Conservative Government of 1955–9 succeeded not only in surviving after the débâcle of Suez, but in winning an increased majority at the next general election. James Callaghan's Government of 1976–9 tried desperately to stay in office until the parliamentary term came to an end in October 1979, in the hope that a good summer would induce the electorate to forget the hardships caused by industrial disruption during the previous winter.

The role of the convention of collective responsibility in British government may perhaps be summarised in the following terms. It does not provide a continuous sanction for the blunders and failures of governments, as it did in the middle decades of the last century. On the other hand, it continues to play a vital role in the British political system, ensuring that governments resign immediately they lose their parliamentary majority in an election. On these admittedly rare occasions when the governing party leads the others by only a hair's breadth the convention may lead the Government to modify its plans, as in 1965 when the Labour Government decided not to go ahead at that time with its declared policy of renationalising the steel industry. At all times the convention gives some procedural advantage to the Opposition: if they put down a motion of censure on the Government, this has precedence over other parliamentary business, and the Government will be obliged to rearrange the time-table to find time for it. And, finally, the convention compels ministers to maintain the appearance of unity: they are expected to resign from the Government if they are not prepared to defend its policies in public. There have been one or two recent instances of ministers disagreeing in public, as in 1975 when Cabinet ministers opposed to British membership of the EEC were permitted to campaign for a negative vote in the referendum on that issue. But there is no general tendency for Prime Ministers to relax their insistence on unity.

INDIVIDUAL RESPONSIBILITY

This convention has two strands, one of which is in full operation, the other of which is something of a myth. The first strand is that the minister in charge of a department is answerable to Parliament for all the actions of that department. As Gladstone said: 'In every free state, for every public act, some one must be responsible, and the question is, who shall it be? The British constitution answers: "the minister, and the minister exclusively".'[1] The positive aspect of this is that Members of Parliament wishing to query the actions of a department, either privately or publicly, know that there is one man who cannot evade the duty of answering their questions. The negative aspect of it is that it protects the anonymity of civil servants and shields them from political controversy. This strand of the convention can be seen each day when Parliament is in session, for the first hour of each sitting is devoted to Question Time, at which ministers answer questions put to them in advance by MPs and have also to deal with supplementary questions which arise out of their answers.

According to the second strand of the convention, ministers must accept responsibility for the actions of their department not only in the sense that they must be ready to explain and defend them but also in the sense that they must resign their appointments if serious blunders or failures are exposed. This, at any rate, is what is implied by many commentators and what is widely thought to be part of the practice of British government.

In fact, resignations of this kind are extremely rare. Mistakes are constantly being made, and from time to time they are exposed or admitted, but it is quite exceptional for a minister to resign on this account. The most conspicuous failures of postwar British governments have led to stormy debates in Parliament and to scathing comments in the press, but they have not led to the resignation of the ministers concerned. The total failure of British policy in Palestine between 1945 and 1948 did not lead the Foreign Secretary to think of resigning, even though he had said in a rash moment that he would stake his political future on his ability to deal with the problem. The fiasco of the groundnuts scheme in 1949 did not lead the Minister of Food to resign, though he was urged to do so by the Opposition and the majority of newspapers. The humiliating collapse of British policy towards Egypt at the time of the Suez expedition was not followed by the resignation on political grounds of any of the ministers concerned, though ill-health forced the Prime Minister to resign a few weeks later. The waste of vast sums of public money on the design of missiles and aircraft which have never been produced has not led to the resignation of any of the Ministers of Aviation and Defence who were responsible for it. The list could be extended to include the various failures of economic policy in the past twenty years, the minor fuel crises that occur whenever the weather is unseasonably cold, the slaughter of eleven prisoners in a Mau-Mau detention camp in Kenya who were clubbed to death by warders acting in pursuance of their instructions to force the prisoners to work, and many other examples.

Looking at the matter another way, S. E. Finer has traced only sixteen cases of a minister resigning as the result of parliamentary criticism of his department between 1855 (when the first case occurred) and 1955.[2] Since there were no cases between 1955 and 1979, this makes sixteen cases in 124 years. The smallness of the number indicates that it is only in exceptional circumstances that failure leads to loss of office, and Finer has shown that what made these cases exceptional was not the gravity of the failures but, in general, the fact that the ministers had lost popularity or respect within their own party. The only clear postwar example of resignation, that of Sir Thomas Dugdale in 1954, is a good instance. Dugdale did not mention resignation when he made his statement to the House of Commons following the publication of the Crichel Down report, and his decision to resign five weeks later was the result of backbench criticism expressed at private meetings of the Conservative Party's Food and Agriculture Committee.

Of course, the exposure of departmental failings may affect a minister's career even though it does not lead to his resignation. In the next Cabinet reshuffle he may find that he is transferred to a less attractive ministry or 'moved upstairs' to the House of Lords. But often failures do not have any such consequence, and whether they do or not depends on the standing of the minister with his party and the Prime Minister, not on the seriousness of the failure or the extent of parliamentary criticism. In view of this, it cannot be said that the convention of individual ministerial responsibility to Parliament renders the minister liable to loss of office if the work of his department comes under fire.

The first part of the convention, however, is of considerable importance. The fact that ministers have to answer for their departments gives MPs the right to demand information about administrative decisions, whether these be related to large issues of policy or to dealings with individual citizens. MPs frequently exercise this right, sometimes by questions in Parliament, more often by private correspondence. It enables Members to investigate the grievances and press the claims of their constituents at the highest level, and knowledge that this has been done is a comfort to constituents even if the decision cannot be changed.

In the second place, there is no doubt that the behaviour of civil servants is affected by the knowledge that, if they make a mistake or offend a member of the public, the matter may be raised in Parliament a few days later. The name of the civil servant will not be publicly disclosed, but no official likes the prospect of having to justify his actions to his superiors in response to an urgent demand by the minister, knowing that the reputation of the department rests, for the moment, on his shoulders. It is true that as the size of the civil service has increased far more rapidly in the past fifty years than the number of questions asked, the chances of any individual decision leading to a parliamentary question must have diminished. But there is no evidence that this has led civil servants to stop worrying about the possibility of a question, and no serious reason to doubt the truth of the following comment by a senior official of the Department of Employment:

> One may say of the British official that, if he is engaged on a job with no immediate outlet to minister and Parliament, he will still be working tacitly with the sort of notions of relevance that would mean something to them; he must try to so order things that, of all that can happen, only those things happen which are susceptible of explanation in the Parliamentary context.[3]

In the third place, the ability to hold ministers to account for their actions in Parliament facilitates the work of the Opposition. They can use parliamentary questions to expose weaknesses in the Government's policies and lack of efficiency in the administration. If the matter which is brought to light is both serious and urgent, the Opposition may be able to secure the adjournment of the House and hold a full debate on the same day. Failing this, the Opposition can move a vote of censure or debate the issue on one of the twenty-six days on which Opposition motions have priority. If the matter is potentially damaging to the Government's reputation, members of the Opposition can return to it time and time again by asking questions on its different aspects. In this way the Opposition can bring the Government's weaknesses to the attention of press and public and so hope to win votes in the next election.

If these three points about individual responsibility are considered in conjunction with the earlier points made about collective responsibility, it is clear that ministerial responsibility to Parliament is one of the central features of the British political system. It does not normally lead to the resignation or dismissal of ministers, but it does mean that they have constantly to explain and justify the work and plans of the administration to a critical assembly, and it provides an important channel of communication between those who govern and those who are governed.

PARLIAMENT AND GOVERNMENT POLICY

Parliament's influence on government policy is limited by three factors. The first is the loyalty and discipline that government leaders can expect from their backbench supporters. This is not only a function of the pressures that the Whips and party organisation can bring to bear on the individual MP but also a function of the team spirit that pervades the two main parliamentary parties. Government backbenchers are normally most reluctant to do anything that would help the Opposition, and when they dislike government policy they tend to voice their criticisms at private party meetings while supporting the Government in public. If they feel strongly about the matter, they may express their dissent during parliamentary debates and may put down a motion of criticism which is not intended to be debated or put to the vote, the object being to see how many signatures they can collect as a demonstration of support for their viewpoint. If the Government's majority is safe, they may occasionally abstain, but it is very rare indeed for a government supporter to go into the division lobbies against his own party. Conservative backbenchers between 1955 and 1964 did not vote against the Government's policy of granting independence to the east African colonies, while Labour backbenchers in the Parliament of 1964–6 did not vote against government policy regarding the war in Vietnam or the control of immigration, though in all these cases backbench criticism was widespread and deeply felt. Since 1966, as has been noted, governments have been let down by some of their supporters on several very important issues, but they can still depend on backbench loyalty and discipline in relation to the normal run of parliamentary business.

A second factor limiting the influence of Parliament on policy is the lack of specialised information available to backbench MPs. Ministers are supported by the whole administrative machine and are briefed by civil servants for every speech and every answer to a parliamentary question. The backbencher is on his own, lacking facilities for research, having no access to government departments except through the minister, and unlikely to be an expert on any subject unless he happens to have personal experience of it or he is well briefed by a pressure group. In domestic affairs pressure groups can instruct MPs on specialised matters and often do so, though this educational role is limited by the fact that the more successful groups deal directly with government departments and do not often think it politic to embarrass ministers by briefing MPs to criticise the Government. In regard to foreign affairs and defence pressure groups are much less knowledgeable and the Government often has a near-monopoly of specialised information.

A third factor is that strand in the British political tradition which insists on the importance of leadership. When people speak of the responsibility of the Government they are often referring to the view that it should be accountable to Parliament and the public for its actions. But at other times they are referring to the fact that the Government has the duty of maintaining the peace and guiding the country towards prosperity. Ministers are responsible for the government of the country, and the British assumption is that they should be given ample powers to do what they think necessary. It is believed that Parliament should criticise them but not that it should try to obstruct them. A President of the United States has to accept that Congress will probably amend his budgetary proposals and will almost certainly cut his requests for the appropriation of money for the various departments of state. A modern British Cabinet, on the other hand, takes it for granted that its budget will go through Parliament without substantial change and that its appropriations will go through without any change at all. This is not just a matter of party loyalty; it is a deeply rooted tradition of political behaviour.

This tradition is reflected in the clichés of political discourse and journalism: time after time MPs are urged not to tie the hands of ministers, to give them powers that are adequate to the needs of the situation, to give them the support they need in difficult circumstances and to suspend judgement until the results of their policies can be seen.

The tradition bridges party-political differences, as can be seen from the following quotations from men of the most diverse opinions. First, L. S. Amery, an elder statesman of the Conservative Party:

> The word 'responsibility' . . . connotes a state of mind, which weighs the consequence of action and then acts, irrespective, it may be, of the concurrence or approval of others. It is the strength of our constitutional system that it encourages and fosters responsibility in that higher sense.[4]

Secondly, Nigel Nicolson, a politician of the centre:

> British democracy has hitherto emerged successful from its most important test: unpopular decisions by a government are, in general, accepted; and popular clamour weighs no more than an ounce or two in the scales of its judgment.[5]

Thirdly, Harold Wilson, Leader of the Parliamentary Labour Party:

> Having been entrusted by the nation with the duties of government, we intend to govern. . . . I think the people of Britain want to see a government acting with firmness and taking the decisions, popular or unpopular, that are called for.[6]

The attitudes reflected in these statements are by no means confined to party leaders: they are shared by most backbenchers, most political journalists, and most members of the public. The preference for decisive executive government is a central feature of modern British politics, and it naturally tends to weaken the influence of backbenchers on government policy.

The combination of these three factors – party discipline, the Government's advantage in terms of specialised information, and the tradition of executive leadership – necessarily limits the influence of Parliament over major questions of policy. The Government can ignore the views of the Opposition, provided it is prepared to withstand a barrage of verbal criticism. It cannot ignore the views of its own supporters, for their attacks can weaken the position of ministers within the party and, in the last resort, they can depose the party leader. But ministers can override the views of a minority within their party if they are sure that it has no chance of becoming a majority and if its leaders lack the power or the will to stage an open revolt. It is therefore possible for controversial policies to be pushed through the House of Commons even though they would be defeated if a free vote were permitted, and occasionally this happens. For instance, it occurred in the cases of the Dock Work Regulation Bill of 1976 and both the Scotland and Wales Bills of 1978.

All the factors indicated in the last few paragraphs shape the extent and nature of parliamentary influence on government policies. The influence varies a good deal according to the nature of the policy, and it is not possible to be precise about this as influence is not susceptible to measurement. One or two generalisations and examples may be helpful, however.

First, it can be said that in the field of defence the Government's position is strongest and Parliament's influence is weakest. The decision to make atomic weapons was taken and implemented without Parliament being informed. Decisions about American bases in Britain have not been influenced by backbench criticisms. The decision to make the TSR2 was implemented despite repeated warnings that the costs would far outweigh the utility of the aircraft. When the Government discovered for itself that the warnings had been justified, the project was abandoned despite parliamentary objections that so much had then been invested in it that cancellation would have a disastrous effect on the aircraft industry.

In the conduct of foreign affairs governments are occasionally subject to criticism by minorities but can usually count on Parliament to give general support to government policy. All parties value the appearance of national unity in diplomatic affairs, and since 1945 the Suez crisis has been the only occasion on which this unity has completely broken down. Sometimes the Prime Minister has private talks with the Leader of the Opposition in the attempt to maintain unity, as happened during the crisis over Rhodesia's declaration of independence, and this was certainly a case in which the influence of parliamentary opinion was greater than could be surmised simply by reading parliamentary debates. This is, indeed, often the case, which is why it is so difficult to assess influence. The government Whips have the task of making constant reports to their leaders about the state of opinion among backbenchers, and in foreign affairs as in home affairs these reports are taken into consideration by ministers.

In home affairs the relationship between Parliament and Government is more complex and more difficult to summarise. Government policy is influenced by pressures from all sides, including pressures from MPs who may be speaking for themselves or may be acting as spokesmen for organised groups or for their constituencies. All that can be said by way of summary is that, while parliamentary views and pressures are always considered when policy decisions are taken, they rarely appear to be decisive when large issues are at stake. A minister's main problem when he wishes to promote a new policy is to get the support of his Cabinet colleagues: if he can surmount that hurdle, he is not likely to be put off his course by parliamentary criticism, even though in minor matters he may trim his sails to the wind. Parliamentary opinion will have more influence on issues which are peripheral to the Government's main concerns, for instance penal reform and cruelty to animals, but this is only because the Government is willing to be influenced on such matters.

THE MP AND THE ADMINISTRATION

The overall weakness of Parliament in relation to the Government does not mean that the MP is a mere puppet. Most MPs are articulate and forceful men and, within the limits of the system, they are able to make themselves felt at Westminster. Backbench supporters of the Government have ample opportunity to express their views at private meetings of the party committees which consider the various branches of government policy. Ministers have to explain their intentions and defend their decisions before these committees, and are undoubtedly influenced by the views expressed there. When Edward Heath announced his intention of abolishing resale price maintenance it was the backbench committee of his own party that provided the most vigorous criticism, though he eventually pushed his measure through. When the Macmillan Government decided to scrap the Skybolt missile the Conservative Defence Committee expressed grave disquiet, and it was to this committee, not to the nation at large, that the Government gave an assurance that the V-bomber force would be strengthened to maintain Britain's independent deterrent in the period before the Polaris system was operative.[7] And it is significant that the Minister for Agriculture at the time of the Crichel Down Affair, who did not feel obliged to resign when the report was published, did so after he had been criticised by his party's backbench committee. Major issues may become the subject of fierce controversy at meetings of the entire Parliamentary Labour Party or the Conservative 1922 Committee, where critics are not silenced by the need to avoid the appearance of disunity, as they frequently are on the floor of the House.

Opposition Members have very little chance to influence the actions of the administration before the event: their role is to expose misjudgements or ambiguities to the public gaze after the event. Within limits, the parliamentary question is a useful device for this purpose. Ministers cannot avoid answering questions, and though their first answer is often a carefully worded piece of camouflage a well-informed MP may be able to penetrate this by skilful supplementary questions. Questions do not lead to debate, for time is strictly limited, but information gathered at Question Time may put the Opposition on the scent of issues which can subsequently be raised in a debate.

The utility of Question Time is limited where the issues are technical and the Government has a near-monopoly of information, for the minister will then reveal only as much as he chooses to reveal. Civil servants are expert at the art of drafting replies which appear to answer the question without actually giving anything away. But when the issues can easily be comprehended and the facts are fairly well known ministers can be given a very difficult time if their answers displease the House. Questions involving civil liberties are particularly apt to rouse the House to anger. Among other examples there was a row over the report that a Scottish policeman had struck a teenage boy who swore at him, which led to an official inquiry, and there was a furore about a West Indian girl who was to be deported for shoplifting, in which parliamentary anger led the Home Secretary to rescind the deportation order.

In assessing the importance of Question Time it should of course be realised that the procedure gives MPs a right to demand information from ministers which is often given privately by correspondence. A Member wanting to know why a constituent has not been given a pension will deal with this privately, and will only consider a parliamentary question on the matter if the behaviour of the ministry is likely to arouse general concern. Question Time is clearly a useful device which fills a number of rather different functions.

Another parliamentary device of some importance is the procedure whereby the normal business of the House can be suspended to make way for an immediate debate on an urgent issue. Under Standing Order 9, the Speaker will allow a motion for the adjournment of the House to be put immediately after Question Time if he is persuaded that an issue has arisen which is of public importance, is within the competence of a minister, could not reasonably have been debated earlier, and could not reasonably be left until room could be found for it in the time-table. These are stringent conditions, and motions of this kind are pretty rare. But occasionally there is a sudden development which arouses the concern of Parliament – a crisis in foreign affairs, a breakdown of public order, a decision to deport an alien at short notice – and in these circumstances the motion may be put. If forty Members support the motion, no matter how many Members oppose it (they are not counted), the motion succeeds and the issue is debated that evening.

SPECIALISED COMMITTEES

The two factors which limit the influence MPs can exert through the channels so far mentioned are the tradition of governmental supremacy (sustained by party discipline) and the Members' lack of specialised knowledge of governmental affairs. To help overcome this second handicap critics have frequently proposed that the House of Commons should establish a full set of specialised committees with power to call for papers and cross-examine civil servants. There can be no doubt that committees of this kind, which have flourished over many decades in the United States and France, are the only channel through which a large representative assembly can exercise effective control over the work of government departments. Without this opportunity to find out for themselves what is being done in departments, members of the assembly are in a poor position to offer detailed and constructive criticism.

Until the changes instituted by the Wilson Government, the House of Commons had only four select committees of a specialised nature, one each on Estimates, Public Accounts, Statutory Instruments, and Nationalised Industries. Of these, the committees on Public Accounts and Statutory Instruments have precise and uncontroversial functions. The function of the Public Accounts Committee is to administer a kind of public reprimand to senior civil servants whose departments are reported to the Committee by the Comptroller and Auditor-General for having transgressed Treasury rules, usually because they have transferred expenditures from one heading to another without seeking Treasury approval. The Select Committee on Statutory Instruments examines the several thousand orders and regulations that are drafted each year by government departments, most of which pass automatically into law after lying before Parliament for a specified number of days unless Parliament takes specific action to prevent this. The Committee's task is to scrutinise all these orders and to draw the attention of the House to any which do not comply with the requirements of the Act under which they were made, or which raise problems of some similar kind. There has been no move either to reduce or extend the powers of these two committees.

The function of what used to be called the Estimates Committee, but now has the much more logical title of the Committee on Expenditure, is to scrutinise Government expenditures with a view to assessing whether or not the taxpayer has got good value for money. Until 1965 the Committee had only a small staff of clerks and could do no more each year than to pick out a few examples of government expenditure for examination. In 1965 the Committee's membership and staff were increased and five specialised sub-committees were established. This move was in line with Whitehall's new emphasis on managerial efficiency in the public services, and in recent years the Committee has produced a stream of useful reports.

The Select Committee on Nationalised Industries was set up in 1956 to examine the reports and accounts of public corporations in charge of the nationalised industries, and it has interpreted its terms of reference in a broad way. Taking one industry at a time, it has conducted fairly thorough inquiries into matters of administration and policy, and has felt free to examine officials of the relevant government departments as well as officials of the public corporations. The Committee has rarely divided on party lines or approached issues in a partisan way, and this has helped it both to secure the co-operation of civil servants and to command respect in Parliament for its reports.

The undoubted success of this committee lent support to those reformers who wished to see the establishment of specialised committees of Parliament covering a wide range of government activities. It was argued that this reform would make Parliament's influence over administration more effective as well as increasing the knowledge and extending the experience of backbench MPs. However, one of several curious limitations of the authority of the House of Commons is that it cannot establish its own committees, any more than it can control its own time-table. In both these respects the House is in the hands of the Government of the day, and the extension of the committee system therefore had to wait for the support of a sympathetic administration.

This support was forthcoming in 1966, when it was announced that several new select committees were to be established on an experimental basis, the experiment to be reviewed after a few years. The first three committees dealt respectively with agriculture, with science and technology, and with education. These were followed in 1968 and 1969 by new committees on race relations and immigration, on Scottish affairs, and on overseas aid.

It is fair to say that this experiment with specialised committees of Parliament failed to justify either the hopes of their more enthusiastic supporters or the fears of their opponents. It would be unreasonable to maintain that the committees did anything but good. But their impact on parliamentary life was not so great as some of their advocates had expected. Many MPs did not wish to serve on the committees, either because they could not spare the time or because they thought it better to conserve their energies for debates on the floor of the House. Not all of the committee meetings were well attended. The reports of the committees attracted little public attention and the parliamentary debates on these reports were very poorly attended. Experience largely confirmed the view that a sceptical academic had put forward in 1966: 'What Members usually want are neat gobbets of information which will be relevant to a particular political occasion. And since this is not what they get from Select Committee reports, it is hardly surprising that they do not read them eagerly.'[8]

Of the new committees, three were devoted to the affairs of particular government departments, while the other three dealt with a broader range of topics. The first three – those concerned with agriculture, education, and overseas aid – made appreciably less impact than the others. Having terms of reference which coincided with the responsibilities of a particular department, these first three committees were inevitably viewed with suspicion by both the senior officials in the departments and the ministers in charge of them. Neither officials nor ministers were happy to see a group of MPs acquire specialised knowledge about departmental affairs which might serve as a basis for penetrating criticisms of departmental policies. These three committees were terminated by the Government between 1969 and 1971. The other committees were more successful. The Committee on Science and Technology has proved particularly valuable. The topics with which it deals are not normally subject to partisan controversy, and some of its members have a good deal of scientific expertise which can be used more effectively in committee than on the floor of the House. The Committee's investigations of alternative designs for nuclear power stations have been welcomed as useful by both officials and politicians.

The Committee on Race Relations and Immigration has been successful for a rather different reason, namely that the topics with which it deals are politically sensitive issues for which the ministers and civil servants concerned are happy to share responsibility. The Committee has made a number of valuable studies and its mandate has been renewed by successive governments.

Two other select committees, both of which will presumably be permanent, have been established to consider, first, the work of the Parliamentary Commissioner for Administration and, secondly, draft proposals for secondary legislation made by the European Commission. The select committees as a whole have won several privileges which they did not enjoy before 1966. They have won the right to appoint outside specialists as advisers; they have been authorised to appoint sub-committees; and they now have financial provision for overseas travel to gather evidence. That committees of Parliament should have to beg the Government for permission to do these things is a striking indication of the relative weakness of the British Parliament. In most European democracies it would be taken for granted both that Parliament could appoint its own committees and that those committees could, if they saw fit, appoint advisers and create sub-committees.

As was pointed out in Chapter 2, the powers of the British Parliament do not conform to the model implied by liberal theories of representative government. But within the confines of the system the new specialised committees are making a modest but significant contribution to Parliament's work in relation to the administration.

NOTES

1 *Gleanings from Past Years* (London, 1879), Vol. I, p. 233.
2 See S. E. Finer, 'The individual responsibility of ministers', in *Public Administration*, vol. XXXIV.
3 C. H. Sisson, *The Spirit of British Administration* (Faber, 1959), p. 123.
4 *Thoughts on the Constitution* (Oxford University Press, 1947), pp. 31–2.
5 *People and Parliament* (Clarendon Press, 1958), p. 11.
6 Speaking to the Annual Conference of the Labour Party, Dec 1964.
7 This example is cited in A. Hill and A. Whichelow, *What's Wrong with Parliament?* (Penguin, 1964), p. 60.
8 Nevil Johnson, *Parliament and Administration* (Allen & Unwin, 1966), p. 145.

FURTHER READING

The conventions governing ministerial responsibility to Parliament are discussed in S. E. Finer, 'The individual responsibility of ministers', in *Public Administration,* vol. XXXIV (1956), and in A. H. Birch, *Representative and Responsible Government* (Allen & Unwin, 1964), pt IV; the work of backbenchers is discussed in P. G. Richards, *The Backbenchers* (Faber, 1972); the role of Parliament in relation to foreign policy is discussed in P. G. Richards, *Parliament and Foreign Affairs* (Allen & Unwin, 1967); the question of parliamentary reform is discussed in Bernard Crick and A. H. Hanson, *The Commons in Transition* (Collins/Fontana, 1970), and in A. Morris and others, *The Growth of Parliamentary Scrutiny by Committee* (Pergamon, 1970).

Chapter 13

Changing the Law

LEGISLATIVE PROCEDURE

The law of Britain consists of Common Law, as interpreted by judges over the centuries, and Statute Law, as enacted by Parliament. In this context the word 'Parliament' signifies the two Houses together with the monarch, for all three must agree to a new law before it can be placed on the Statute Book. The procedure is for a Bill to be introduced in one of the Houses, where it must pass three readings and a committee stage, for it to be sent to the other House for the same treatment, and for it then to be presented to the monarch for assent. In constitutional law the monarch retains the right to refuse assent but in practice she has no choice in the matter. After the Royal Assent the Act is entered in the Statute Book and immediately becomes part of the law of the land.

Parliamentary Bills are of two kinds. The great majority, in the present century, are 'public Bills' which affect the community generally. The others are 'private Bills' which relate to a matter of purely private or local interest: for instance, an individual may promote a private Bill to free his property from some legal restriction as to its disposal or a local authority may do so to acquire the powers necessary for the damming of a river or the conversion of a burial ground into a park. There is a special procedure for private Bills which is quasi-judicial in nature. First, the promoters of the Bill must notify all persons and organisations whose interests may be affected by the Bill. After a formal first reading there is a second reading which is also formal unless someone objects to the Bill in principle, as might happen, for example, in the case of a Bill which would extend the power of a municipal authority to engage in trade. If the Bill passes the second reading, it is then referred to a special committee of four or five Members, before which the proponents and opponents of the measure argue their case with the assistance of counsel. This is the important stage, and if the Bill gets through this committee it is usually passed without further amendment.

In the case of public Bills the second reading in the House of Commons is the most important stage. The first reading is a pure formality. On the second reading there is a debate on the principles and purpose of the Bill, which may last for several days. The Bill is then referred to a committee which considers it clause by clause. Finance Bills and some other Bills of exceptional importance are heard in committee of the whole House. Bills relating only to Scotland are referred to the Scottish Committee and other public Bills are normally referred to one of the six standing committees of the House, which are not specialised in function or title and are known simply as Standing Committees A, B, and so on through to F.

Each standing committee deals with Bills on a wide variety of topics, and for this reason it is commonly thought that there is only a random relationship between the subject of a Bill and the interests and expertise of the members of the committee which considers that Bill. The truth is very different. Each committee is composed of a nucleus of twenty members, chosen by the Committee of Selection in proportion to the strength of the parties in the House, together with up to thirty members who are appointed for the consideration of one Bill only and are chosen for their interests and qualifications. Given the nature of party management in Parliament, these additional members are also chosen in rough proportion to party strengths, but they are people who have an active interest in the Bill to be discussed. Furthermore, the Committee of Selection does not appoint the twenty nuclear members of a standing committee until after it is known what Bill will first be discussed by that committee, and the choice is usually influenced by that knowledge. If the subject of the second Bill is markedly different, several of the nuclear members may resign from the committee and be replaced by others who are better qualified to discuss the second Bill, and so on through the session. It follows that the standing committees of the House of Commons are much more specialised in composition than appears at first sight. The minister responsible for the Bill in the House always sits on the committee, advised by his officials, while the Attorney-General and Solicitor-General are entitled to take part in the proceedings of all standing committees so as to advise on legal points. The standing committees are therefore usually well-informed bodies. They consider each Bill clause by clause, though they are sometimes limited by shortage of time. In order to keep up the pace of legislation which is required in modern Britain, the Government has occasionally to use the closure in committee, together with other procedural devices known as the guillotine (which stops debate on a clause after a predetermined time) and the kangaroo (which takes the committee in jumps from one important clause to another).

When a Bill comes out of committee it is reported to the House, at which stage the House discusses and occasionally reverses the amendments made in committee, as well as having the chance to add detailed changes of its own. There quickly follows the third reading, at which only changes in wording are permitted, and the Bill is then sent to the House of Lords for similar (though briefer) treatment, unless it is one of those non-controversial Bills which go through the Lords before they are presented to the Commons.

THE ORIGINS OF LEGISLATION

A century ago most Bills were initiated by Private Members. However, since 1867 governments have progressively increased their control over the legislative process so that Private Members are now given only the most limited opportunities to introduce Bills. Every alternate Friday in the first twenty weeks of each session is reserved for Private Members' Bills, and as the House rises early on Fridays this means that in practice Private Members have no more than 10 per cent of parliamentary time at their disposal for legislation. This is often regarded as an inevitable consequence of the great extension of government activities that the past century has seen, but in fact the British Parliament is dominated much more completely by the Government than are the legislatures of most other liberal democracies. In the United States Congress all Bills are technically introduced by Private Members and most Bills are actually initiated by them; in Sweden Private Members' Bills usually outnumber government Bills (though they do not deal with such important subjects); in the Fourth French Republic the ordinary Deputy had a good deal of room for initiative; and even in the Fifth Republic the members of the National Assembly enjoy somewhat more scope for legislative enterprise than do their British counterparts. It is hard to find another democratic system in which the legislative rights of backbenchers are curtailed as severely as they are in the Mother of Parliaments, where strict party discipline is accompanied by tight control of the parliamentary time-table by the government of the day.

The present practice in Britain is for backbenchers to ballot for the opportunity to introduce Bills. Only twenty of the 635 MPs win a place in the ballot each session, and a Member does not have much chance of getting his Bill a decent hearing unless he is in the top half of this twenty. Some MPs have draft Bills in their pockets to introduce if they win, while others use the opportunity to sponsor a Bill drafted by a pressure group or by one of their colleagues. Success in the ballot entitles a Member to introduce a Bill for its first and second readings, but progress beyond this stage depends upon the goodwill of the Government. In an average session only about eight or nine Private Members' Bills pass into law. To get a Bill enacted requires skill, patience, determination, a measure of support from more than one party, and the sympathy of the ministers most directly affected. An interesting example is the Obscene Publications Bill, which was originally drafted by Roy Jenkins in the autumn of 1954. In the spring of 1955 this got a brief first hearing in the House but lapsed at the end of the session. In the following winter it was reintroduced by a friendly MP who had won a place in ballot, but was 'talked out' by the Under-Secretary for Home Affairs, who spoke for so long that the House passed to other business without there being time for a vote. A year later a third Member sponsored it and it was passed on second reading, after which it would normally have been referred to a standing committee which was so choked with other Bills that it would never have got round to discussing this one. The Bill was saved from this fate by R. A. Butler, the new Home Secretary, who arranged for a select committee to be established to discuss the Bill in detail. This took time, and the committee did not produce its report until the spring of 1958, by when the Bill had once again lapsed, as all uncompleted legislation does at the end of each session. In the ballot the following autumn none of the twenty successful Members proved willing to sponsor the Bill and the whole operation was back to square one, from which it was rescued a few months later by the Home Secretary, who offered government time for a new second reading, on the understanding that the principles as well as the details of the Bill would be open to debate. What emerged from this was a compromise Bill which was not unacceptable to the Government and which eventually passed into law, after a good deal of hard bargaining in the committee and report stages, in July 1959. The whole process has been likened to a game of snakes and ladders lasting five years.[1]

Although Private Members' Bills are not numerous, some of them are very important. Recent examples include the 1967 Sexual Offences Act, which legalised homosexual practices between consenting adults, the Act which authorised abortion more or less on demand, and the Act which abolished censorship in the theatre.

Government Bills are much more numerous, and their passage through Parliament is more certain. In an average session about seventy are introduced and nearly as many are enacted. Their origins are various, and may be discussed under the headings of: (*a*) party policy; (*b*) Cabinet decisions; (*c*) committee reports; (*d*) outside pressures; and (*e*) administrative needs.

(*a*) Legislation based directly on policy statements put out by the parties normally occurs only after a general election has led to a change of government, and there tends to be more of it when a Labour government takes office than after a Conservative victory. The 1945 election brought a government into office which was committed to a set of reforms that had been under discussion for many years. In the following five sessions Parliament passed more major Acts than it has ever passed in a period of comparable length. The coal, gas, electricity and transport industries were nationalised, the civil airlines were established, the National Health Service was set up, national insurance was reorganised, and an elaborate Act regarding town and country planning was passed. But this was altogether exceptional. When the Conservatives regained power in 1951 the only major Acts which followed from their party programme were those to denationalise road transport and the iron and steel industry. Some other important changes were made, such as the abolition of petrol rationing, but these did not require legislation apart from the making of orders under powers already granted to ministers.

The Labour victory of 1964 produced a Bill to extend rent control and a number of financial measures to deal with the balance-of-payments crisis, but Labour's electoral programme was reflected more in administrative changes and the appointment of committees than in the passage of legislation. The Conservative victory of 1970 led to the Industrial Relations Act, the Housing Finance Act, and the enabling legislation consequent upon Britain's entry to the EEC. But when Labour returned to power in 1974 the main legislative consequences of its election manifesto were simply the repeal of the Industrial Relations Act and the Housing Finance Act. Over the whole period since 1945, only a small proportion of government Bills have had their immediate origin in party policy statements.

(b) Many other bills, however, are party-political in origin in the sense that they are sponsored by ministers or by Cabinet committees who become convinced that changes are needed. For instance, Conservative Cabinets between 1951 and 1964 decided to grant independence to a large number of British colonies, to disband the Central African Federation, to abolish resale price maintenance, to establish machinery for economic planning, and to extend the control of restrictive practices in trade. The annual Finance Act is also a highly political measure, as are the various legislative attempts to control prices and incomes.

(c) Other bills are based on the reports of committees of inquiry. Examples are the Clean Air Act which followed the Beaver Committee on Air Pollution, the Act to reorganise the government of Greater London which followed the report of the Herbert Commission, the Act to liberalise the laws regarding gambling which followed the report of the Royal Commission on Betting, Lotteries and Gaming, the Act designed to drive prostitutes off the streets which followed the report of the Wolfenden Committee, and the Local Government Act of 1972 which drew on the analysis (though not the conclusions) of the Redcliffe-Maud Commission. Each of these was a matter of policy rather than party policy, and the Government would have welcomed the support of the Opposition for a measure which an impartial committee had recommended. In most cases, though not in the case of London government, Opposition support was secured for the principle of the Bill even if not for its details.

(*d*) Some Bills result from outside pressures, usually overt but occasionally covert. The Act which led to the establishment of commercial television is an outstanding example of a piece of legislation promoted largely as the result of the activities of a well-organised pressure group who acquired influence through friends and contacts in the governing party and the Cabinet. The parliamentary debates on this Bill were frank, lively and well publicised, but the previous negotiations had been devious and fairly secret. However, this example is exceptional. Most legislation which has its origin in outside pressures results either from open campaigns by promotional groups, such as the RSPCA or the Abortion Law Reform Society, or from frank discussions between government departments and spokesmen for economic interests.

The RSPCA is without question the most successful promotional group in Britain. It has keen supporters in both main parties and enjoys the great advantage that animal welfare is not a cause to which anyone objects, so long as it is not taken to the length of interfering with a traditional sport like hunting. Other promotional (as opposed to interest) groups that have attempted, successfully or not, to promote legislation since 1949 are the National Campaign for the Abolition of Capital Punishment, the Marriage Law Reform Society, the League Against Cruel Sports, the Abortion Law Reform Association, and the National Temperance Federation.

Interest groups also propose legislation from time to time on behalf of their members, sometimes by drafting a Bill for introduction as a Private Member's Bill, sometimes by approaching the government department most directly concerned. In 1951 the British Veterinary Association drafted a Bill to make the use of anaesthetics compulsory for operations on domestic animals, which was eventually passed as a Private Member's Bill in 1953. In 1954 the Society of Authors was partly responsible for the first draft of the Obscene Publications Bill, discussed above. An initiative taken by the Joint Committee of Ophthalmic Opticians resulted in the passage of a Bill requiring opticians to be registered. A similar initiative taken by a society representing estate agents has led to a good deal of debate but has not so far resulted in legislation, because there are differences of view within the profession, and the Government, while willing to find time for a Bill which meets the wishes of the profession, has not been willing to impose its own view on the profession. A good deal of legislation, over the years, has resulted directly or indirectly from proposals made by trade unions. The Catering Wages Act of 1948 was introduced by the Government to meet long-standing complaints by unions about the treatment of workers in the catering trades. The Offices Act of 1960 was designed to meet some of the complaints by white-collar unions about the conditions of work in offices. The Trade Disputes Act of 1965 was passed at the request of the unions to remove the possibility that a union might be sued for damages if it broke a contractual agreement for the purpose of injuring a third party.

(*e*) A good deal of legislation has its origins within the administration. Government departments find that problems arise which cannot be solved without a change in the law, and the officials persuade their minister that a Bill must be drafted. Many of the minor Bills that go before Parliament have administrative origins, and so do some of the major Bills. The Commonwealth Immigrants Act of 1962, for instance, had its origins in the evidence reaching Whitehall that the arrival of ever-increasing numbers of Commonwealth immigrants was causing serious social problems with which local authorities could not cope unless some check were put on the flood. The Transport Bill introduced (but not passed) in 1965 was based on the continuing efforts of the Ministry of Transport to reduce road accidents. Both Bills proved highly controversial, but each might have been introduced in substantially similar terms had the other party been in power. And each year there is a substantial body of legislation about fairly technical matters which is essentially 'administrative legislation', drafted by government departments after consultation with the affected interests, and controversial only in so far as spokesmen for groups which are not entirely happy with it try to get it amended in Parliament. Examples are Bills dealing with wage negotiations, with conditions of work, with weights and measures, with national insurance, with public health.

FROM A PROPOSAL TO A LAW

After a government department has decided to sponsor a piece of legislation, there is much work to be done. The minister and the senior officials concerned with the Bill will have agreed upon its general principles, and the latter should 'know the minister's mind' sufficiently well to be able to negotiate with affected groups without having constantly to refer back to their chief. Consultation with all the groups likely to be affected by the Bill is essential, and is recognised as an integral part of the British system of government. A minister whose department omitted to consult a significant group would undoubtedly be criticised in Parliament for this omission, for the group would not fail to find a backbencher willing to express their objections.

Of course, consultation with groups does not imply acceptance of all their suggestions and criticisms. The Government's task is to balance group claims against one another and to assess them in terms of the national interest. But a wise minister will give group spokesmen every chance to press their claims, for three reasons. First, he needs to know all the practical difficulties involved in the proposal so as to get the details right, to avoid ambiguity, and to reduce the opportunities for evasion of the law. Secondly, he will want to get as much support as he possibly can for the Bill from those directly affected by it and to assess the arguments and strength of any probable opposition. Even when groups dislike the proposal in principle, it will pay the minister to put his case to them, if they are influential, and perhaps to moderate their opposition by offering them concessions on points of detail. If he does not do so, his Bill will have a more difficult passage through Parliament and his party may lose a certain amount of public support. Thirdly, the minister will be concerned about future relations between his depart-ment and the groups. For better or worse, government departments and interest-group spokesmen have to live with one another, and both sides normally do everything they can to keep the relationship harmonious.

It is an established convention that a Bill is not published in advance of its presentation to Parliament. These consultations and negotiations therefore normally take place on the basis of either a report of an official committee or a White Paper explaining the Government's intentions. In the case of Bills which are unlikely to arouse party controversy the whole prócess may be based on discussions and departmental papers, without anything being published in advance of the Bill. The following quotation from the 1948 *Year Book* of the National Farmers' Union illustrates the kind of detailed discussion that often takes place before a Bill sees the light of day, though (as noted earlier) the NFU is more fortunate than most interest groups in that it does not have to contend with rival or hostile groups of any signifi-cance. The degree of influence claimed may therefore be untypical, but the extent of discussion is not unusual.

The Agriculture Bill was introduced . . . in December 1946. For as long as two years before this date discussions had been going on between the Union and the Ministry of Agriculture as to the form which this Bill was to take. . . . When the Bill was introduced it represented, in substance, the result of discussion and a large measure of agreement. . . . There were, however, still many points upon which the Union wished to see the Bill amended, and during the first six months of the year an intensive campaign was conducted inside and outside Parliament to persuade the Government to adopt these amendments. On three points only were we unsuccessful.[2]

When the draft Bill is in shape the minister must get Cabinet approval for it, together with a firm place in the parliamentary time-table. He will previously have secured provisional support for the Bill and some promise of parliamentary time, but the time-table is crowded and draft Bills are sometimes delayed from one session to the next for this reason. The political climate also changes, and Bills may be deferred if the Government is going through an anxious period or if the Bills seem likely to provoke more controversy than had previously been anticipated. Occasionally a measure which has been given provisional approval by the Cabinet alarms government backbenchers, who communicate their feelings through the Whips and at meetings of the specialised party committees. Many Conservative backbenchers disliked a 1957 proposal to liberalise the law regarding shop-closing hours and substantially the same group were opposed to a later proposal to abolish resale price maintenance. In the former case the Government dropped the Bill; in the latter case the minister concerned defended his policies before the party committee and then before the whole 1922 Committee, gaining enough support for his Cabinet colleagues to let him continue with the Bill, which was subsequently passed.

Bills which are deferred by a government or are left stranded by a change of government are consigned to the pigeon-holes of Whitehall. But the majority avoid this fate and, after Cabinet approval, are put into legal shape by the parliamentary draftsmen and duly presented to Parliament for a formal first reading. As noted, the main debate occurs on the second reading, which lasts for three or four days if the Bill is important. This tends to take the form of a set battle between Government and Opposition, with the backbenchers on each side supporting their leaders and the final vote being entirely predictable.

Most Bills then go to a standing committee, at which party discipline is not quite so rigid. The minister steers his Bill through committee and expects the support of his party colleagues when he is attacked by the chief spokesman for the Opposition. But government backbenchers will feel free to make criticisms and suggest amendments on points of detail. Standing committees do not hear evidence from expert witnesses, as Congressional committees do, but members of the committee may bring advisers into the room with them to hear the proceedings. The minister brings civil servants, who will have briefed him in advance and will pass notes of advice to him during the hearings. Other Members may bring group spokesmen of various kinds, who will sit on the public benches but may withdraw into the corridor to advise

Members if points arise that have not been covered by their earlier discussions or briefs. Of course only a proportion of the members of a standing committee have this kind of relationship with group spokesmen, but many of the most effective proposals for amendment arise in this way.

The report stage is often brief and formal, but is sometimes an occasion for sharp controversy. If the Government dislikes some of the amendments made in committee, these may be reversed at the report stage. More commonly, the minister may have agreed in committee to consider a proposed amendment and discuss it at report stage, and his comments then may arouse the ire of the Opposition. Occasionally the closure is applied in committee, and Members use the report stage to propose amendments for which there was no time in committee. Very exceptionally, the Government itself uses the report stage to amend its own Bill in the light of second thoughts. When the Transport Bill of 1947 reached the report stage ninety-seven government amendments were put and carried without any time being allowed for discussion, and in the case of the Town and Country Planning Bill of the same year 168 government amendments were carried in the same way. But these were quite exceptional occasions, resulting from the unprecedented number of important legislative changes which the Labour Government pushed through between 1945 and 1950. ·

With the conclusion of the report stage the main hurdles have normally been cleared. The third reading deals only with wording, and the influence of the House of Lords on legislation is limited in the ways discussed in Chapter 4. It remains only for the Clerk of the Parliaments to announce the Royal Assent, which he does in medieval French, and for another Act to be entered in the Statute Book.

NOTES

1   See Roy Jenkins, 'Obscenity, censorship, and the law', in *Encounter,* Oct 1959.
2   Quoted in Allen Potter, *Organized Groups in British National Politics* (Faber, 1961), p. 207.

FURTHER READING

A full account of the legislative role of Parliament is given in W. Ivor Jennings, *Parliament* (Cambridge University Press, 1957); parliamentary procedure is illustrated with examples in A. H. Hanson and H. V. Wiseman, *Parliament at Work* (Stevens, 1962); a short guide is provided by S. A. Walkland, *The Legislative Process in Great Britain* (Allen & Unwin, 1968); recent developments are discussed in S. A. Walkland and Michael Ryle, *The Commons in the Seventies* (Collins/Fontana, 1978).

Chapter 14

Local Government

Many of the most important public services are administered by local authorities, each of which is controlled by its own elected council. In England and Wales there are 54 county councils, 402 district councils, and about 11,300 parish or community councils. Between them these councils employ over 900,000 staff together with nearly 700,000 teachers and over 100,000 construction workers.[1] These figures do not include Scotland, where the same services are provided through a slightly different system.

The structure of the local government system is rather complex and has been frequently changed, most recently in 1974. Since a brief outline of the structure would not be meaningful, and an explanation of its rationale and problems would require more space than is available, it is intended in this chapter to take structure for granted and to focus attention on two questions which relate local government to national government. These are, respectively, the character of central–local relations and the character of local democracy.

THE CHARACTER OF CENTRAL–LOCAL RELATIONS

The relationship between local authorities and the national government is extremely complex, and cannot be characterised as easily as can either the centralised system which exists in France or the decentralised system of the United States. France has a system of local administration. The country is divided into ninety departments and in each of these administration is controlled by a prefect, who is an official of the Ministry of the Interior and is moved from one area to another in the course of his career. The prefect and his staff are responsible not only for the administration of local services, which vary only a little from one department to another, but also for the enforcement of the law, the collection of taxes, and the administration of a number of national services in the area. They are influenced by local politics and local pressures, but they are part of the government of France.

The United States, on the other hand, has a system of genuine local self-government. The government of an American city is not a part of either the state government or the federal government. In most states a city government has a considerable measure of independence, with power to levy taxes, to raise loans, to decide on the level of services it will provide, and to change its own form of organisation, provided the electors agree (and within limits set by the state constitution). The result is that American local authorities vary a great deal in their mode of organisation and their policies in regard to housing, town planning, and other matters.

British local government does not fit neatly into either of these categories. It has the appearance and trappings of a system of local self-government but not much of the reality. The Corporation of the City of Hull, for instance, cannot be said to be part of the British Government; it is an independent corporation which was established in the fifteenth century, which owns a great deal of property, and which appoints its own Sheriff and Lord Mayor; it does not administer national services and it has, indeed, very little contact with the various branch offices of government departments that are established in the city. On the other hand, the Hull Corporation cannot change its own constitution, which is regulated by Act of Parliament; it cannot exercise any powers other than those delegated to it by Parliament; and it is subject to constant regulation and inspection by government departments. A city council which cannot impose a speed limit or create a one-way system without the consent of the Department of the Environment cannot be said to have much genuine autonomy in dealing with its traffic problems, even though the Department would say that these are under local rather than national control.

National control of local government determines how local authorities are organised, what services they must provide, what other services they may provide if they choose to do so, and how most of their services must be administered. The services they must provide include education, police, sanitation, and public health. If an authority fails to provide one of these services at a level which meets the minimum standards set by the relevant ministry, the ministry may take powers to act in default, at the expense of the local authority. In 1954, for instance, the Coventry City Council refused to organise a civil defence service on the ground that civil defence, as understood in England, would be quite irrelevant to the problems of nuclear warfare. The Home Office thereupon took powers to organise a civil defence force in Coventry and send the bill to the City Council, a move which eventually persuaded the Council to fall into line.[2] In 1957 the St Pancras Borough Council decided to abandon its civil defence department for the same reason that had motivated Coventry, and with exactly the same result.

Some other services are optional, but the limits of a council's activities are set by the doctrine of *ultra vires,* according to which no authority is entitled to engage in any activity unless it has been specifically empowered to do so by Parliament. An authority which tries to exceed its legal powers may be stopped from doing so by a court order, as happened in 1921 when the Fulham Borough Council proposed to establish a municipal laundry under its power to provide public washhouses. Local laundry firms objected and the Council had to abandon the project. If an authority proceeds unheeded in an activity which is *ultra vires,* the sanction is applied at the end of the financial year when the authority's accounts are audited by an official of the central government known as a District Auditor. If he finds that certain expenditures were unjustified, his duty is to disallow their payment from public funds, in which case those members of the authority who voted for the expenditures have to pay for them out of their own pockets. To avoid this fate, local authorities who are in doubt about the legality of a proposed measure often ask the relevant government department for a ruling before a final decision is taken.

The best-known example of disallowance occurred in 1921–2 when the Poplar Borough Council paid some of its workmen a wage considerably higher than the standard wage, on the ground that the Council wished to be a 'model employer'. The District Auditor's view was that councillors had no right to be generous at the ratepayers' expense and the councillors had to pay the difference between the standard wage and the actual wage paid.[3] Another interesting example occurred in the 1950s in Manchester. It was the custom for one of the local theatres to present a performance of the Shakespearian play that was included in the GCE syllabus each year and for the Manchester City Council to send schoolchildren of the appropriate age-group to see this. One year no performance was offered. The Council thereupon decided to commission a performance for the special benefit of their pupils, thinking that this expenditure would be covered by their two powers: (*a*) to commission and subsidise theatrical performances; and (*b*) to pay for schoolchildren to see educational plays. When they asked for a ruling, however, they were told that this plan would be *ultra vires,* as the first power could only be invoked if the performances were open to all members of the public and the second power only covered the purchase of tickets for a play that was in any case being given. A more trivial example occurred in 1963, when the District Auditor forced members of the Castle Donnington District Council to pay the cost of two telegrams they sent during the Cuban crisis, one to Kennedy and one to Khrushchev, appealing for peace. A much more serious and controversial example occurred in 1972, when the majority of councillors in a Derbyshire town called Clay Cross refused to raise the rents of council-house tenants in accordance with the requirements of the Housing Finance Act. They were subsequently ordered to pay the difference between the two levels of rent themselves, though the sums involved were so large (because the councillors insisted on defying the national government over a protracted period) that it was impossible for the money to be collected.

Control over the way in which services are administered rests on the fact that the authorities derive over half of their income from government grants. These grants are conditional, and the central government is prepared to suspend them at very short notice if an authority refuses to comply with the conditions. As an example, the grant given for the maintenance of local police forces carries with it as one of many conditions the proviso that appointments to the post of Chief Constable should be approved by the Home Office. In 1947 this post fell vacant in Salford and the City Council decided to promote their Deputy Chief Constable to the vacancy. The Home Office refused to approve the appointment because it was a matter of Home Office policy that Chief Constables should always be appointed from some other police force. When Salford confirmed the appointment in spite of this their grant was immediately cut off and after a few weeks financial pressure forced them to give in.

Needless to say, things rarely come to this pass. Local authorities accept control by Whitehall as a condition of life and their conduct of local affairs is shaped by ministry regulations, by a constant stream of ministry circulars, and by the reports of ministry inspectors. Their schools are inspected by the Department of Education and Science; their health services are inspected by the Department of Health and Social Security; their housing plans are subject to the approval of the Department of the Environment; their plans for traffic control and pedestrian crossings have to be agreed by the Transport Division of the Department of the Environment; their police forces are inspected by the Home Office. In so far as there is variety and experiment in local government, it can be said to be by permission of Whitehall. Nevertheless, there is in practice a good deal of variety. Government departments vary considerably in the extent to which they use their powers to foster national uniformity. The Department of Health and Social Security, for instance, is said to have a *laissez-faire* attitude to local authorities, believing that, provided they meet the requirements of the law, they should be allowed to enjoy a good deal of freedom in the way they develop local health services.[4] A recent example is the Department's attitude to the fluoridation of water supplies: the Department believes this to be a desirable development and has sent a number of circulars to local authorities advising them to undertake it; but though some councils have not accepted this advice the Department has taken no steps to make them do so. On the other hand, the Department of the Environment exercises a great deal of control over local authorities, and the Department of Education and Science uses its powers to minimise differences in the standards of educational provision.[5] To this end, the Department controls the output of teachers from Colleges of Education, the number of teachers each authority may employ, teachers' salaries, investment in school buildings, and the provision of ancillary services. It also has a large staff of inspectors who advise local authorities on teaching methods.

Local authorities naturally differ in the use they make of their discretionary powers. Thus, they are required by law to dispose of sewage but some do so cheaply, by pumping it into the sea, while others do so expensively, by installing a sewage plant. Authorities vary widely in the services they provide for old people, for mentally defective people, and for the deaf and the blind. Authorities also differ in their policies for the provision of council houses or flats to be let at subsidised rents. A great deal of argument takes place about the rate and method of building, the location and the rents of council housing. In many areas housing is the most controversial service provided by local government.

Another area in which there is scope for local initiative is in the provision of recreational and cultural facilities. Some authorities spend a lot on parks and recreation grounds; some run repertory theatres and subsidise symphony concerts; some have spendid art collections; some have libraries of gramophone records as well as books and a few have loan collections of lithographs and artists' prints. There is ample opportunity here for councillors who want to improve the amenities of their town. The short answer to questions about the character of central–local relations, therefore, is that local authorities have the appearance and to some extent the legal status of independent authorities; that despite this the degree of practical independence they enjoy at any time depends almost entirely on the policies of central government departments; and that at the time of writing, although their activities are much more tightly restricted than they were fifty years ago, they nevertheless retain a fair degree of initiative in fields which can make a real difference to the lives of their citizens.

THE CHARACTER OF LOCAL DEMOCRACY

In the context of the British parliamentary system, the idea of local democracy presumably implies three things. First, it implies that elected councillors should have effective control of decision-making in local government. Secondly, it implies that the councillors should be fully accountable to the electorate and responsive to public opinion, through competitive elections and a fairly high level of communication between councillors on one hand and electors and pressure groups on the other. Thirdly, it implies what J. S. Mill called civic education, meaning widespread knowledge of local government activities and a reasonably high degree of popular participation in community affairs.

The first of these conditions has clearly been achieved in England. Control of policy rests with the council, in which the members are elected for three-year terms of office. Councils operate through a set of specialised committees such as the Education Committee, the Housing Committee, the Parks Committee and so on, each of which keeps a continuing watch on its branch of local administration and reports to council each month. The chief officers of the authority act as secretaries of their respective committees and can expect to have a good deal of influence on what is decided, but they are not entitled to vote. The council as a whole is limited in its freedom of choice by the requirements of the central government, but within these limits the power to make decisions rests clearly in the hands of the councillors.

There is much more doubt about the second condition. There is not a great deal of competition to serve on local councils and in many areas elections are normally uncontested. In England and Wales as a whole about 40 per cent of the councillors were returned unopposed at their last election. Those elections that are contested arouse remarkably little interest. Whereas in general elections between 75 and 85 per cent of the electorate turn out to vote, in local elections the proportion voting varies between 25 and 50 per cent, with an average of under 40 per cent. The county councils and the Greater London Council, which control many of the more important services, attract less public interest than the district councils. Voting in the larger towns and cities reflects the national popularity of the parties so faithfully that local issues cannot, as a general rule, have much influence on the results. It follows that very few councillors are kept on their toes by the prospect of vigorous election campaigns: many councillors expect to be returned unopposed, many more have safe seats, and where there is a genuine contest the campaign is apt to be very quiet and the voting to turn upon national rather than local issues.

Nor is there usually a great deal of communication between councillors and their constituents. In Glossop it was found that 15 per cent of the electors had at one time or another in their lives approached a local councillor,[6] but this must be regarded as a small proportion in view of the fact that local services have a daily impact on people's lives and must in the nature of things give rise to frequent feelings of dissatisfaction. In Glossop most councillors were known by name to the townsfolk, but this is not the case in large cities and over the country as a whole the general custom is for people to address their complaints about local services to officials in the town hall, not to their local councillors. Another factor in this situation is the relative scarcity of well-organised local pressure groups. There are few British equivalents of American organisations like the League of Women Voters, the Community Chest, the Elks, the Kiwanis, and the Parent–Teachers' Associations, all actively concerned with local affairs.[7] Local organisations in Britain tend to send resolutions to their national headquarters rather than apply pressure to their local authorities, just as local party branches tend to alternate between organising whist drives and discussing national policy, rather than pressing local councillors to improve the schools or the parking facilities. There are exceptions, of course, but as a general rule it does not seem that councillors are besieged by public demands and complaints which they pass on to the council. This aspect of local democracy does not appear to flourish in England.

Nor can it be said that local government contributes to civic education in the way that was anticipated by Victorian reformers. For one thing, many local authorities are secretive about their activities. Local authorities are required by law to admit the press and the public to their council meetings, but need not admit them to committee meetings. For many years some authorities avoided publicity by holding their most important debates in a General Purposes Committee, to which all councillors belonged, the debate at the council meeting proper being merely a brief ratification of the decision reached in committee.

This practice was banned by the Public Bodies (Admissions to Meetings) Act of 1961, which stipulated that the public must be admitted to any committee which includes all members of the council. A ministerial circular was sent to all authorities when this Act came into force, telling them that in order to facilitate the reporting of council affairs the local press should be supplied with copies of committee reports well in advance of council meetings, and that no restriction should be placed on press comments. However, when a survey was made of fifty local authorities in the Midlands in the autumn of 1962 it was found that twenty-seven of them had refused to accept this advice. *The Times* reported that eleven of the authorities 'either do not issue committee reports before their council meetings or forbid the press to print any portion of them. Sixteen of the authorities allow factual stories to be written about proposals but attempt to ban newspapers from commenting upon them in any way.'[8]

Another factor in the situation is the state of the local press in England. As noted in Chapter 1, it is less important than in other countries because almost everyone in England reads one of the national papers. Local papers are read partly for their advertisements and partly as evening papers, in which case they tend to give prominence to national news because what people want is a follow-up to the news items they have read in the morning. Very few local papers try to make a story out of the activities of their local council, so they do not complain when the council is secretive. The result is that only a small minority of citizens have any knowledge of what their local authority is doing, and even fewer know the names of local politicians. Whereas most New Yorkers know the name of the Mayor of New York, very few Londoners know the name of his equivalent, the Chairman of the Greater London Council.

In this situation local government cannot be said to contribute much to the civic education of the masses. Most people are neither knowledgeable about nor interested in local affairs. As noted in Chapter 8, relatively few people want to participate in local government and the parties in most areas have to exert themselves to find candidates. Those people who do take part benefit from the experience, but they are a tiny minority of the electorate.

For these reasons, it is difficult to write with confidence about local democracy in England. It is significant that a Fabian Tract entitled *Why Local Democracy?*[9] was able to produce only one clear argument in answer to the question posed. This was that local authorities fulfil a useful function as pressure groups in national politics, acting particularly on behalf of consumers. While this may be a fair point, it does not constitute a defence of the local government system itself, and the greater part of the discussion of that system in the pamphlet was devoted not to local democracy but to the problem of defining administrative areas. The basic question raised by the pamphlet remains unanswered.

THE CASE FOR LOCAL SELF-GOVERNMENT

It has been suggested that the English have an 'ethical commitment' to the idea of local self-government but only the vaguest notion of what this means in practice.[10] If it means local democracy, as defined above, it would appear that the English system is not very successful. But it does not follow that the country would be better governed if the functions of local authorities were henceforth taken over by the civil servants. 'Self-government' and 'democracy' are not synonymous terms, as the recent history of Africa makes clear. And several plausible arguments can be put forward in support of the rather muddled English system of local self-government.

First, since services do vary from area to area, people can exercise choice by moving from one authority to another. If parents dislike the schools in the city, they can move out to the suburbs: an expensive way of exercising choice, but much better than having no choice to exercise. And when people move for other reasons (and about 10 per cent of the population move each year) the quality of the local schools and other services is certainly one of the factors they take into account. The level of local rates is another factor: when the writer moved to Yorkshire he had a choice between living in the city of Hull, with excellent public services but very high rates, and living in the East Riding, with poorer public services and much lower rates. If freedom can be defined as the maximisation of choice, the local government system can be said to extend freedom. The only service to which this does not apply is housing, where the habit of local authorities of giving priority to residents of long standing makes it more difficult for council tenants to move than it would be if housing were nationally controlled.

A second argument has been put by Enoch Powell. Writing about his experiences as Minister of Health, he draws an interesting contrast between the National Health Service, which is financed entirely by the Exchequer, and the health and welfare services which are financed and organised by local authorities with the assistance of government grants, government advice and (to some extent) government instructions. One of the features of the Health Service, he observes, is 'the continual, deafening chorus of complaint which arises day and night from every part of it',[11] not so much because it is inefficient (in Powell's view) but because it is financed by a remote authority which can be blamed for all shortcomings and whose resources appear to be limitless. When the Minister meets people concerned with the local health and welfare services, on the other hand, he 'is surprised and delighted by the change of climate. *They* do not run their services down; they praise them, and though they recognize deficiencies and objectives still far from being obtained, they recognize them as stimuli and incentives, not as material for moaning.'[12] This different attitude, Powell suggests, is based partly on local pride and partly on the knowledge that improvements in the service would cost money, part at least of which would be a burden on the local rates.

As it happens, there is one service which offers a more direct comparison, because the identical service is provided in one area by the local authority and elsewhere by the national government. This is the telephone service, provided in Hull by the City Council and in the rest of the country by the Post Office. Everywhere except in Hull this service is the subject of constant complaint. There is a long waiting-list for telephones; when you get one you may have to share a line; the operators are often slow to answer; mechanical defects give wrong connections and produce clicks while one is talking; and so on and so forth. All these complaints except the first could be made in Hull also, but in nine years in the city the writer never heard one. On the contrary, the people of Hull are conspicuously proud of their telephone service and frequently congratulate each other upon it.

This local pride has got nothing to do with local democracy: the telephone service is not an issue in local politics and if things go wrong subscribers complain to the staff, not to their local councillor. In part it is simply localism: a feeling of pleasure that the service is controlled by Hull people instead of by anonymous officials in London. Beyond that it is a matter of finance. Telephone charges in Hull are appreciably lower than elsewhere, and subscribers know that all their payments are spent on the service. Telephone users elsewhere know (if they read the papers) that the Post Office makes an enormous annual profit on the telephone service which is used to offset the annual loss normally made on postal services. Subscribers outside Hull probably also suspect that they are helping to pay for communications satellites and other expensive gadgets which enable the Post Office to boast about scientific progress but which bring no perceptible benefits to the average telephone user. It is a good principle that the relationship between costs and benefits should be visible, and this constitutes an argument for local control of those services which will not suffer thereby.

A further advantage of local self-government is that it provides a sphere of political activity which is open to almost everybody who wants to take part. Very few people feel that they could enter Parliament, with the financial insecurity and the disruption of normal life that this involves, quite apart from the difficulty of finding a seat. But almost anybody could become a local councillor, both in the sense that it is easy to get elected and because the work need not disrupt a man's career (though it may well absorb nearly all his spare time). It follows that a would-be politician in England need not feel frustrated, or at any rate not for long: there is an opening for his talents on his doorstep. For the councillors, at least, local government *does* provide a valuable form of civic education.

If these arguments are put together, it can be seen that there is a strong case for local self-government. The English system is not very successful as a form of local democracy, it has never found a satisfactory solution to the problem of defining administrative areas, and it sometimes seems to be in the hands of small-minded men interested in their own privileges and power. But, when all this is said, it remains true that it provides a large range of services with reasonable efficiency, that more would be lost than gained if these were transferred to central control, and that the task of reformers is to invigorate the system, not to abolish it.

NOTES

1   See Jeffrey Stanyer, *Understanding Local Government* (Collins/Fontana, 1976), pp. 289–94.
2   The civil defence in Coventry was run by the Home Office from July 1954 to Aug 1955.
3   The matter was taken up through the courts to the House of Lords, which endorsed the decision of the District Auditor. See Herman Finer, *English Local Government*, 4th edn (Methuen, 1950), p. 333.
4   See J. A. G. Griffith, *Central Departments and Local Authorities* (Allen & Unwin, 1966), pp. 515–18.
5   ibid., pp. 521–4.
6   See A. H. Birch, *Small-Town Politics*, p. 96.
7   There is a growing number of PTAS in England, but they are rarely effective as pressure groups.
8   *The Times*, 8 Jan 1963.
9   L. J. Sharpe, *Why Local Democracy?*, Fabian Tract 361 (1965).
10 See W. J. Mackenzie, *Theories of Local Government*, pp. 5–7.
11 J. Enoch Powell, *A New Look at Medicine and Politics* (Pitman Medical, 1966), p. 16.
12 ibid.

FURTHER READING

W. J. M. Mackenzie, *Theories of Local Government* (London School of Economics, 1961), is brief but brilliant; Jeffrey Stanyer, *Understanding Local Government* (Collins/Fontana, 1976), provides an analytical account of the contemporary system; P. G. Richards, *The Reformed Local Government System*, 3rd edn (Allen & Unwin, 1978), gives a more descriptive version; A. H. Birch, *Small-Town Politics* (Oxford University Press, 1959), is a study of local politics and government in one northern town; J. G. Bulpitt, *Party Politics in Local Government* (Longman, 1967), is a comparative study of political behaviour in six local authorities; G. R. Rhodes and S. K. Ruck, *The Government of Greater London* (Allen & Unwin, 1970), describes the unique system of the metropolis; Dilys M. Hill, *Democratic Theory and Local Government* (Allen & Unwin, 1974), is interesting and helpful. G. W. Jones (ed.), *New Approaches to the Study of Central–Local Government Relationships* (Gower Press, 1980), contains some useful articles.

Part V

The Citizen and the Government

Chapter 15

The Rights of the Citizen

In Part III of this book we considered the roles played by citizens as voters, as party members and as members of pressure groups, and discussed the opportunities open to citizens to stand for election. In these chapters the citizen was viewed as an active or potentially active participant in the political process. This final Part of the book will deal with the position of the citizen in his more passive role as a person who is governed. In the present chapter we shall consider his individual liberties and his rights in relation to the administration and the agencies for law-enforcement. In the following chapter an attempt will be made to provide a more generalised assessment of the relations between the British public and their government.

The rights and liberties of the citizen in Britain will be discussed in the following order: first, the basic civil rights of free speech and freedom of political action; secondly, the rights of the citizen in relation to the police and the courts; thirdly, the rights of the citizen in relation to government departments and other administrative authorities; and, fourthly, the right of ethnic minorities to be protected against discrimination.

THE LEGAL BASIS OF CIVIL LIBERTIES

British civil liberties rest on a quite different basis from those in most other countries. Elsewhere, civil rights are normally specified in writing, either in constitutional declarations of rights or in provisions of the legal code of the country. In the United States the fundamental civil liberties are set out in the constitution, the ten constitutional amendments that were added in 1791 (which are collectively known as the Bill of Rights), and the amendments that were passed after the Civil War with the intention of extending equal rights to negroes. In France civil rights were first specified in the Declaration of the Rights of Man and the Citizen of 1789, and the continuing French attachment to these rights is shown by the references to the Declaration in the preambles of the constitutions of both the Fourth and the Fifth Republics. In other countries guarantees of rights are much more recent, depending on the dates on which regimes purporting to be liberal were first established.

The position in Britain is different because Britain has not gone through the common experience of overthrowing an oppressive system of government by force of arms and establishing a constitutional regime more or less *de novo*. Britain has enjoyed the rule of law for at least three centuries, since long before its political system was in any sense democratic, and the rights of citizens have been established not by the declarations of politicians but by the decisions of judges, interpreting the Common Law of the land. It follows that one could search the Statute Book in vain for acts conferring upon citizens the rights of free speech, freedom of association, or freedom of movement. These rights rest simply on the age-old assumption by British courts that a citizen is free to do as he likes provided he does not commit any specific breach of the law. A consequence of this situation is that the extent of civil rights can be assessed only by considering particular types of freedom and particular limitations that have been established over the years on the exercise of these freedoms.

Freedom of Speech
It is assumed by the courts that anyone is free to say or write what he likes provided he does not break the laws designed to protect the rights and security of his fellow-citizens. The laws of libel and slander are one check on this freedom: if a statement is made by A about B which is untrue and defames B's character, B may sue A in the civil courts and may be awarded substantial damages if he wins the case. But it is not libellous to publish a true statement unless malice can be established; nor is it libellous to hold a man up to ridicule, as is done in satirical programmes on television; nor is it libellous to say that a manufacturer's products are useless, as is done by consumers' associations.

A case lies for libel or slander only if an individual is named. What protection does the law afford to a group of citizens who are the collective victims of defamatory statements? One possibility is that the Director of Public Prosecutions may launch a prosecution for seditious libel. However, the last occasion on which this was done was in 1947, when the editor of a Lancashire local paper was prosecuted for publishing an anti-Semitic leading article. When the case was heard both judge and jury were so reluctant to restrict the freedom of the press that the result was an acquittal.

Another possibility, if the statement is made in a public place, is that the speaker might be prosecuted for using insulting language. This was done in 1937, when a fascist speaker in the East End of London was successfully prosecuted for a speech at a public meeting in which he said that 'Jews are the lice of the earth and must be exterminated from our national life'. But the police generally lean over backwards to avoid prosecuting political speakers, no matter how offensive their remarks.

The legal situation has been somewhat changed by the passage of the Race Relations Act of 1965, which makes it a criminal offence to stir up racial hatred in a public place by written or spoken words. This led to a good deal of comment arising from the ingrained British dislike of anything approaching political censorship, and *The Times* observed that

> the clause can be seen to set the criminal law moving once again towards a position from which it has been retreating in Britain for about 300 years: judging the criminality of utterances by reference to their subject matter and content rather than by reference to their likely effect on public order.[1]

However, the British police share the values underlying this comment, and less than ten cases have so far been brought under this section of the Act. Of these the most publicised case was against a speaker at a public meeting who described coloured immigrants as 'niggers and wops' and made some singularly unpleasant remarks about them. At the trial the jury failed to agree, and at the retrial the speaker was acquitted.

Other restrictions on freedom of speech are the laws against blasphemy, obscenity and incitement to violence. The law against blasphemy is a relic from earlier times which is now virtually obsolete. The law against obscenity has been liberalised by the passage of the Obscene Publications Act of 1959, under which a charge of obscenity can be successfully countered by proving (with the aid of expert witnesses) that the publication has literary merit. It was on this ground that the publishers of the unexpurgated edition of *Lady Chatterley's Lover* successfully withstood a prosecution alleging that this was an obscene publication. The law against incitement to violence will be discussed below, in connection with public meetings.

Freedom to March in Procession
It is both traditional and common in Britain for people wishing to demonstrate their views on a political issue to march in procession bearing placards. For many years members of the Labour movement have done this on May Day. In the 1930s unemployed workers drew attention to their plight by marching from the north of England to London. In the 1960s tens of thousands of people tramped about the country to indicate their dislike of nuclear weapons.

People are entitled to do this because the Queen's highway exists to facilitate travel from one place to another, and as each citizen enjoys the right to use the highway it necessarily follows that 10,000 citizens have the right to do so together. They have to be careful about stopping, because that may constitute obstruction, but so long as they keep on the move they are within the law.

There are two limitations on this right, one dating from the eighteenth century and one fairly new. The former is that no processions or public meetings may be held within one mile of the Houses of Parliament while Parliament is in session. In practice it is common for meetings to be held with official permission in Trafalgar Square, but the one attempt made in recent years to move off from the Square towards Parliament was broken up by the police in a most brisk and effective way. The other limitation arises from the Public Order Act of 1936, which was passed because of the disorders caused by fascist meetings and processions in London. The Act gives any chief of police power to change the route of a procession if he has reason to think that it may otherwise lead to serious disorder, or to impose other conditions on the marchers to prevent disorder. This means that organisers of marches are wise to give the police notice of their intentions.

This arrangement protects the rights of demonstrators even though it may compel them to change their proposed route, for once the police have agreed to a march they are obliged to protect the marchers against hostile counter-demonstrations. Since about 1970 the National Front, a fringe organisation motivated mainly by hostility to coloured immigrants, has staged numerous marches which have been attacked by left-wing groups of an extremist kind. The National Front marchers are entitled to police protection, and the result has been a series of violent clashes between left-wing demonstrators and the police, often leading to hundreds of injuries.

A particularly nasty confrontation of this kind occurred during the 1979 general election campaign, when the National Front put up a candidate in a west London constituency populated largely by Indian immigrants. The Front could muster only fifty-nine supporters for their election rally, but it took four thousand policemen to protect them from a hostile crowd of about five thousand, consisting partly of immigrants who lived in the area and partly of left-wing demonstrators from outside the area. The police were attacked with stones, bricks and fireworks; they retaliated with baton charges; and at the end of the day one demonstrator (a New Zealander) had been killed, nineteen demonstrators and twenty-one policemen had been taken to hospital, and hundreds of minor injuries had been suffered by both sides. In this kind of situation the costs of protecting the right of free speech can be tragically high.

Freedom of Meeting

Since individuals are free to talk with one another, it follows that large numbers of them are free to gather together in a public meeting, provided they can find a place to meet. If they can hire premises, there is no problem. If they gather on the public highway, however, they will be guilty of obstruction, unless they have police permission. As motorists know to their cost, the highway is intended only for movement, and a motorist who parks in a cul-de-sac is technically guilty of obstruction although a procession of demonstrators holding up traffic on a main road are innocent of any such thing. It is commonly thought that people enjoy a legal right to hold meetings in public parks, but in fact meetings of this kind are dependent on the permission of the authorities who control the parks: the Department of the Environment in London and local authorities elsewhere. However, in practice such permission is fairly freely granted and, one way or another, groups who wish to hold a public meeting rarely find it difficult to do so.

The general principle governing public meetings is that people may say what they like provided it is not likely to lead to a breakdown of public order. If this likelihood arises, the police may ask the speaker to desist or in some circumstances they may arrest him. The offences with which he may be charged include disturbing the peace, inciting others to commit a breach of the peace, behaviour with intent to provoke a breach of the peace, behaviour whereby a breach of the peace is likely to be occasioned, insulting behaviour, and (if he refuses a request to stop) obstructing a police officer in the execution of his duty. As a form of shorthand it is convenient to group these offences under the heading of incitement to violence.

The law regarding incitement to violence is generally administered in a liberal way, though the following examples show that there is a slight area of uncertainty at the margin. In 1914 George Lansbury was arrested after a meeting at which he had urged suffragettes to continue their militant tactics and was subsequently found guilty of inciting others to commit breaches of the peace. In 1961 Bertrand Russell and other leaders of the Committee of One Hundred were condemned on the same charge when they tried to hold a meeting in Trafalgar Square without official permission, though on other occasions members of this Committee advocated civil disobedience without prosecution.

In 1936 a Mrs Duncan proposed to hold an open-air meeting to protest against government treatment of the unemployed in a street outside a training centre for unemployed workers. When she had held a similar meeting in the same place fourteen months earlier this had been followed by a disturbance in the centre. Believing that the same result might follow again, a police inspector told her that she must move 175 yards away if she wished to hold the meeting. When she ignored this instruction she was charged with obstructing a police officer in the execution of his duty and was subsequently fined. This case caused some public concern because it was felt that it gave the police too much discretion. In fact it was necessary for the court to be convinced that the police officer had reasonable grounds for believing that the meeting might cause a breach of the peace, for otherwise the order he gave Mrs Duncan would not have been 'in the execution of his duty'. But it is clear that persons proposing to hold a meeting on the public highway are well advised to get police permission in advance. The police are usually co-operative, but if they have no advance notice and they ask the speaker to 'move on', either because they fear a disturbance or on grounds of obstruction of the highway, the speaker has no choice but to obey the instruction or face arrest.[2]

Another interesting example is that of the series of fascist meetings in Dalston, north London, in 1947. These were held in a cul-de-sac with police permission, but they caused violent reactions from the audience, many of whom came to the meetings with the express intention of breaking them up. The speeches were full of abusive and provocative anti-Semitic remarks which could be regarded as an incitement to violence when uttered in an area with some Jewish residents. But all the violence was directed towards the speakers and the police took the view that, although a speaker should be prosecuted if he incites his audience to violence against a third party, he is entitled to take the risk of provoking violence against himself. It was felt that the traditional right of uttering unpopular opinions should be defended, and in the later meetings of the series the speakers were accordingly surrounded by a cordon of policemen facing outwards towards the audience. On the other hand, in 1963 a fascist speaker in another area was successfully prosecuted for provoking a breach of the peace among an audience which was almost entirely hostile to him,[3] and it is clear that the application of the law in this field depends very much on the attitudes of the police.

Freedom of Political Association

There have been no restrictions on the organisation of voluntary associations in Britain since the repeal of the Combination Acts in 1824. Trade union leaders had to engage in a long struggle to secure immunity from court actions over the organisation of strikes which have an injurious effect on the interests of other people, but the right to form unions has not been curtailed and pressure groups and political parties have been completely free from legal restrictions. As noted in Chapter 5, political parties are not known to the law and their organisation and activities are entirely untrammelled. The Communist Party has never been banned, as has happened in France and some other democratic countries. Neither has the British Union of Fascists been declared illegal, though during the last war some of the leading members of the Union were interned because the Government regarded their loyalty to the nation as suspect.

What is almost equally important, individual members of parties have not suffered persecution or hardship on account of their views. Britain has never seen anything like the McCarthyite period in the United States, when men were driven from their jobs and sometimes driven to suicide by the lack of tolerance for their suspected sympathies or connections (past or present) with the Communist Party. Nor would the British have any truck with a variety of practices that are accepted as normal in the United States, such as the inquiries that FBI men address to university teachers about the political views of their students, the screening of applicants for a wide variety of posts that could not possibly be 'classified' for security reasons, or the occasional suspension of teachers or professors for expressing heretical views on political or religious matters.

Of course the British Government has to exercise some control over internal security. In 1948 the development of the Cold War led the Government to initiate a new policy of screening civil servants in posts involving security risk. Five years later it was reported that 17,000 officials had been screened, which was rather less than 2 per cent of the total number of civil servants at that time. Of these 111 were regarded as possible risks to security and nine were still under consideration. Of the 111, sixty-nine were transferred to equivalent posts elsewhere in the civil service, nineteen resigned, and 'only twenty-three were dismissed, and these because their qualifications were such that they could be employed only in secret work'.[4] In the two years following there was only one resignation and three transfers. This is not a disturbing record, and there is no evidence or suggestion that civil servants with extreme political views suffer in their careers if they are engaged in non-secret work. Outside Whitehall, the only reported case of a man being penalised on political grounds occurred in 1956 when a lawyer working for Imperial Chemical Industries was dismissed because the Government refused to place secret contracts with the firm unless he were denied access to the secrets. The case created such a furore in Parliament and the press that it is unlikely that any similar incidents have occurred.

These facts underline the general tolerance of British society, as does the unemotional way in which the British receive news that scientists or public servants have given secrets to potential enemies. The cases of Klaus Fuchs, Nunn May, and Burgess and Maclean created interest, a measure of understanding, and in the last case a good deal of amusement, but little or no sense of moral indignation.

Maclean's family went to join him in Moscow, Fuchs was allowed to work for East Germany after he was released from prison, and Nunn May was offered a post in industrial research a few weeks before his sentence ended.

The British take their liberties and their tolerance so much for granted that they do not always realise how rare these conditions are in the world or how much they contribute to the quality of British life. They are among the most precious fruits of three centuries of political stability and security.

FREEDOM FROM ARREST AND IMPRISONMENT

This is a field in which it is difficult to be specific in short compass because of the complexity of the law and the very large number of relevant cases that could be cited. However, it is possible to establish one or two general points.

In the first place, it is a principle of British law that all persons are presumed to be innocent until they are found guilty by a court. This has various implications. For instance, it implies that persons suspected of a crime should not be physically harmed by the police before they are brought to trial. The extensive guarantees of fair treatment by American law are of no use to those who are killed while being arrested, to say nothing of the fact that each year in New York several innocent pedestrians are killed or wounded because police bullets miss their mark. Nothing like this has happened in Britain because, at least until the late 1970s, British police have been unarmed. This makes them almost unique among the police forces of the world, and has only been possible because of the relative lack of violence in British society. Unfortunately, the situation changed during the 1970s. It became necessary to train special squads of police marksmen to protect embassies and airports against international terrorists, and the considerable growth in the propensity of armed robbers to open fire on the police forced the authorities to adopt the policy of issuing guns to the police in dangerous situations. At the time of writing about 20 per cent of the British police are trained marksmen, to whom guns may be issued in special circumstances on the authority of a senior officer. However, arms are not carried normally and when they are issued the police have to account for every bullet used.

Secondly, the principle implies that people should not be detained without trial. In fact, a person other than a suspected terrorist cannot legally be detained in Britain unless he is charged with a specific offence, and if he is then kept in custody he must be brought before a magistrate within twenty-four hours. In the great majority of cases he will then be released on bail until the time of his trial. Since November 1974 (the month when IRA bombs killed over twenty people in a Birmingham pub), it has been possible for the police to detain suspected terrorists for questioning for up to seven days at a port of entry to Great Britain and up to three days within the country, a provision which has been used against both Irish and Arab suspects. In the first forty-two months after this provision was introduced 3,259 persons were detained, 2,299 at ports and 960 within Britain. However, only about 10 per cent of these suspects were detained for more than forty-eight hours and only about 4 per cent were charged with criminal offences.[5]

Thirdly, the principle implies that there should be some method whereby a person kept illegally in custody may secure his release. This method is the writ of *habeas corpus,* which can be issued by any High Court judge at any time, on his being informed that a person is being kept in custody without authorisation. An application for such a writ takes precedence over all other business in court and application may also be made directly to a judge in chambers. This writ, incidentally, is of use not only against detention by the police but also against detention in, say, a mental home.

Another principle is that 'the Englishman's home is his castle'. The police are only entitled to enter a house if they have secured a search warrant after making a sworn statement regarding the need for it, unless they are in hot pursuit of a criminal. If the police exceed their powers they can be sued for damages. Thus, in the case of *Peters v Shaw* (1965) a merry-go-round proprietor sued a policeman who had entered his caravan without permission while looking for persons suspected of committing a felony on the fairground: the proprietor was awarded damages and costs against the policeman.[6] In another case a policeman entered a garage to inquire about a lorry there which had previously been obstructing the highway. The owner ordered the policeman off the premises, but instead of leaving immediately he started to produce a document to prove he was a police officer. The owner then ejected him by force, was prosecuted by the policeman for assault, but was acquitted because the policeman had no right to stay on the premises after he had been told to leave.[7]

Another principle is the right to a fair trial before an impartial judge or jury. British judges are appointed for life from the ranks of successful barristers, so that they cannot be subjected to any kind of political pressure. The right to trial by jury has been firmly established for a very long time, and juries are independent bodies who cannot easily be bullied or persuaded into taking a decision which they do not consider right. There have been numerous cases, from the eighteenth century onwards, of juries acquitting an accused person in spite of the strongest advice given by the judge that the facts pointed towards a conviction. Further provisions designed to ensure a fair trial are the provision of legal aid to persons who cannot afford to pay for representation by counsel and the right of appeal to the Court of Appeals and, with permission, to the House of Lords (where the case is heard by a small group of Law Lords appointed for this purpose).

Of course the police have some powers not granted to ordinary citizens, but these are strictly limited. They have no right, for instance, to take a person to a police station or detain him there for questioning, against his will, unless they arrest him. The papers frequently report that a person has spent some hours at a police station 'assisting the police with their inquiries', but this happens either because the man wishes to co-operate with the police or because he thinks it will pay him to appear to co-operate with the police or because he does not know his rights and was not told of them.

This last point draws attention to one of the problems of assessing police behaviour, namely that researchers cannot interview a scientific sample of people who have been taken in for questioning in regard to a criminal offence. Among the population at large, the British police are highly regarded. An international survey conducted in 1959 and 1960 showed that 74 per cent of British people expected that the police would give serious consideration to their point of view in an encounter, compared with 59 per cent in West Germany, 56 per cent in the United States, 35 per cent in Italy, and 12 per cent in Mexico. Moreover, Britain was the only one of these countries in which the expectations were just as favourable among people who had left school at 14 or 15 as they were among the better educated.[8] However, it would be rash to conclude from these figures that British police behaviour is always beyond criticism when dealing with suspected criminals.

The difficult period is that between the time when a suspect is taken to the police station for questioning and the time when he appears in court. In this period the behaviour of the police is supposed to conform to a pattern determined partly by the Judges' Rules and partly by police regulations. According to this ideal pattern, the police must permit the suspect to call a lawyer unless this is likely to interfere with the administration of justice; must respect his right not to answer questions unless he freely chooses to do so; must ensure that he is provided with reasonable comfort and refreshments; must not tell the suspect that the police believe him to be guilty; must not use threats or promises or any undue pressure to induce the suspect to make a statement; and must give the suspect a clear warning that any statement he makes may be taken down and used in evidence.

The police have to deal with some pretty rough characters in circumstances of considerable tension, and it would be surprising if this code of conduct were always followed exactly. In practice it is clear that the police sometimes trade on the ignorance of the people they examine and sometimes engage in verbal bullying or cajolery in order to secure information, or even a confession, on which they can base a charge. Occasionally they also resort to intimidation and the milder forms of violence. People do not suffer torture or broken bones in British police stations, but they are sometimes punched and bruised. Moreover, there are grounds for believing that police behaviour is tending to deteriorate. Given the general increase in violence during the 1970s, this is not surprising. The police now have to cope with armed robbers, with terrorists bent on murder, with violent political demonstrations, with mass picketing which frequently produces violence, with mugging in the streets of London, and with repeated crowd violence at football matches. Only twenty years ago, these phenomena hardly existed in Britain. Now the police are increasingly obliged to use their fists and batons in the course of their duty and there is a danger that some of them may become coarsened by this experience. In any assessment of police behaviour, it is essential to realise that the great majority of the police are not heroes or saints, not bullies or pigs, and not disembodied instruments of the law, but men and women doing a difficult job whose performance is inevitably influenced by the cumulative impact of their experiences.

The rules of police conduct should not therefore be taken as an infallible guide to practice. Their great value is that they constitute a norm to which appeals can be made. If the police deviate from them, the matter may be raised in court. If the defence can show that a statement was involuntary in the sense that it was induced by threats or promises, the statement may not be admitted as evidence; and if it is the basis of the prosecution's case the result is likely to be an acquittal.

There can be no doubt that the existence of these rules is a considerable protection against intimidation by the police and a distinct asset to persons suspected of breaking the law. It has indeed been said that some of the rules unduly weaken the hands of the police in their dealings with professional criminals, and in 1972 the Commissioner of Police at Scotland Yard suggested that the right not to answer questions should be abolished on the ground that innocent people have no reason to be afraid of helping the police with their inquiries. This proposal got a mixed reception: there is clearly a case for it in a period when the crime rate is rising sharply and the rate of detection is falling, but it would seem a serious infringement of individual freedom to abolish the right to keep silent unless special safeguards were created.

CITIZENS' RIGHTS IN RELATION TO THE ADMINISTRATION

The rights so far discussed in this chapter are essentially rights to be left alone by agents of the State. The development of social and economic legislation in the twentieth century has given citizens rights of a different kind: the right to a pension, to benefits while unemployed or sick, to housing at a controlled or subsidised rent, to tax relief in respect of some kinds of expenditure. The disputes about rights of this kind could not appropriately be settled by the ordinary courts, for a variety of reasons. First, the courts would be hopelessly clogged by the vast number of cases which arise. Secondly, the citizen needs a remedy which is quicker and cheaper than court procedure makes possible: it would be useless for an unemployed man to have to hire a lawyer to make a claim for a few pounds benefit. Thirdly, the issues are administrative rather than judicial: it is desirable for those hearing the case to have some technical knowledge and it is often thought appropriate for them to be guided by departmental policy when reaching decisions.

For these reasons, disputes of this kind go not to the ordinary courts but to a variety of administrative tribunals. It is almost impossible to generalise about the composition and procedure of these tribunals because they are so varied. Some are chaired by lawyers, others by ordinary administrators. Some contain members appointed to represent interested groups such as trade unions or employers, while others do not. At some the appellant may be represented by a lawyer, at others he may bring a friend but not a lawyer.

This kind of variation is confusing but may be inevitable if each body is organised to deal with a particular set of problems. By and large, the tribunals are quick and cheap, and the people who have most to do with them are not dissatisfied. What sometimes causes concern, however, is that they violate the elementary principle that no man should be a judge in his own case. The members of tribunals which hear appeals against the decisions of a ministry are nearly always appointed by the minister concerned, and aggrieved citizens are apt to think that they would have got fairer treatment from a court of law. This kind of complaint is also levelled against public inquiries, which differ from tribunals mainly in the fact that a tribunal takes a decision whereas the chairman of a public inquiry submits advice to the minister. Proposals to change the use of a piece of land frequently lead to public inquiries at which all the interested parties can testify. But the result of the inquiry is simply a report to the minister which he must consider but is not bound to accept. Since in many cases the reason for the inquiry is the dislike of citizens for the minister's proposed developments, this procedure is not calculated to make them feel that they have had a fair hearing.

Criticisms of this kind led to the passage of the Tribunals and Inquiries Act of 1958, which extended the rights of appeal and obliged tribunals to inform appellants both of the reasons for their decisions and of the possibilities for further appeal. The most common situation is that it is possible to appeal to a court on points of law but further appeals on questions of fact or interpretation have to go to another administrative tribunal or to the minister himself. It is therefore not surprising that, although in general the system works tolerably well, there remains a minority of cases which leave citizens with a deep feeling of grievance. British civil servants enjoy a well-deserved reputation for tolerance and fairness, but they wield such extensive powers that some people are bound to get bruised. A former Conservative minister has said in his memoirs that:

> For every Crichel Down that comes to the ears of the public there are literally thousands that are buried in the archives of Whitehall and in the hearts of the people. Every MP and social worker knows of men and women who are living with a sense of grievance at the hands of authority, some of whom have had their lives ruined by persecution complexes.[9]

For this reason many critics have looked to foreign experience to see if any other countries have lessons for Britain in this field.

The general conclusion has been that they have. In many other democratic countries the citizen's rights against the administration are more thoroughly protected than they are in Britain, and in some countries people can appeal against acts of administrative discretion against which the British citizen has no appeal whatsoever (except to write to his MP). For instance, if a British citizen is refused an allocation of foreign exchange which he needs for a business trip, there is nothing he can do about it. Nor can an industrialist appeal against a decision forbidding him to build a new office block in London, or a taxi driver appeal against a decision of the Metropolitan Police Commissioner to revoke his licence.

Two main examples have been recommended as ones which might be followed. One is the French system of administrative justice. In France cases involving the way public servants use their powers are heard in a special administrative court (which has many branches) known as the Conseil d'Etat. This court has succeeded in doing what British courts have never tried to do, namely to apply the rule of law to the whole field of administrative discretion. For instance, there are in both countries numerous statutes which give a minister the power to make orders, issue licences, revoke licences and so forth 'if he is satisfied that' it is in the public interest to do so. British courts have always taken the view that if the minister declares himself to be satisfied he has complied with the condition, so that his decision is beyond challenge by the court. The Conseil d'Etat, on the other hand, takes the view that the minister has complied with the condition only if his satisfaction is based upon reasonable grounds which can be explained and justified in court. The Conseil has the power to require the minister or his officials to justify their decisions in this way, supplemented by power to declare the decisions null and void if the attempted justification is unsatisfactory and to award damages to the aggrieved citizen if this is thought appropriate.

Decisions about town planning make an interesting example. Whenever a local authority or government department in Britain plans to acquire property by compulsory purchase to make room for a new development the property-owners have the right to ask for a public inquiry into the scheme. Such an inquiry will be conducted by an inspector who is appointed by the minister and is usually an official of the department concerned. The inspector makes his recommendations in a report which the minister is bound to consider, under the terms of the Town and Country Planning Act. But, having considered the report, he may accept or reject the recommendations as he thinks fit, and his decision is final. Under this procedure an objector may well feel that the scales are doubly weighted against him: the inquiry is conducted by a member of the department most closely involved in the plan, and even if the result of the inquiry should be favourable to the objector the minister could still decide to ignore the inspector's advice and go ahead with the plan. The procedure gives ample time for lobbying and counter-lobbying, which indeed is its main purpose, but it does not bring the minister's actions under judicial or quasi-judicial control.

If Britain had a system of administrative justice like the French system, the situation would be quite different: the objector would be able to appeal against the minister's decision and the latter would be required to justify it to the satisfaction of the administrative court. Numerous other examples could be cited but it is unnecessary to do so, for there can be no doubt that French citizens have recourse to a more effective system of control of administrative actions than British citizens enjoy. However, it has never been likely that a British government would institute a system of administrative courts in this country: the civil service would put up the strongest resistance to such a reform and ministers could not be expected to go out of their way to create a rod for their own backs.

A much more modest form of check on administrative behaviour operates in Denmark and Sweden. In these countries there is an officer known as an Ombudsman who has the specific task of investigating grievances against the administration. He is appointed by Parliament after each general election but he then enjoys security of office till the next election. His main function is to investigate complaints against the behaviour of the central administration. He has power to call for persons and documents and if he concludes that the complaint is justified it is his duty to inform the parties to the case and to publish his findings. He has no power to nullify the decision or to award damages to the complainant, but the press takes a keen interest in his reports and if a department were to ignore his recommendations this would immediately create a public outcry.

In 1965 the Government decided to create an office of this kind in Britain, with the title of Parliamentary Commissioner for Administration. The Commissioner is appointed by the Crown but is at the service of Parliament. The main difference between his position and that of the Scandinavian Ombudsman is that the Commissioner acts only on the request of an MP. Citizens wishing to complain must therefore find an MP (not necessarily their own) who is willing to pass the matter on to the Commissioner. The Commissioner has power to call for oral or written evidence and to examine departmental files – a major concession by the Government. If he finds that the complaint is justified and the department responds to his invitation to put the matter right, that is the end of the matter; if the department does not so respond, the Commissioner reports the whole matter to Parliament, which has established a select committee to consider such reports.

The jurisdiction of the Parliamentary Commissioner was at first very limited, for his original terms of reference made it impossible for him to criticise the exercise of administrative discretion provided all the forms had been correctly complied with and there had been no error in the interpretation of the facts. However, in the first year of his work the Commissioner found an instance of maladministration which attracted nationwide publicity and gave both legitimacy and prestige to his office. For over twenty years the Foreign Office had refused to pay the compensation due to concentration-camp victims to a group of ex-servicemen who had been incarcerated in the notorious Sachsanhausen camp as prisoners of war, on the ground that their treatment had been less severe than that meted out to the other inmates. Though numerous previous appeals had failed, the Parliamentary Commissioner found that the Foreign Office had no good reason for the position it had taken and his report resulted in substantial compensation for the men involved. With his prestige strengthened by this case, the Commissioner was able to secure a substantial extension of his terms of reference in 1968, which enabled him to criticise the exercise of administrative discretion if its consequences were clearly unfortunate and to criticise administrative rules if a complainant had sustained hardship through the correct application of a rule which the Commissioner deemed to be unfair.

This constitutional innovation has proved to be a success. The work of the Commissioner has led to a significant extension of the rights of the citizen in relation to the administration. As a consequence of this success it was decided in the 1970s to appoint Commissioners with similar powers to deal with complaints about the National Health Service and complaints about the activities of local authorities.

THE RIGHTS OF ETHNIC MINORITIES

The British tradition in regard to civil rights is that these rights inhere in the individual citizen as a subject of the Crown. The object of judges and legal reformers over the past two centuries has been to ensure that these rights are adequately protected against encroachment by agents of the State and that the protection is afforded equally to all citizens, irrespective of class, sex, religion and political opinion. Until very recently there has never been any suggestion that particular groups of citizens needed legal protection against discriminatory treatment by other private citizens.

The situation has changed in recent years as a consequence of the arrival since the late 1950s of large numbers of Commonwealth immigrants from Asia, east Africa and the Caribbean. By 1979 these immigrants and their children constituted a group of ethnic minorities comprising 1·8 million people, a total which is expected to increase to nearly four million by the end of the century. Sadly, but almost inevitably, problems of racial discrimination have developed and have created a need for special measures to protect the minorities.

The Government first promoted legislation to this end in 1975, this action being undertaken (in the words of an American lawyer) 'very promptly by American standards, precipitously according to British tradition'.[10] It was an entirely new field of legislation for Britain, and the minister responsible for it made an important change in response to public pressure after the Race Relations Bill had been published. In its first draft the Bill provided for criminal sanctions against anyone found guilty of racial discrimination in public places. However, the Campaign against Racial Discrimination, an organisation which spoke on behalf of the main immigrant groups, joined forces with a group of Labour lawyers and numerous MPs to urge that criminal sanctions be dropped from the Bill and replaced by a conciliation process for which a Statutory Board or Commission would be responsible. This change led to the creation of the national Race Relations Board and a number of local committees, and it was undoubtedly an improvement on the original proposal. Criminal sanctions would have been difficult to enforce and dysfunctional because of their unpopularity with the general public, whereas the revised procedure was well received and established a body of public officials with a duty to conciliate and educate. In another section of the Act criminal sanctions were included for the new offence of incitement to racial hatred but, as noted earlier, there have been few prosecutions under this section and even fewer convictions.

The 1965 Act was limited in its scope, covering only discrimination in public places, discrimination in tenancies, and incitement to racial hatred. However, in 1968 the second Race Relations Act extended the scope of the law to cover employment, housing, the sale and rental of business premises, the sales of all goods at both wholesale and retail levels, the provision of all services, and membership of trade unions and professional associations. It was also decided to introduce a complete ban on racially discriminatory advertisements and to establish a new body called the Community Relations Commission, with responsibility for improving race relations by education and the co-ordination of voluntary activities in this field.

If these British arrangements for protecting the rights of ethnic minorities are compared with American arrangements, some interesting differences emerge. First, British law-makers moved much more quickly than their American counterparts, enacting comprehensive legislation within ten years of the first emergence of a problem of race relations. Secondly, British legislation is more comprehensive than American, for American laws do not cover the sale and rental of business premises, do not cover all commercial transactions, and do not ban discriminatory advertisements.

On the other hand, British legislation makes much less use of criminal sanctions and does not give the person discriminated against the same right of redress that he enjoys under some American laws. Thus, an American employer who has refused to employ a person on grounds of race can be forced to employ him by court order, whereas a British employer can only be forced to abstain from discriminatory activities in the future. Since racial discrimination in employment undoubtedly exists in Britain (though its extent is difficult to measure), it is common for American observers to recommend that British law be remodelled on American lines.[11] However, American racial conflicts have been far more serious than any experienced in Britain, and the general British view is that the more drastic American methods are unnecessary and would be dysfunctional in the British context.

A final difference between British and American practice is that there is no equivalent in Britain of the positive discrimination that has become common in some fields of American life since the 1960s, with employers and various public institutions (including universities) being compelled to give preferential treatment to ethnic minorities. This kind of policy would be completely contrary to the British tradition that rights inhere in the individual and that all individuals should be treated as equal by courts and government authorities. The object in Britain is not to confer special privileges on particular ethnic groups but simply to ensure that individuals are not discriminated against on racial grounds.

NOTES

1   *The Times,* 8 April 1965.
2   Both of these pre-war cases, and several others, are mentioned in ch. 2 of Harry Street, *Freedom, the Individual and the Law.*
3   See *Jordan v. Burgoyne* (1963), Two Weekly Law Reports 1045.
4   Street, *Freedom,* p. 222.
5   *The Shackleton Review of the Operation of the Prevention of Terrorism (Temporary Provisions) Acts 1974 and 1976,* Cmnd 7324 of 1978, app. E.
6   Reported in *The Times,* 6 May 1965.
7   *Davis v. Lisle* (1936), cited in Street, *Freedom,* p. 24.
8   See Gabriel Almond and Sidney Verba, *The Civic Culture* (Little, Brown, 1965), p. 66.
9   Reginald Bevins, *The Greasy Pole* (Hodder & Stoughton, 1965), p. 66.
10 Louis Claiborne, *Race and Law in Britain and the United States* (1974), p. 11.
11 See ibid., and Donley Studlar, 'Political culture and racial policy in Britain', in Richard Rose (ed.), *Studies in British Politics,* 3rd edn (Macmillan, 1976), pp. 105–14.

FURTHER READING

The legal basis of British civil liberties is outlined clearly in Harry Street, *Freedom, the Individual and the Law* (Penguin, 1963); the best practical guide to the situation is Anna Coote and L. Grant, *Civil Liberty: the NCCL Guide* (Penguin, 1972); some essays on the activities of the police will be found in C. H. Rolph (ed.), *The Police and the Public* (Heinemann, 1962); a survey of public attitudes to the police is analysed in William Belson, *The Public and the Police* (Harper & Row, 1975); police behaviour in political demonstrations is discussed in R. L. Clutterbuck, *Britain in Agony: The Growth of Political Violence* (Faber, 1978); a perceptive essay on maladministration will be found in K. C. Wheare, *Maladministration and Its Remedies* (Stevens, 1973); the work of administrative tribunals is discussed in H. J. Elcock, *Administrative Justice* (Longman, 1969), and in R. E. Wraith and P. G. Hutcheson, *Administrative Tribunals* (Allen & Unwin, 1973); the position of the Parliamentary Commissioner for Administration is described in Frank Stacey, *The British Ombudsman* (Oxford University Press, 1971); the French system of administrative justice is explained in C. J. Hamson, *Executive Discretion in Judicial*

Control (Stevens, 1954); the most illuminating short guide to the protection of the rights of ethnic minorities is Louis Claiborne, *Race and Law in Britain and the United States,* revised edn (Minority Rights Group, 1979); the fairest account of the disadvantages from which minorities nevertheless suffer will be found in David J. Smith, *Racial Disadvantage in Britain* (Penguin, 1977).

Chapter 16

Characteristics and Problems of British Democracy

Previous chapters have given a brief account of the way Britain is governed. The aim of this final chapter is to provide a tentative assessment of this system of government in terms of democratic values. This is not easy because democracy is a rather vague concept subject to a variety of interpretations. It is therefore necessary to say a word about the basic values which all democrats have in common and then to outline the main characteristics of the British version of democratic government. The chapter will conclude with some discussion of the recent developments which have led a number of critics to allege that British democracy is in a state of decline or even of crisis.

Some basic values are common to all societies with a reasonable claim to be democratic. These include a commitment to freedom of speech and freedom of political association; a belief that the representative system should offer equal opportunities of participation to all citizens and should provide a fair method of choosing between alternative candidates for political office; a belief that those in power should have to justify their decisions in a forum which gives their opponents ample opportunity for criticism; and a commitment to the view that the rights of the citizen should be protected by an independent judiciary and by adequate procedures for the redress of grievances against the administration.

Beyond this, values and institutions vary from one country to another. American democratic values, for example, are permeated by the belief that the people should as far as possible govern themselves. In this view, which can indeed be traced back to the origins of the term 'democracy' in ancient Greece, representative government tends to be seen as a substitute for the unattainable ideal, which would be direct government by the masses. Tom Paine reflected this view in 1792 when he described representative government as the best form of government for a nation 'too extensive and populous for the simple democratic form'.[1] The Founding Fathers reflected the same view when they constructed a system of constitutional checks and balances to prevent any one set of political leaders from acquiring too much power and when they decided that members of the House of Representatives should be elected for only two years, a shorter term of office than that adopted in any other country. The frequent use of the initiative and referendum in state and municipal government demonstrates the enduring strength of this belief in popular sovereignty.

The British democratic system has a rather different foundation. The constitutional source of political authority is not the people, but the Crown in Parliament. Criminal cases are characterised as 'Regina v. Smith', in contrast to the American style of 'The People v. Smith'. Political power is not divided between institutions and levels of government, but highly concentrated. Ultimate responsibility for all political decisions taken in the country rests with the Prime Minister and the Cabinet, governing with and through Parliament but normally able to rely upon parliamentary support for their measures. As noted in Chapter 2, constitutional theorists differ in emphasis in their accounts of the proper relationship between Parliament and the executive. But in practice it is clear that the effective power of decision-making is concentrated in the hands of a small group of ministers, and the essence of British democracy is that this small group gain office as a result of a general election, act in accordance with certain conventions and understandings while in power, and may be dismissed from office when the next election comes round. The system, like most European systems, assumes a greater willingness on the part of the people to trust their political leaders than is normally assumed in the United States.

SOME CHARACTERISTICS OF BRITISH DEMOCRACY

The main democratic aspects of the British system of government can be summarised quite briefly, and doing this will provide a framework for the assessment of recent criticisms. It will be useful to give this summary a logical order by adopting the common and convenient assumption that the process of government can be divided into three stages, known respectively as inputs, decision-making and outputs. The inputs include demands, pressures and elections. The decision-making is concentrated in Parliament, the Cabinet, and the government departments in Whitehall. The outputs include laws, regulations, administrative techniques, public services and government subsidies. These stages will be discussed *seriatim*.

(1) On the input side, the British democratic tradition lays stress on the maintenance of a set of largely unwritten rules which permit free competition between political parties and associations. It is taken for granted in Britain that civil liberties will be preserved and that no

peacetime Government will attempt to curtail freedom of speech and association. Since 1974 the Irish Republican Army has been proscribed on the ground that it is a terrorist organisation relying on violence, but political associations with similar objectives to the IRA have not been proscribed.

It is also assumed that no government will take advantage of its temporary majority in order to change the electoral system for its own benefit. It is true that the recurring need to adjust constituency boundaries creates opportunities for political manipulation and it has been suggested in Chapter 5 that there would be some advantage in tying the Boundary Commissions more tightly to a numerical formula so as to increase equality of representation. But the Commissions are impartial bodies, the partisan pressures put on them are normally small, and governments since 1945 – with the important but solitary exception of the Labour Government in 1969 – have been entirely fair in their handling of recommendations emerging from the Commissions. The registration of electors is also conducted in a scrupulously fair way, and in the twentieth century there have been hardly any complaints about the conduct of elections.

Political parties have complete freedom to organise and are not subject to any legal controls regarding their procedures or activities. Extremist parties have never been banned (as they are in West Germany); their candidates are given the same privileges and (where necessary) protection as other candidates; and their members are not excluded from government jobs (as they would be in the United States). At the same time, parties opposed to the existing democratic regime receive very little support from the electorate. Two Communist MPs were elected in 1945, but since the 1950s the various Marxist and fascist candidates have received only a derisory number of votes. To date the British system has successfully combined the advantages of toleration and stability. The main parties alternate in power much more frequently than is the case in some democratic systems (e.g. France, Italy, Sweden, Canada, Israel, India), which must be counted an advantage on democratic grounds provided the costs in terms of policy upheavals are not too great. To date (or, as some would say, until the 1970s) the British parties have had enough in common for these costs to be relatively small.

All the parties, and particularly the major ones, act as channels for the communication of public opinion to the policy-makers. The head offices of the parties receive a constant stream of communications about party policy from local branches, discussion groups, youth sections, and organisations like the Fabian Society, the Bow Group and PEST (Programme for Economic and Social Toryism). British parties and their affiliated organisations publish pamphlets and articles about policy issues to an extent that is unknown in many other democracies, such as the United States and Canada. Party conferences are also occasions for the expression of rank-and-file opinion and, though party leaders do not always feel obliged to follow the policies favoured by conference, it would be a mistake to think that leaders are not influenced by the views of their supporters.

Pressure groups are another vital channel for the communication of public opinions and demands. They are highly organised and extremely active in Britain and can easily gain access to political decision-makers. Differences in their financial resources play a relatively small role in the extent of their influence, for policy-makers are hardly ever bribable and the most effective channels of communication are fairly inexpensive. As noted in Chapter 6, it is a convention of the system that spokesmen for affected interests should be consulted by civil servants when government policy is formulated. Many MPs have connections with pressure groups and all MPs get a flood of correspondence from them. Each day the average MP gets at least fifteen letters from pressure groups and their members, giving information about various causes and interests. The propagation of ideas about government policy is also greatly helped by the existence of weekly journals of opinion, such as *The Economist,* the *New Statesman,* the *Spectator* and *New Society,* which have no real equivalents in North America.

(2)   The decision-making process can be said to satisfy democratic criteria if policy changes involving legislation are publicly debated, with a real possibility of amendments being made; if the grounds on which administrative decisions are taken are made public, so that informed criticism is possible; and if the overall programme of the Government takes account of popular wishes.

The first of these criteria is fairly well satisfied in Britain. The drafting of legislation is normally preceded by an elaborate process of consultation with spokesmen for affected interests. Legislative procedure in Parliament ensures that Bills are freely debated. It is possible to criticise the legislative process, however, on the ground that in recent decades governments have become excessively reluctant to accept detailed amendments at the committee stage or in the House of Lords. Party discipline is valued in Britain and few would dispute the proposition that a Government is entitled to expect its supporters to see most of its legislative proposals safely through Parliament. However, it might be thought that a Government would be satisfied if nine-tenths of its Bills got through unscathed rather than insist on winning every skirmish as well as the main battle. The resentment with which some ministers in recent years have reacted to the loss of a vote on an amendment might lead an overseas observer to wonder whether they accept the legitimacy of any legislative role for Parliament other than that of a rubber stamp.

The second criterion raises the whole question of governmental secrecy. The British system has frequently been criticised on the ground of undue secrecy, and it is undoubtedly vulnerable to this criticism. There have, however, been improvements in recent years which are cumulatively of some importance. The new specialised committees of Parliament, now armed with research staff, have secured information for backbench MPs. The Parliamentary Commissioner has power to call for Whitehall files. The new practice of publishing consultative documents (known as Green Papers) on policy questions has opened up some issues for discussion before governmental decisions are finalised.

The Official Secrets Act has been somewhat liberalised and investigative journalists have been able to secure and publish fascinating accounts of the way in which particular administrative decisions were reached. They have been helped by the increasing tendency of ministers to leak information about interdepartmental disputes and even Cabinet meetings, and Granada Television was able to produce an apparently authentic reconstruction of secret Cabinet meetings about the future of Chrysler Motors in Britain. All in all, it can no longer fairly be said (as it could be in the early 1960s) that British administration is wrapped in an undemocratic veil of secrecy; but some senior officials have conducted such a dogged rearguard action to protect Whitehall from publicity that the criticisms have inevitably continued.

The third of these criteria is the most difficult to define precisely, for it involves the whole problem of what is meant by governmental responsibility. All democrats believe that governments should be responsible, but this term has three meanings which are not always compatible with one another. It means, first, that governments should be responsive to public wishes and demands. It means, secondly, that governments should be answerable and accountable for their actions, and should be liable to suffer politically for policies which are shown to be unsuccessful. It means, thirdly, that governments should act in a consistent fashion, pursuing policies which are mutually compatible and likely to advance the public interest.

Much of the difficulty of assessing the decision-making process in government derives from the fact that responsibility in the first of these senses is sometimes incompatible with responsibility in the third sense. People want higher incomes but they also want stable prices. They want lower taxes but they also want higher public expenditures. They want freedom to drive to work in city centres, want to avoid traffic congestion, but do not want to disfigure their cities with urban motorways. They want freedom to go on strike but they do not want public services to be disrupted by other strikers. A Government that responded to all the demands put upon it would produce policies that were inconsistent and therefore, in the third sense of the term, irresponsible. Decision-makers in government have not only to balance the claims of conflicting groups but also to weigh the long-term consequences of pursuing short-term popularity.

It cannot be said that postwar British governments have been very successful in this regard. The art of political leadership in a democracy is to persuade people to accept policies that will be beneficial in the long run, even though they may involve what appear to be short-run sacrifices. In Britain there has been much talk about planning for progress and growth, but in many areas of policy the reality has been a succession of electoral bribes and concessions to sectional interests. Rent subsidies and tax allowances for housing are granted to millions of people who do not really need them, while many of the poorest families live in private rented accommodation without any subsidies at all. Regional economic policies have poured money and directed industry into areas of industrial decline, although the economic benefit to these areas has been greatly outweighed by the loss to areas of potential growth. Most of the massive government grants for industrial development have gone not to the promotion of new industries which might make Britain more prosperous but to the protection of jobs in industries that can no longer compete profitably in international markets. The financial arrangements for the Health Service make it a burden on the national exchequer without giving it enough X-ray equipment or kidney machines, or enabling it to make the salaries and conditions of work for doctors and surgeons sufficiently attractive to prevent the profession being weakened by large-scale emigration.

In summary, it appears that the decision-making process in British government has been excessively responsive to the immediate demands of the public to the detriment of economic and social progress in the long run. The political leaders of the postwar era must bear an appreciable part of the blame for the fact that since 1945 Britain has declined from being the third most prosperous country in Europe (surpassed only by neutral Sweden and Switzerland) to its present (1979) position of thirteenth. Economic decline and fiscal overload have political consequences which have led some critics to suggest that British democracy has entered a critical period, and this question will be discussed in a later section of this chapter.

(3) On the output side of government, democratic tradition requires honest administration, which does not discriminate between citizens. It requires an adequate machinery to remedy grievances against the administration. It requires that the law-enforcement agencies show a proper respect for individual privacy and freedom and

that citizens should generally comply with the law, not because of fear but because they recognise it to be fair.

The honesty and impartiality of British public officials has hardly been called into question in the twentieth century. The civil service appears to be virtually incorruptible and, although there is evidence of corrupt practices in local government in regard to architectural and building contracts, this appears to be on a small scale compared with what is taken for granted in many democratic regimes.

British administration is also marked by strict adherence to the principle that there should be no discrimination between citizens, not even in a good cause. The French economy has benefited considerably from the practice adopted by government planning agencies of discriminating between industrial firms in terms of their efficiency and probable contributions to economic growth, offering capital grants at low rates of interest to promising firms which are willing to accept certain conditions. Most British officials would regard this practice as slightly improper because the benefits are selective, even though the policy does not interfere directly with the rights of other firms.

Two examples indicate the force of British traditions in this regard. In 1966 controversy arose over the Prices and Incomes Act, which gave the minister power to issue orders which would prevent particular firms from raising their prices or paying higher wages. The acquisition of this executive power to discriminate between firms was followed by an incident in which some trade unionists and businessmen who had negotiated a wage increase in the printing industry were summoned to the office of a Cabinet minister, who told them he would not allow the increase to be paid. A minister has, of course, no power to summon citizens to see him, but in the circumstances they could hardly refuse. This incident led critics to regard the Act as not only a break with tradition but also a diminution of liberty, and there was a general sigh of relief when controls on prices and incomes were abandoned in 1969.

A somewhat similar incident occurred in 1978, when the Ford Motor Company awarded its workers a wage increase in excess of the government norm. Ministers had no power to prevent this being paid, but it was announced that the Government would punish Ford for ignoring its advice about wages by ordering public authorities throughout the country to boycott Ford products. This policy was challenged in Parliament by the Conservative Opposition and defeated. These two incidents have tended to strengthen the tradition that administration should in no circumstances be discriminatory.

The remedies for individual grievances against the administration have been discussed in Chapter 15 and need not be recapitulated. The protection of individual liberties has been discussed in the same chapter and no more need be said about it except to stress the point that was made in Chapter 1, namely that in all kinds of ways Britain is a land of freedom, where the privacy and rights of the citizen are accorded more respect than in almost any other country.

The other side of the coin is public compliance with the law because it is regarded as fair. The British record of compliance has always been remarkably high, but in recent years certain danger signals can be detected. The crime rate is going up, the use of guns by criminals is increasing, there has been an increase in casual violence, and tax evasion (minimal until recently) is becoming common. However, crimes of violence are still relatively rare by international standards and the rise in tax evasion is a reaction to particular economic problems (which will be discussed below) rather than a sign that the law is held in general disrespect.

CURRENT PROBLEMS OF BRITISH DEMOCRACY

During most of the twentieth century British attitudes towards their system of government have been marked by a high degree of complacency. The system has been viewed as liberal, democratic, stable, and productive of policies which were well intentioned and generally defensible even if not always successful. Since the early 1960s disappointment with the outputs of the system has punctured this complacency and eventually replaced it with cynicism and (in some quarters) with alarm. The realisation round about 1960 that Britain's rate of economic growth was appreciably poorer than that of its industrial competitors, and that the Government was partly responsible for this, led to the belief that institutional reforms were needed to improve the performance of the system. The following decade was marked by a succession of reforms and experiments, some of which have been mentioned in earlier chapters, but the country's economic performance did not improve and by the early 1970s it was clear that Britain was suffering from a deeper malaise, which could not be cured by tinkering with institutions.[2]

When Edward Heath took office in 1970 he promised to introduce 'a new style of government' and to revitalise the economy by new policies. But in 1972 some of his new economic policies were abandoned, and from then onwards Britain has experienced little but a succession of crises: confrontation with the trade unions over the Industrial Relations Act; the 1973 oil crisis and the quadrupling of oil prices; the miners' strike of 1974 which brought down the Government; runaway inflation which increased prices by 25 per cent in the twelve months of 1975; a high rate of unemployment; and a devaluation of sterling which forced the Government in 1976 to accept external controls on public expenditure as a condition of getting a loan from the International Monetary Fund.

Since 1976 the development of the North Sea oilfield has led to a recovery in the value of sterling, but in 1979 Britain was poorer than it had been six years earlier and is the only industrial country in the world to have experienced an absolute decline in industrial productivity. At the time of writing a Conservative government has just been elected and Margaret Thatcher has promised a more far-reaching revision of economic policies than that promised by Heath in 1970. It is quite uncertain whether these policies will be successful. It is indisputable, however, that unless drastic changes of some kind are made Britain will enter a period of irreversible decline.

A protracted period of economic crisis is bound to have an impact on the operation of the political system. Only two decades ago it was commonly asserted that democracy could not survive an inflation rate of more than 10 per cent per annum. This was clearly an alarmist view, but there are tendencies in recent British political behaviour which have led numerous writers and politicians to assert that the British democratic tradition is endangered, and it would be unduly complacent to write these off as alarmist without discussion. The main arguments can be summarised quite briefly.

First, a number of critics have suggested that the British democratic system is threatened by a growing ideological gap between the two main parties. It has been pointed out that the 1974 Labour Government did something that no previous British Government had done, namely that it repealed nearly all the legislative reforms introduced by its predecessor. The prospect that the Conservative Government elected in 1979 might follow the precedent set by the Wilson Government raises the possibility that the gradual evolution of policy that has hitherto characterised British government may be replaced by sharp oscillations as the parties take turns in office. This concern has been supplemented by fears that the Conservative Party has become a party of reaction and that the Labour Party may fall into the hands of extreme left-wingers.

Concern about the rightward turn of the Conservative Party has been voiced by numerous Labour politicians, by the leader of the Liberal Party, and by a number of independent critics. It is based on repeated statements by Margaret Thatcher and Sir Keith Joseph that they will not share the reluctance of previous Conservative leaders to undo Labour reforms in economic and social matters. They believe that this reluctance has created a ratchet-like progress towards socialism in postwar Britain which must be stopped if the private sector of the economy is not to be sapped of its remaining vitality. This clearly represents a change, but it must be noted that the kind of mixed economy and welfare system that Conservative leaders advocate puts them a little to the left of the Christian Democrats in Germany, the Liberals in Canada, and the Democrats in the United States. It would be absurd to call this an extreme position and it cannot in itself be a threat to British democracy.

Concern about extremism in the Labour Party has been expressed not only by Conservatives and independent critics but also by active Labour politicians. These include the following: Woodrow Wyatt, a Labour MP for twenty-one years who now recommends people to vote Conservative because the Labour Party is adopting Marxist policies; Reginald Prentice, the former Labour Education Minister whose local constituency party disowned him after it had come under the control of a group of Trotskyites; Paul Johnson, a former editor of the *New Statesman*; and Stephen Haseler, a political scientist and Labour member of the Greater London Council who has written a book about extremist tendencies in the Labour Party under the title *The Death of British Democracy*. There are a number of policy issues which have contributed to the disillusionment of this distinguished quartet, but the reasons which they and others have given for concern about the future of British democracy can be reduced to three, given below in ascending order of importance.

First, Marxists of various kinds, who are not interested in the preservation of British democracy, have gained control of several constituency Labour parties and have induced their management committees to repudiate sitting Labour MPs of moderate views in favour of radical candidates. Sir Harold Wilson has warned the Party about the dangers of this development, which has only been possible because the sharp decline in party membership has enabled small groups of extremists to take over local committees. However, only three MPs lost their seats in this way between 1975 and 1979 and it is hard for the impartial observer to regard this as very serious. It is certainly a breach of the British tradition that sitting Members are automatically entitled to renomination, but there are other countries in which a struggle for renomination is regarded as a normal and desirable feature of the democratic process.

Secondly, the National Executive Committee (NEC) has been dominated by a left-wing majority since 1975. It was more of an embarrassment to the Labour Party than a threat to British democracy when the NEC refused to intervene on behalf of the MPs rejected by their local parties or when they appointed a self-proclaimed Trotskyite as National Youth Organiser (a development that so outraged the permanent staff at Labour Party headquarters that they at first refused to speak to him or let him see any papers). However, a legitimate concern about the democratic process developed when the NEC tried to give orders to the Cabinet and the Parliamentary Labour Party about matters of policy. The NEC is an extra-parliamentary body which is not responsible to the electorate. So far as is known, Labour governments have rarely yielded to pressures applied by the NEC, but the prospect that possible changes in the internal organisation of the Labour Party might put a future Labour Government under the control of such an unrepresentative body is a reasonable cause for alarm. It should be said, however, that such a prospect is still entirely hypothetical.

Thirdly, in recent years the Annual Conference of the Labour Party has been dominated by left-wingers. The 1976 Conference adopted a radical policy statement entitled *Labour's Programme for Britain 1976* by a massive vote of 5,838,000 to 122,000. This statement proposes the nationalisation of the main banks and insurance companies, the largest industrial firms and all land, the appointment by trade unions of half the directors of those companies left under private control, a massive reduction in defence expenditures, and plans to control the press by nationalising printing plants. It can well be understood why numerous critics, within the Labour Party as well as outside, feel that the enactment of such a programme would spell the end of liberal democracy in Britain. Both Wyatt and Haseler have written about their fears that Britain may go the way of Czechoslovakia or East Germany.[3]

The immediate prospects for the enactment of this programme are slender. Very few British citizens have Marxist sympathies. When the *Economist* commissioned an opinion survey on the proposal to nationalise banking and insurance, this showed that only 23 per cent of Labour Party supporters were in favour while 63 per cent were opposed.[4] The majority of Labour MPs are firmly opposed to this kind of programme, partly because they object to it in principle and partly because they regard it as a certain vote-loser. When James Callaghan was presented in 1979 with an election manifesto drafted by the NEC which included a number of these policies, he was able to get it redrafted by a small committee of which he was chairman, and in the final version most of the radical proposals were watered down. It would be argued that the main significance of the adoption of this extreme programme is the evidence it provides of the unrepresentative nature of the Labour Party Annual Conference.

Those who take a more pessimistic view of the situation have two arguments at their disposal. The first is that, because the radical programme was adopted by a two-thirds majority, it will remain the official programme of the Party indefinitely, unless it is rescinded by the same majority. The second is that the whole political balance would be transferred if the leader of the Parliamentary Labour Party were to be elected by a process which involved the Annual Conference and/or the NEC instead of being chosen simply by Labour MPs. It is to be presumed that radicals within the Party will try to secure this change of procedure.

A second focus of concern for those worried about recent developments is the type of method used by pressure groups to advance their aims. It is an important convention of democracy that those seeking to influence political decisions should do so through the normal democratic channels of communication and should limit their methods to lobbying, propaganda and other forms of verbal or written persuasion. It is not democratic to use physical forms of persuasion which make it impossible for non-sympathisers to carry on with their normal activities, or to use industrial power for political purposes.

There have been previous periods in British history when physical forms of persuasion were used in the attempt to secure political reforms, in the main by people who were then denied the right to participate through the ballot box. The contemporary reversion to these tactics began in the late 1960s, with university students organising 'sit-ins' because they disapproved of government policy, and thousands of squatters occupying other people's houses to draw attention to housing problems. In the 1970s the use of this kind of technique became more widespread. Mothers who wanted a ban on heavy traffic in a residential area sat down in the road with their babies. Anti-apartheid demonstrators disrupted rugby matches to induce the Government to ban sporting fixtures with South African teams. Campaigners who wanted a criminal case to be reopened dug up a cricket pitch in the middle of a match between England and Australia. People who objected to highway developments in residential areas disrupted public inquiries and won the day because it was legally impossible for the developments to go ahead until the inquiries had been completed.

Industrial action for political ends by trade unions is not different in principle from these examples but is much more important because the unions wield more power and the effects of their actions are often more widespread. A small example illustrates the point of principle rather well. In 1976 hospital porters prevented food and other essential supplies from reaching private patients because their union, the National Union of Public Employees, disapproved on ideological grounds of private medical practice in hospitals. Arguments can be mustered both for and against the union's attitude to this question, but they are quite irrelevant in this context. The point of principle is that in a democracy political issues of this kind should be settled through the ballot box and through the ample constitutional channels that enable group spokesmen to lobby for their preferred policies. For hospital porters to employ physical sanctions against the patients in an attempt to force politicians to adopt a certain policy is a clear breach of democratic legitimacy. A rough sporting equivalent would be the decision of a losing team in cricket or baseball to substitute a hand grenade for the ball in an attempt to determine the outcome of the match.

During the 1970s industrial action for political purposes became widespread and often achieved its aims. In 1971 the Trades Union Congress instructed its members to sabotage the Industrial Relations Act and boycott the Industrial Relations Court. This was a deliberate defiance of the law which rendered an important piece of legislation unworkable, though the Act had been passed by a newly elected government which had a clear mandate for it. In 1972 the National Union of Mineworkers called a strike to break the Government's pay policy, and brought about a serious disruption of public services by the use of mobile pickets who stopped traffic entering or leaving power stations, docks and coal depots. During this strike thousands of pickets from various industries and areas converged on the Saltley coke depot, near Birmingham, and forced the Chief Constable of Birmingham to shut the gates of the depot as the only alternative to bloodshed.[5]

In February 1974 another miners' strike disrupted electricity supplies and brought down the Government. This unprecedented triumph of industrial power was emulated three months later in Belfast, when militant Protestant workers organised a general strike in order to force the resignation of the only Government Northern Ireland has ever known in which power was shared between Protestants and Catholics. Between 1977 and 1979, when opinion polls showed the Conservative Party to have much more support in the country than the Labour Party, it was repeatedly suggested that if a Conservative Government were returned at the next general election this would be followed by industrial chaos. The threat was itself an illegitimate intervention in the democratic process, and if it were to be translated into practice and were to succeed there would be little hope for the survival of democracy as it has been known to date in Britain.

It is sometimes suggested by union apologists that the use of union industrial power for political purposes is justified because (a) it is employed in a good cause and (b) the unions are themselves democratic institutions. The first of these arguments is irrelevant. The issue is not whether the cause is good or bad but whether the methods are compatible with the conventions of a democratic system. The second argument is also irrelevant, because undemocratic tactics by a pressure group cannot be justified by referring to the internal organisation of the group.

In any case, the argument would not survive scrutiny of union practices. Participation in union elections rarely involves more than 10 per cent of the membership. The institution of the closed shop in many

British industries forces workers to join in a strike called by their union, on pain of losing their jobs and being excluded from similar employment elsewhere by expulsion from the union. What union militants can do even in the absence of a closed shop was vividly illustrated by a strike at a film-processing plant in north London in 1977, where the majority of workers were not union members and refused to join the strike. Day after day, over a period of several months, hundreds of pickets (mostly recruited from other industries) tried to prevent workers entering the factory by attempting to overturn the buses in which they arrived. The pickets failed only because the workers were protected by hundreds of policemen, scores of whom were injured and one of whom lost the sight of an eye as the result of having acid thrown in his face.

When sizeable groups of people in a democratic state take power into their own hands, the rule of law is in jeopardy. It is therefore essential for the survival of British democracy that unions abandon these practices, either voluntarily or as a result of laws being enacted and enforced which restrict their powers. Opinion polls indicate that such measures would be widely popular. In the words of Anthony King of Essex University, who has analysed repeated polls on this issue, 'the message of all the available evidence is that the British people deeply resent trade union power'.[6] A majority of union members believe that union leaders and organisers have too much power. Among voters who reported a stable identification with the Labour Party in 1974, only 23 per cent said they generally sympathised with strikers and only 29 per cent were in favour of retaining close ties between the trade unions and the Labour Party.[7] The problem for Mrs Thatcher's new government is whether they will be able to mobilise this large-scale but passive support for a modification of union behaviour in the face of the entrenched power of union militants.

A quite different problem for British democracy has arisen in the area of policy-making and implementation. This problem is commonly given the shorthand title of 'overload'. It has a fiscal aspect which can be measured and a qualitative aspect that can only be discussed in rather speculative terms.

The fiscal aspect of the problem is that the extension of government activities and public services in recent years has created a built-in tendency for public expenditures to increase more rapidly than national wealth. The crux comes when the increase of public expenditure over a period eats up more than the total increase in national wealth during the same period, with the inevitable result that people employed in the private sector experience a net reduction in the real value of their take-home pay. This crux has already been reached in Britain. Between 1971 and 1977 the increase in governmental expenditure absorbed 131 per cent of the increase in gross domestic product.[8] This is an insupportable trend, for when people find that the real value of their after-tax income is eroded year after year they tend to strike for higher wages (which achieve a temporary improvement in their own position at the expense of general inflation), to engage in tax evasion, to emigrate, or to become disillusioned and alienated from the political system.

The problem is not unique to Britain. Italy and Sweden are in a similar position, and other advanced industrial countries are working their way towards it. The problem can only be cured by improving the rate of economic growth or cutting public expenditures, or a combination of the two. Japan and West Germany hope to avoid or postpone the problem by rapid economic growth. Italy has been in a state of political crisis since 1976. In the United States citizens are taking the matter into their own hands, true to the populist tradition of American political culture, by measures such as the famous Proposition 13 of California which put a fixed upper limit on taxation. In Britain and France the national governments are attempting to reduce public expenditure.

In Britain the main parties agree on the need to cut back public expenditure but differ in their preferred methods of attempting this. Between 1976 and 1979 the Labour Government imposed 'cash limits' on Treasury payments to local government and other public authorities, while insisting that staff should not be dismissed and public services should not be cancelled. This technique minimised political controversy while maximising inefficiency, for it meant either that the same number of staff were providing poorer services or that staff reductions were achieved by the haphazard process of natural wastage (i.e. not replacing staff who resign or retire, no matter how important they might be to the organisation). The new Conservative government apparently plans to reduce public expenditure by axing some services and making planned reductions of staff, a technique which would probably be more efficient but would certainly arouse more controversy. Whichever party is in power, the problem of reducing the burden of public expenditure is intrinsically very difficult.

The qualitative aspect of 'overload' has been well described by Anthony King. He argues that the government of Britain has become more difficult in recent years because public expectations of government services have increased markedly while the capacity of government to fulfil these expectations has decreased. King does not blame individual politicians or officials for this, believing instead that the increased demands put upon government combined with the increased complexity of modern industrial society have made governments dependent on behaviour which they cannot control.

The result of successive failures by government to meet public expectations is to reduce confidence in the political system and its leaders. 'Once upon a time . . . man looked to God to order the world. Then he looked to the market. Now he looks to government.' And when things go wrong the public blame 'not "Him" or "it" but "them"'.[9] If this rather depressing analysis is correct, the consequences may be an increase in public cynicism regarding political leaders, a decrease in the willingness to comply with the requirements of public authority, and a readiness to use non-democratic methods to promote sectional interests.

There is scattered evidence of all these developments. As noted in earlier chapters, party membership has fallen off and electoral turnout is lower than it used to be. As reported earlier in this chapter, sectional groups have increasingly turned to practices of doubtful legitimacy. There has been a marked increase in tax evasion and it is reported that 'Britain has the worst non-compliance record in the EEC for value-added tax'.[10] Bills for services are increasingly paid in cash, with the tacit understanding that no tax declarations will be made. Political satire, as exemplified by the popular journal *Private Eye*, has a biting and bitter edge not equalled in other democratic countries. The police are increasingly subject to violent assault, not only by criminals but also by political demonstrators and pickets. No sensible observer could now say that British political behaviour is characterised by deference, as was commonly said by American political scientists in the 1950s.

To mention these trends is not to suggest that the British democratic system is in serious danger of collapse. A system which is so deeply rooted in history and culture has an immense capacity to withstand strains and tensions. French democracy survived the strains of the Algerian war, American democracy survived those of the war in Vietnam, and it is to be expected that British democracy will survive the rather different strains put upon it by economic decline and the inept handling of some domestic policies by recent governments. Moreover, Britain has significant assets which are steadying influences in a period of political difficulty. The British people are rightly noted for their tolerance and sense of proportion. British politicians, though not always successful, are conspicuously honest and well intentioned, so that the heat of political controversy is moderated by an underlying respect for the leaders of the opposing party.

The best prediction, therefore, is that the British democratic system, though slightly frayed at the edges, will retain most of its essential characteristics intact. It is, however, vital to realise that within a generation Britain has changed from being a rather relaxed society to being a rather tense one, and from being a society that was relatively easy to govern to being one which is increasingly difficult to govern. If the traditional analogy of a ship of state were to be invoked, the appropriate image would be of a somewhat elderly sailing ship which is wallowing in heavy seas, affected by adverse currents, and giving its passengers an uncomfortable ride. However, its design gives it an unusual degree of stability, it has some elegant furnishings, and it is manned by an experienced crew. The prospect of its capsizing is almost as remote as the prospect of its keeping pace with its more modern competitors.

NOTES

1   *Rights of Man,* pt II, ch. II.
2   See Richard Rose and William Gwyn (eds), *Britain: Progress and Decline,* for a number of essays on the theme.
3   See Woodrow Wyatt, *What's Left of the Labour Party?* (Sidgwick & Jackson, 1977), chs 9 and 10, and Stephen Haseler, *The Death of British Democracy* pp. 198–220.
4   *The Economist,* 24 July 1976, p. 19.
5   For a lively account of the incident by one of the miners' leaders, see Arthur Scargill, 'The new unionism', in *New Left Review,* no. 92 (1975).
6   *The Observer,* 7 May 1979.
7   ibid.
8   Richard Rose and Guy Peters, *The Juggernaut of Incrementalism* (University of Strathclyde, 1978), p. 19.
9   Anthony King, 'Overload: problems of governing in the 1970s', in *Political Studies,* vol. XXIII (1975), p. 288.
10   *The Economist,* 23 Dec 1978, p. 92.

FURTHER READING

Almost any general book on British politics contains some discussion of the characteristics of British democracy. Discussions of the particular problems of the past decade will be found in Stephen Haseler, *The Death of British Democracy* (Paul Elek, 1976), in R. Emmett Tyrrell (ed.), *The Future That Doesn't Work* (Doubleday, 1977), in R. L. Clutterbuck, *Britain in Agony: The Growth of Political Violence* (Faber, 1978), in Anthony King, 'Overload: problems of governing in the 1970s', *Political Studies,* vol. XXIII (1975), and in William Gwyn and Richard Rose (eds), *Britain: Progress and Decline* (Macmillan/Tulane University Press, 1980). Some of these problems are put into theoretical and comparative perspective in Samuel Brittan, 'The economic contradictions of democracy', *British Journal of Political Science,* vol. 5 (1975), in Richard Rose and Guy Peters, *Can Government Go Bankrupt?* (Basic Books, 1978), and in Mary Kaldor, *The Disintegrating West* (Allen Lane, 1978). A new study by Stephen Haseler is *The Tragedy of Labour* (Blackwell, 1980).

Appendix

NOTES ON THE POLITICS OF NORTHERN IRELAND

1. The character of politics in Northern Ireland differs sharply from the character of politics in the remainder of the United Kingdom. While in Britain power alternates between the two main parties, in Northern Ireland the Ulster Unionist Party enjoyed power continuously from 1922 to 1972. In Britain religion is of little political significance whereas in Northern Ireland it dominates the political scene. In Britain the main opposition parties are completely loyal to the constitutional system whereas in Northern Ireland their aim is to transform or overthrow it. Above all, British politics is almost entirely free from violence whereas Northern Ireland has been the scene of violent protests, political assassinations and intermittent guerilla warfare for the past sixty years.

2. The extraordinary character of Irish politics can only be explained in historical terms. While political attitudes in other countries are influenced by history, political attitudes in Ireland seem to be imprisoned by it. For this reason some of the main events in Irish political history will be outlined in the following paragraphs. For reasons of space, the treatment will be extremely sketchy, but it is hoped that readers may find it throws some light on Irish attitudes and behaviour.

3. Ireland was dominated by England from the twelfth century to the twentieth century. There was never an independent Irish state until 1921. There were local communities and local rulers, provinces and provincial governors, but the sovereign of Ireland – in so far as it could be said to have a sovereign – was the King of England. The Roman Catholic religion of the Irish people was not affected by the Reformation, but in the late sixteenth and seventeenth centuries a substantial number of Protestant settlers migrated to Ireland from Britain, settling mainly in the northern part of the country.

4. 1641 saw the 'Ulster Rising', which was a revolt of the native Irish against British government and against the Protestant settlers in the northern counties (nine of which constituted the Province of Ulster). It was a bloody affair, and troops had to be sent from England to suppress it. King Charles was weakened doubly by this episode. In the first

place, the rebellion increased anti-Catholic feelings in England. Secondly, the need to finance a military expedition forced Charles to convene Parliament, which set in train the events leading to the English Civil War.

5. After the Civil War Cromwell's army took their revenge against the Irish. In particular, they attacked the Catholic Church, killing priests and despoiling the churches. However, after the Restoration in 1660 there was a reversal of fortunes. Ireland became a Roman Catholic country once more, an Irish army was recruited which was almost entirely Catholic in composition, and all Protestant judges, officials and aldermen were thrown out of office.

6. In the bloodless revolution of 1688 James II fled from England without putting up a fight against William of Orange, his invading army and his English supporters. However, in Ireland only the Protestants recognised William and Mary as legitimate rulers. In March 1689 James landed in Ireland from France and took command of the Irish army, and what was in effect a war for the English throne was then fought out on Irish soil. An attack on Londonderry was frustrated by the courage of the Protestant minority in the city – an event which has been celebrated annually ever since by the 'Apprentice Boys' March' – and on 1 July 1690 James came face to face with William in the Battle of the Boyne. In this famous encounter James's Irish and French troops were defeated by a mixed force of Ulster Protestants, Scots, Englishmen, Dutchmen and Danes and this victory ensured the supremacy of the Protestant religion in Britain.

7. From 1690 to 1800 Ireland was ruled by its Protestant minority through a Parliament in Dublin. This Parliament was notable for the 'Penal Laws' with which it discriminated against Roman Catholics. Under these laws, Catholics were not allowed to bear arms, Catholic priests were forbidden to celebrate mass, and Catholics were not permitted to send children abroad to be educated (to stop them going to Continental seminaries). In an attempt to help Protestant landowners extend their estates, Catholics were not permitted to buy land, except on a lease of up to thirty-one years, and were not permitted to bequeath their land by will. When a Catholic landowner died his land was divided equally between all his sons, which in a country of large families ensured the fragmentation of Catholic estates. And, as a final twist of the knife, it was decreed that if the eldest son of a Catholic landowner joined the Protestant Church he would immediately be given ownership of the whole estate, with his father remaining simply as tenant for life and his brothers disinherited.

Edmund Burke said that this period degraded the character of the Irish Catholic peasant, and an Irish historian has elaborated the same view:

His religion made him an outlaw . . . and whatever was inflicted on him he must bear, for where could he look for redress? To his landlord? Almost invariably an alien conqueror. To the law? Not when every person connected with the law, from the jailer to the judge, was a Protestant. . . .

In these conditions suspicion of the law, of the ministers of the law and of all established authority worked into the very nerves and blood of the Irish peasant, and since the law did not give him justice he set up his own law. The secret societies which have been the curse of Ireland became widespread . . . dissimulation became a moral necessity and evasion of the law the duty of every God-fearing Catholic.[1]

8. In 1800 Ireland was made an integral part of the United Kingdom and a sizeable contingent of Irish MPs arrived at Westminster. The Penal Laws were gradually abolished and Catholics achieved equality of status with Protestants. The last quarter of the nineteenth century saw the growth of the Irish nationalist movement and from 1886 onwards the question of Irish Home Rule became a lively issue in British politics.

9. In 1912 Asquith's Liberal Government introduced a Home Rule Bill which was designed to give a substantial measure of internal self-government to the whole of Ireland, under the control of an Irish Government and Parliament in Dublin. The Ulster Protestants objected passionately to this proposal, being quite unwilling to accept the rule of what would inevitably be a Roman Catholic regime. As loyal subjects of the Crown they claimed that the United Kingdom Government had no right to place them at the mercy of their historic enemies. In this they had the support of British Conservative leaders and large sections of British public opinion. An armed fighting force, under the title of the Ulster Volunteers, was established to resist the proposed change by force and it is possible that a civil war would have developed had not the outbreak of war with Germany given the British Government the opportunity to put the whole reform into cold storage.

10. Frustrated by these events, the Irish Nationalists turned from moderate leaders to extremists. In 1916 a group of the latter staged the 'Easter Rebellion' in Dublin, seized the main Post Office, and proclaimed an Irish Republic. The rebellion was put down by the British, sixteen of the leaders were sentenced to death, and fifteen of them were executed. The sixteenth was Eamon de Valera, an Irishman born in the United States, who was reprieved to placate American public opinion. The Republican Movement subsequently came under his leadership and that of Michael Collins, a brilliant revolutionary organ-

iser who directed the activities of the Irish Volunteers, who were reconstituted as the Irish Republican Army in 1919. From 1916 until the end of 1921 the Catholic counties of Ireland were the scene of demonstrations, boycotts and growing violence, with the Republicans escalating their attacks to a campaign of guerilla warfare and the authorities responding in kind.

11. In November 1920 the British Government accepted what had become almost inevitable and passed the Government of Ireland Act, establishing a Parliament in Dublin for the twenty-six Catholic counties and a Parliament in Belfast for the six largely Protestant counties of the north-east. Provision was made for a Council of Ireland, to consist of twenty representatives elected by each Parliament, which could legislate for all Ireland on any subject which both Parliaments delegated to it. Powers such as defence, foreign affairs and the coinage of money were to be retained by the Westminster Parliament, in which all Irish counties would enjoy a reduced representation. The Ulster Unionists accepted this arrangement, which until 1972 provided the legal basis for the Parliament at Stormont (in Belfast), but the Republicans refused to accept it and continued their struggle.

12. In December 1921 a treaty was signed between the British Government and the leaders of the elected (though illegal) Irish Assembly, among whom was Michael Collins. It constituted the twenty-six counties as the Irish Free State, which although acknowledging the British Crown would have complete political independence of Britain, as did Canada and the other self-governing Dominions. The six counties remained in the United Kingdom and the partition of Ireland was henceforth a fact in international law.

13. Not surprisingly, the conflicts of 1912–21 engendered bitterness among Irish politicians of almost all opinions. The Catholics won independence from Britain and the Protestants achieved independence of the Catholics, but the former did so by violence and the latter did so by the threat of violence. The intransigence of Irish attitudes in this period can be illustrated by two episodes, each of which cast shadows over the following half-century.

(*a*) The proposal to partition Ireland naturally raised questions about the location of the border. The nine counties of the Province of Ulster included three which were overwhelmingly Catholic, three which were overwhelmingly Protestant, and three where the religions were fairly evenly balanced. The Protestant leaders claimed these three divided counties but the moderate Catholic leaders (the only ones willing to discuss partition) claimed two of them. When Asquith and Lloyd George proposed that these two counties should be divided so that the border could follow religious lines as nearly as possible both Catholic and

Protestant leaders rejected this idea out of hand. In Asquith's words: 'The extraordinary feature of the discussion was the complete agreement (in principle) of Redmond and Carson. Each said "I must have the whole of Tyrone or die; but I quite understand why you say the same".'[2]

(*b*)   When the Irish Free State came into being after so many years of struggle the leaders who had fought for independence immediately plunged into a savage quarrel about whether the new government should take a formal oath of allegiance to the Crown. De Valera and his friends attacked Collins as a traitor for agreeing to this and led a sizeable proportion of the IRA into a new campaign, this time against their own former colleagues. The Free State thus began life with a bitter civil war which lasted for over twelve months before a cease-fire was agreed.

14. The new Province of Northern Ireland was (and is) by no means homogeneous in its population. Thirty-four per cent of the inhabitants were Catholics in 1920 and (despite rumours to the contrary) this proportion has remained virtually static ever since. (It increased from 34·2 per cent in the 1911 Census to 34·9 per cent in the 1961 Census.) The two communities are highly segregated. They are served by different schools, which are equally supported by government funds. The schools teach history in a different way and they play different sports, so that Catholic and Protestant children never meet on the sports field. There is considerable segregation in areas of residence and in clubs and pubs visited. There is little intermarriage, which is condemned by both communities. Looked at in a sociological perspective, Northern Ireland is more like a bi-tribal society than a society divided between two branches of the Christian religion. Like tribes, each community in Northern Ireland has its own myths and heroes, its own songs and its own symbols – the orange and green sashes, the Union Jack and the Irish tricolour. Each community also has its own ritual marches, which by celebrating past victories are designed to rub salt in the wounds of the other side.

15. In an open society (i.e. one which is not governed on totalitarian lines) which contains more than one religious or ethnic community there are only three possible patterns of political behaviour. One pattern may be called the politics of integration, in which the differences between religious and other groups have no direct bearing on the competition for political power. A good example is England, where there are only a handful of parliamentary constituencies in which a candidate's religion has any perceptible effect on his electoral support (these all being constituencies with a considerable number of Irish electors). A second pattern is best called the politics of accommodation. In this kind of system a deliberate and conscious attempt is made

to ensure that each community or group has a reasonable share of political power. In Canada, for instance, there is a firm convention that, no matter which party holds office, the federal cabinet should contain so many French-speaking Catholics, at least one English-speaking Catholic, and representatives from each province of the country. The third pattern is the politics of group dominance, in which each community or group is associated with its own political party and a policy of 'winner take all' is adopted.

16. From the beginning, politics in Northern Ireland followed the pattern of group dominance. The Ulster Unionist Party, which has close relations with a Protestant society called the Orange Order, won every general election and made no attempt to share any of its power with Catholics. At the same time, Catholic politicians made no attempt to win the support of Protestant voters and deepened the antagonism of the Unionists by refusing to recognise the legitimacy of the Stormont regime. For fifty years Northern Ireland had a political system in which a permanent majority nursed their power and a permanent minority nursed their grievances.

17. Until 1973 the Protestants were always more united than their opponents. The Ulster Unionist Party was well organised and well financed, benefited from the fruits of office, and had the advantage of a clear objective – to maintain the constitutional position. This was advantageous to Northern Ireland in some ways, for over a whole range of social affairs the Stormont Parliament had the option of either adopting British legislation or introducing its own variations. By normally adopting British legislation on social and economic affairs the Unionists not only deprived their opponents of the possibility of appealing to the voters with a programme of progressive social policies but also ensured a very heavy concealed subsidy from the British taxpayer. In 1972 this was running at the rate of about £200 million a year, quite apart from loan advances, subsidies to local industries, and the cost of the security forces. Given a population of 1·5 million, this means that the average family of four, with earnings of between £1,500 and £2,500 per annum, benefited to the tune of at least £500 per annum from the status of Northern Ireland as part of the United Kingdom. The sum involved is now two or three times as great as this.

18. The Catholics, in contrast, have always been somewhat divided. It is demoralising to be in a permanent minority and not surprising that Catholics have differed among themselves over tactics. Should they, for instance: (a) fight elections and if successful put up a vigorous opposition in Parliament; (b) fight elections but if successful boycott Parliament; (c) boycott elections; (d) offer passive resistance to the Stormont regime; (e) take every step, including violence and terrorism, to erode the authority of Stormont; (f) engage in guerilla warfare

with the hope of internationalising the conflict and securing the intervention of the Irish Republic? All six tactics have had their supporters and these differences of view have fragmented the political activities of the Catholics. This has been reflected in the multiplicity of political organisations supported by the Catholic community, which in the past twenty years alone have included Sinn Fein, the Nationalist Party, the Republican Party, the Social Democratic and Labour Party, the Civil Rights Association, and both the Official and the Provisional wings of the IRA.

19. The IRA, with over sixty years of intermittent guerilla warfare to its credit, is one of the most experienced and hardened revolutionary organisations the world has ever known. Its original enemy was the British Government and its first and most successful campaign induced the British to grant independence to the twenty-six counties in 1921. However, the IRA has never accepted the legitimacy of partition and its stated *raison d'être* since 1921 has been to bring about the reunification of Ireland. The Official IRA has also acquired another *raison d'être*, namely to organise a socialist revolution in the Irish Republic. Both branches of the IRA (which split in 1969) are well equipped with arms from overseas, and the Provisionals are financed to a large extent by donations from American sympathisers. The relations of the IRA with the government of the Republic are somewhat ambiguous. Since 1931 the IRA has been an illegal organisation, but it has commanded such a mixture of sympathy and fear among the public that when its members have been prosecuted they have nearly always been acquitted by Irish juries. In practice the IRA has therefore been tolerated by the Dublin government and has operated training camps in various parts of the Republic. In Northern Ireland it has organised several campaigns of violence, and in 1938–9 it extended its activities to Britain with small-scale bomb attacks in several English cities.

20. August 1969 saw the outbreak of the longest and most intensive period of political violence in Northern Ireland since the Province was established. The most plausible explanation of this is that the reforming ambitions of Captain O'Neill (Prime Minister at Stormont from 1963 to 1969) loosened the political situation. It can be argued that they encouraged Catholic leaders to demand a much quicker pace of reform; that they produce a minor backlash among Protestant extremists; and that this in turn created the conditions for a resumption of armed IRA activities. Like all general explanations of historical events, this is an oversimplification of a very complex story, but it contains an important kernel of truth. The build-up to the crisis was a series of demonstrations and marches by Catholic supporters of the Civil Rights Association, which were sometimes attacked by Protestant crowds and sometimes stopped or dispersed by the Royal Ulster Constabulary (a

predominantly Protestant force which was distrusted and disliked by Catholics). The crisis broke on 12 August 1969, when the annual Apprentice Boys' Parade was held in Londonderry to celebrate the Protestant victory there 279 years earlier. Catholic demonstrators gathered in the Bogside (a fairly self-contained Catholic area) to stage a counter-demonstration; the RUC surrounded the Bogside to prevent the demonstrators marching to the city centre; the demonstrators bombarded the police with stones and petrol bombs and could not be subdued, even when (after eight hours) the police used tear gas. After forty-eight hours of fighting the British Army were called in to restore order. Within days there was much more serious rioting between Catholics and Protestants in Belfast, with houses burned and several deaths, and again the Army were called to the scene.

21. This serious breakdown of law and order drew the problems of Northern Ireland forcibly to the attention of the British Government and people. It could well be argued that the British should have paid more attention to these problems before 1969, but having devolved much of the responsibility to the Northern Ireland Parliament, and having in any case no clear views about what should be done, British governments understandably steered clear of the problems until violence broke out. Since 1969 successive British governments (in each case with all-party support) have pursued four different strategies in regard to Northern Ireland, none of which has been particularly successful.

22. The first strategy was to press the Stormont Government to speed up its programme of political reforms, so as to remedy the political grievances of the Roman Catholic community. Within a few months, steps were taken to meet virtually all the demands which the Civil Rights Association had made. The RUC was disarmed and put under the control of a Chief Constable from England. It was decided to disband the B Specials, a part-time paramilitary force, consisting almost entirely of Protestants, which had been available to help the police. The City Council of Londonderry (which had always been dominated by Protestants although more than half the population were Catholic) was replaced by a commission on which the communities were equally represented. Since Catholics had alleged that they were discriminated against in the allocation of municipal housing, it was decided to introduce a points system for allocation. Subsequently housing management was taken out of the hands of local authorities altogether and given to a non-elected central housing authority, which was free from political and sectarian pressures. The property qualification was removed from the local government franchise, which henceforth included all adult citizens. A Minister of Community Relations was appointed and a Community Relations Commission was established.

23. The response to these reforms was discouraging. In London and at Stormont the reforms were regarded as sweeping, rapid and calculated to remedy all the legitimate grievances of the Catholic community. Many Catholic politicians, on the other hand, regarded the reforms as belated concessions which would not have been made in the absence of violence, and drew the conclusion that militancy was the best policy. Civil rights leaders said little about the reforms and discovered new grievances. The Catholic members of the Londonderry Development Commission refused to take part in administration. More and increasingly aggressive demonstrations were held, complete with the use of petrol bombs and firearms. The Army was soon being denounced as an instrument of British oppression and Catholic children took to throwing stones at British soldiers instead of playing football. Effective control of the Catholic community passed into the hands of the IRA, who put road-blocks round several Catholic areas and declared them 'no-go' areas to the police and the Army. Catholics who opposed the IRA or who were thought to be disloyal to them were threatened, beaten, tarred and feathered, 'knee-capped' (i.e. crippled by a bullet through the knee), and in some cases murdered.

24. In August 1971 the British Government adopted a second strategy, namely to smash the IRA. This could not be done by means of normal prosecutions in the courts, because IRA intimidation effectively deterred potential witnesses from giving evidence, and juries were also apt to be intimidated. It was therefore decided (at the suggestion of the Stormont authorities) that IRA suspects should be interned without trial. This decision, followed by house-to-house searches for arms in Catholic areas, infuriated the Catholic community and had the effect of increasing IRA recruitment. Although several hundred IRA members were interned, IRA violence increased and became more indiscriminate and brutal as the months went by. In 1971 there were 173 known deaths from political violence and in 1972 there were 467 such deaths.

25. The third British strategy was to work for what became known as 'a political solution'. In 1972 the Stormont Parliament and Government were suspended and power was concentrated in the hands of a British Cabinet minister holding the office of Secretary for Northern Ireland. In the next year, following prolonged negotiations, a new Northern Ireland Assembly was established with election by proportional representation and with fewer powers than those previously exercised by the Stormont Parliament. Control of elections, law and order, courts and the police was kept in the hands of British ministers. It was agreed that a Northern Ireland Executive could regain some of the powers that had previously been exercised by the Stormont Government, but only on condition that the Executive included members of both Protestant and Catholic communities. The British also

insisted that each government department should be controlled not only by a member of the Executive but also by a committee of the Assembly whose membership would reflect the balance of the parties.

26. In December 1973 the Conservative Government took their pursuit of political accommodation a stage farther by persuading members of the new Executive and the Prime Minister of the Irish Republic to take part in a conference at Sunningdale (near London) with members of the British Government. This was the first occasion that leading members of the three governments had ever met together and the resulting agreement was hailed in London and Dublin as the beginning of a new era of co-operation.

Under the terms of the Sunningdale Agreement the Government of the Republic made clear that they had no desire to incorporate Northern Ireland against the wishes of the majority of the people of that Province and also agreed (in rather vague terms) to reconsider the position of men who committed murder and other acts of terrorism in the North but were immune from prosecution once they had crossed the border into the Republic. The Northern Irish and British representatives reaffirmed their intention to protect the rights of the Catholic minority in the North and to give their representatives some share in the government of the Province, and also agreed that they would accept the incorporation of Northern Ireland into the Republic if a majority of Northern voters expressed a wish for this and satisfactory arrangements could be made to protect the rights of the minority. Both sides agreed to the creation of a Council of Ireland (an echo of the British proposal in 1920), which would have rather loosely defined powers to make recommendations on matters of common concern. The intention was that the actual powers of this Council would be very small in the first instance but would be capable of expansion if the habit of co-operation developed.

27. This Agreement got a very mixed reception in Northern Ireland. It was welcomed by the Catholic community but resented by most of the Protestants. In January 1974 the Ulster Unionist Party disowned their leader, Brian Faulkner, who had become leader of the new Executive. The Party (which had splintered a few months earlier) then split completely. Of the fifty Unionist Assembly members, only twenty-two continued to support the Executive. The other twenty-eight were divided between three rival groups, all opposed to the power-sharing experiment and known collectively as the Loyalists. In the United Kingdom parliamentary election of February 1974 Faulkner and his supporters were completely defeated, eleven of the twelve Irish seats being captured by Loyalists while the other seat went to the leader of the main Catholic party. A total of 366,000 votes were cast for Loyalist candidates but only 96,000 for Faulkner and his supporters.

This vote undermined the political legitimacy of the power-sharing Executive and in May 1974 it was effectively destroyed by a general strike of Protestant workers in Belfast. The Ulster Workers' Council set up barricades on the roads and anyone trying to go to work was prevented from doing so. The supply of food, electricity, gas and petrol was controlled by the strikers and very severely restricted. The Workers' Council made it clear that unless the power-sharing experiment was abandoned all essential services in the Province would be cut off, including water supplies and sewage disposal. On the fourteenth day of the strike the Executive resigned in the face of this threat.

In this way all the hopes for reconciliation and compromise were destroyed. It was made clear once again that the majority of Protestants would not accept any move that opened the possibility of their incorporation into the Republic and were unwilling to see Catholic politicians whom they regarded as disloyal have any share in the government of Northern Ireland. The British Government recognised defeat and the power-sharing experiment was abandoned.

28. Since 1974 Northern Ireland has been governed as an integral part of the United Kingdom, with no regional assembly or Parliament. The British strategy in this fourth phase has been to normalise the situation as far as possible. Internment has been abolished and the majority of the former internees have been released. The others (both Catholic and Protestant) have been successfully prosecuted in the normal courts and sent to prison, where they are treated in the same way as other prisoners. The Army has transferred security duties to the police as far as is possible and the number of troops engaged in security work has been reduced from 15,000 to about 11,000. It has been agreed (in 1979) to give Northern Ireland five more seats in the London Parliament so as to bring its representation up to parity with other parts of the United Kingdom, a logical and necessary decision since its representation was reduced by a third in 1920 in recognition of the fact that the Province also has its own Parliament.

29.   With the abandonment of special status for Northern Ireland and the abolition of representative institutions at the Provincial level, the volume of political debate has declined markedly. There are fewer issues to argue about, there is no representative forum in which to argue, and most of the men who previously drew a salary as elected representatives now have to earn a living in other ways. But this does not mean that the Province has been reduced to colonial status, for its citizens have the same rights and duties as those of Scotland, Yorkshire, or London.

30. Tragically, the political violence continues. Although somewhat weaker than it was, the IRA continues its campaign of largely indiscriminate arson and murder, and Protestant extremist groups have

responded by killing Catholics who for one reason or another are marked out for assassination. Between 1969 and 1979 approximately 2,000 people died from political violence in Northern Ireland – not a large number in itself but equivalent to about 71,000 deaths in Britain or 310,000 in the United States. The IRA has also extended its campaign to England, where about seventy people have so far been killed.

31. It is difficult to see what the British Government can do to end this violence. The IRA cannot be crushed without: (*a*) the reintroduction of internment and other measures that are distasteful in a democracy; and (*b* the active co-operation of the Republic, which now provides a sanctuary for IRA terrorists and shows no inclination to change this policy. The IRA cannot be starved of arms so long as it gets ample funds from American sympathisers and bank robberies and can get weapons from the United States, Libya, Palestinian groups, and the Soviet Union. It is impossible to come to terms with the IRA, for their objectives are the incorporation of Northern Ireland into the Republic followed by the overthrow of the government of the Republic. It is even impossible to negotiate a cease-fire or a temporary truce, both because there are three rival groups to deal with (the Official IRA, the Provisional IRA, and the new Irish National Liberation Army) and because they have not observed the terms of such local cease-fire agreements as have been made.

32. The final question is whether some new political initiative might improve the situation. Politicians in the Republic apparently think that the British Government should try something fresh and so do American politicians who take an interest in Irish affairs. The options for change can easily be listed:

(*a*)   The re-establishment of devolved government through the Stormont Parliament, this time with proportional representation. Unless and until new parties of a non-sectarian kind develop in strength, this would mean a reversion to government by Protestants and would be less acceptable to the Catholic community than the present system of government from London.

(*b*)   Another attempt to impose a power-sharing government. This was a failure in 1973–4 and, since there has been no change in political leadership apart from the death of Brian Faulkner, there is no reason to believe that another attempt would be any more successful.

(*c*)   The incorporation of Northern Ireland into the Republic. This is an impossible solution, advocated only by the most ignorant overseas observers. The Republic does not want the North and could not possibly cope with the problems it would present, either in terms of security or in terms of the need to subsidise Northern industries, many of which now depend upon large grants from the British Government. The citizens of Northern Ireland would suffer a drastic reduction in the level of their social services, which are now kept up to British mainland standards by courtesy of the British taxpayer. The only people who would gain from this move (apart from the IRA) would be the British, and they could not possibly deprive a million loyal citizens of their rights by bargaining over their heads with a foreign government. In practice it is likely that any British attempt at this kind of betrayal would be followed not by the ending of partition but by the emergence of an independent and defiant Protestant state in the North, controlled by para-military forces.

(*d*) It is sometimes suggested by people who like to play with constitutions that the Republic and the North and Britain could somehow be linked in a vague confederation, without any real transfer of power. As this would make no difference to the situation on the ground, it would almost certainly be a waste of time, and might be doubly dysfunctional. This is suggested, first, because Irish politicians have no incentive to draw support from across sectarian lines, so that they are virtually forced to act as sectarian spokesmen and it would seem dysfunctional to create further institutions for them to air their hostilities in. Secondly, any constitutional arrangements involving the Republic would sharpen the fears of the Protestant community that the British Government might eventually abandon them. If the Protestants are to become more tolerant they must first be given a greater sense of political security.

33.   If the view is taken that a drastic political problem requires drastic solutions, this author's belief is that the best hope would be to try to modify the attitudes of future generations. When Americans decided in the 1950s that drastic measures were needed to improve race relations, they did not set about this by insisting that half the members of the President's Cabinet should be black. Very wisely, they started by abolishing segregation in schools. If this example were followed in Northern Ireland it would be necessary to abolish religious instruction in state schools, to ban private schools operated on sectarian lines, and to bus children around Belfast so as to ensure that the schools were not segregated by the accident of geography.

Such a novel policy would involve all kinds of problems. It would be attacked by the churches as a gross violation of religious freedom. The schools would have to be guarded against bomb attacks. Many of the existing teachers would be so incapable of providing a non-sectarian education that they would have to be dismissed. Bussing would be highly unpopular with parents and would involve major problems of security. But, with all the problems, this policy is probably the only one which offers hope (in the long run) of ending the bigotry and communal hatreds which now poison Northern Irish society. Sceptics should note that the only major institutions in the Province where Catholics and Protestants now have happy relationships are the two universities.

NOTES

1   C. Woodham-Smith, *The Great Hunger* (Hamish Hamilton, 1962), pp. 27 ff.
2   Quoted in Roy Jenkins, *Asquith* (Collins/Fontana, 1967), p. 358.

FURTHER READING

Short guides to the development and recent history of British policies in regard to Ireland will be found in Nicholas Mansergh, *The Irish Question, 1840–1921,* 3rd edn (Allen & Unwin, 1975) and in A. H. Birch, *Political Integration and Disintegration in the British Isles* (Allen & Unwin, 1977), chs 4 and 5; the best analysis of the political system of Northern Ireland is that in Richard Rose, *Governing Without Consensus* (Faber, 1971); a careful account of discrimination is provided by D. P. Barritt and C. F. Carter, *The Northern Ireland Problem,* rev. edn (Oxford University Press, 1972); invaluable insights into the psychology of the situation will be found in Harold Jackson, *The Two Irelands,* rev. edn (Minority Rights Group, 1979); a lively commentary from a Dublin perspective is given in Conor Cruise O'Brien, *States of Ireland,* (Hutchinson, 1972); and a good analysis from an Ulster perspective will be found in T. E. Utley, *Lessons of Ulster* (Dent, 1975). A useful new study is Paul Arthur, *The Government and Politics of Northern Ireland* (Longman, 1980).

1981 Addendum

In this addendum (written in July 1981) brief comments will be made on the developments since the book went to press which seem most likely to have a significant impact on the operation of the political system.

DEVELOPMENTS IN THE PARTY SYSTEM

1. In the winter of 1980–1 left-wingers in the Labour Party secured changes in the rules so radical that they surprised nearly all commentators. At the 1980 Annual Conference it was decided to change the method of electing the Leader of the Parliamentary Labour Party so as to involve the constituency parties and the trade unions, the details of the new method to be decided by a special conference convened for that purpose in January 1981.

This was a crushing defeat for the existing Leader, James Callaghan, who resigned immediately after the Conference. Operating under the old rules, the Parliamentary Labour Party elected Michael Foot, a popular left-winger who is a committed parliamentarian and seemed better placed than any other candidate for the leadership to ensure that MPs retained a dominant role in the new procedure for selecting the Leader. However, Foot's efforts to achieve this object failed completely, and of the various methods canvassed the January conference chose the one which gave least power to MPs. Under the new procedure, trade unions affiliated to the Labour Party will have 40 per cent of the votes for the Parliamentary Leader, constituency parties will have 30 per cent and Labour MPs themselves will exercise the remaining 30 per cent.

In assessing this new procedure, it has to be remembered that the Labour Party has no power to control the way in which the many affiliated trade unions will determine their votes. It is likely that the methods will vary considerably and the one common factor about them is apt to be their involvement of only a minute proportion of union members. A second point is that the determination of union votes will not be confined to Labour Party members or supporters. Union officials and members who are Communists, Trotskyites, or Conservatives will have just as much right to cast votes on the leadership of the Parliamentary Labour Party as union members who happen also to be Labour Party members. As Marxists are highly influential in several large unions, the understandable fear of moderate Labour MPs is that this procedure will give an unfair advantage to left-wing candidates for the leadership. This fear is enhanced by the fact that some constituency Labour parties have also come under the influence of left-wing extremists. For most of its life the Party has had a 'Proscribed List' of organisations whose members were ineligible for membership, but this list was abolished in 1973 and since then Trotskyite groups have pursued a policy of 'entryism', meaning the infiltration of constituency Labour parties so as to influence or control their policies. In the first six months of 1981 thirteen Labour MPs felt so strongly that their party would inevitably be captured by extremists that they abandoned it to join the entirely new Social Democratic Party.

2. The Social Democratic Party was formed in the spring of 1981 by four prominent Labour Party leaders, namely Roy Jenkins (formerly Chancellor of the Exchequer and then President of the European Commission), David Owen (formerly Foreign Secretary), William Rodgers (formerly Minister of Transport) and Shirley Williams (formerly Minister of Education). They were quickly joined by other Labour MPs and they entered into discussions with Liberal Party leaders with the object of securing an electoral alliance between these two parties of the centre.

This development is likely to change the whole structure of the British party system. In July 1981 the Social Democratic Party contested its first by-election, in the northern working-class constituency of Warrington where the voting record was solidly Labour. It would have been hard to find a less promising arena for the electoral debut of the new party, but in the event Roy Jenkins secured 42 per cent of the vote for the Social Democrats. Computer analyses showed that if there were an equivalent swing to the Social Democrats and Liberals at the next general election, these parties would secure an overwhelming majority in the House of Commons.

There are, of course, reasons to doubt whether this new alliance of centre parties will be as successful as all that. First, the Liberal Party has commonly done better at by-elections than at general elections, mainly because of tactical voting by electors who return to their normal allegiance when the composition of the government is at stake. Secondly, the Social Democratic Party has only a rudimentary organisation and a weak financial basis. Thirdly, the development of a pragmatic alliance which would maximise electoral gains may be handicapped by the fact (already noted in Chapter 7) that many

Liberal Party members appear to be more concerned to promulgate Liberal ideals than to make the compromises that are necessary to secure political power. Nevertheless, the emergence of a sizeable political force in the centre of the ideological spectrum seems almost certain, and it is the most significant development in the party system since the displacement of the Liberal Party by the Labour Party in the years 1918–24.

3. The Conservative Party, though securely in power, is experiencing internal tensions over policy of a kind that have hitherto been more common in the Labour Party. Mrs Thatcher's economic and fiscal policies have been attacked by Edward Heath and criticised more or less openly by some of her Cabinet colleagues. The 1981 Budget was unpopular with many Conservative backbenchers, one of whom left the party in protest to join the Social Democrats. Mrs Thatcher is a controversial Leader and if the Conservatives lose the next general election her position as Leader may be precarious.

DEVELOPMENTS IN POLICY-MAKING

The interesting developments in this field have all resulted from the style and policy preferences of Margaret Thatcher, who has proved to be a quite remarkable Prime Minister. She dominates her Cabinet to a greater extent than any other peacetime Prime Minister, doing so by a combination of exceptionally hard work, a brilliant intelligence and an iron will. At the same time, she does not mind Cabinet disagreements being aired in public, and on several occasions has referred to them herself, even going to the length of describing her softer colleagues (in terms of economic policy preferences) as 'wets'. She is impatient with the tendency of civil servants to resist change and is said to have shocked top administrators by her brusque comments on their memoranda. In short, she is a radical with exceptional powers of leadership.

Although Mrs Thatcher's critics have inevitably accused her of a tendency to dictatorship within the Cabinet, it would be a mistake to think that she always gets her own way. She has so far carried the day on economic and fiscal policies, but her colleagues have evidently persuaded her to accept a gentle and moderate approach to the reform of the laws governing industrial relations. She took a much tougher line than her diplomatic advisers recommended in regard to Britain's financial contributions to the EEC, and scored a personal victory by doing so. On the other hand, she was persuaded to take a much more progressive line over the problems of Rhodesia than anyone had expected, and achieved success in this area also.

Whether her economic and social policies will be as successful as her diplomatic initiatives is an open question at the time of writing. They have reduced inflation at the cost of increasing unemployment, and cut the resources going into inefficient enterprises at the cost of driving a number of efficient smaller firms into bankruptcy. What can be said about both her economic and her social policies is that they display a consistent preference for confining the role of central government to that of overall strategy, leaving others to decide how their institutions and enterprises can best adjust to the impact of government policies. Thus, government grants to local authorities have been reduced, but local councils have been left to decide for themselves whether to meet the deficit by increasing property taxes or cutting services. The overall grants to universities have been drastically reduced, but the University Grants Committee was left to decide how the cuts should be apportioned between the forty-eight universities and each university has been left to itself to decide how to deal with the ensuing problems.

This decentralised manner of implementing policy decisions has led to conflicts and inconsistencies. The differences between the services provided by individual local authorities have been accentuated, and some local councils are coping with their financial difficulties in ways that are clearly at odds with the Government's ideological preferences. Equally, the University Grants Committee decided in 1981 that the most severe cuts should be borne by three relatively new technological universities, notwithstanding the fact that the aim of successive governments in recent years has been to develop technological universities. The Government has shown considerable equanimity in the face of these developments and it seems that in the field of social policy, as in economic policy, Mrs Thatcher's Government is remarkable for its rejection of the view that 'the man in Whitehall knows best'.

CIVIL DISORDER AND ITS CONSEQUENCES

The summer of 1981 saw the most serious civil disorders of the twentieth century, with the outbreak of rioting and looting in over twenty urban areas of England. The three main causes of this disorder were tension between West Indian immigrants and the police, conflict between Asian immigrants and white gangs and resentment of the high level of unemployment. Subsidiary factors were provocation by political extremists of both left and right, and the inflammatory influence of television news programmes, which unintentionally encouraged disaffected groups in peaceful areas to emulate the excitement and looting they saw on their screens. It would be a complete mistake to isolate any one of these factors as the main cause. As the following brief outline of the July riots indicates, the causes and character of the disorders varied from one area to another.

The first riots of July 1981 occurred in Brixton (south London) and were a repetition of earlier riots in the same area. Brixton is an area with a high concentration of West Indian immigrants and a notoriously high crime rate among these immigrants. In 1981 the police launched an intensive campaign to cut this crime rate, which was naturally resented by the immigrants as a discriminatory form of harassment. In both April and July police attempts to detain a West Indian suspect led to violent attacks on the police by immigrants armed with bricks and petrol bombs. Large numbers of police were injured, police cars and other vehicles were set on fire and shops owned by whites were looted and/or burned.

A slightly different scenario developed in Toxteth (Liverpool) and Moss Side (Manchester), both decaying urban areas with a high rate of unemployment and prostitution and mixed populations of British, Irish and West Indians. In both these areas whites joined with blacks to attack the police and loot shops.

Thirdly, a very different situation developed in Southall (west London), an area inhabited mainly by Asian immigrants from India and East Africa. Several hundred skinheads arrived by coach to attend a pop concert in a large pub. Some of the skinheads wore swastika badges, made insulting remarks to Asian residents and broke the windows of an Asian shop. Gangs of Asians then attacked the skinheads and eventually burned down the pub. The police arrived while the battle was in progress and attempted to separate the groups.

After three days of disorder in these areas the trouble spread elsewhere, with the important difference that in these other areas the great majority of the participants were unemployed white youths and their primary motive was looting. In some of these areas pamphlets were found issued by extreme left-wing groups encouraging lawlessness.

The development of these disorders confronts both the police and the Government with appalling problems. If the police continue to combat bricks and fire bombs with fists and batons they will continue to suffer a high rate of injury and may lose control of the situation (as they did for a time in Liverpool). But if they arm themselves with tear gas, water cannon and plastic bullets they will embitter their opponents and may endanger the high regard in which they are held by the general public. The Government is also in an awkward dilemma: if it strengthens police powers by legislation it will be accused of infringing civil liberties; if it announces a dramatic crash programme to reduce youth unemployment the lesson will be drawn that violence pays dividends; and if it does neither of these things it will be accused of complacency.

THE PROBLEMS OF NORTHERN IRELAND

There have been two developments regarding Northern Ireland, each of which has confirmed the intractable nature of the problems of that Province. First, the Government has created an Advisory Council consisting of politicians from Northern Ireland who have been elected to the European Parliament, the British Parliament and Northern Irish district councils. This new body is scheduled to meet in the winter of 1981–2, but leading spokesmen for the Protestant parties have already expressed scepticism about this initiative. The Deputy Leader of the Democratic Unionist Party has said: 'We would like to be at the Council to strangle the mis-shapen child at birth.'

Secondly, a number of IRA stalwarts, imprisoned for terrorist offences in Belfast, went on hunger strike in the spring of 1981 to support their demands that they be treated as political prisoners rather than as ordinary criminals. No British Government can agree to this and Michael Foot has made it entirely clear that the Parliamentary Labour Party supports the Conservative Government's position. The hunger strikers have rejected the attempts of a Swiss team from the Red Cross to mediate and as all parties involved are opposed to forcible feeding there is nothing for it but to leave the prisoners to starve themselves to death if they wish to do so.

This sad episode has been successfully exploited by the IRA to revive its flagging fortunes. Up to 10,000 Catholic sympathisers have marched in the funeral processions of the hunger strikers; violence following their deaths has caused several more deaths (mainly of police and British troops); in the 1981 general election in the Irish Republic several sympathisers with the hunger strikers were elected on this one issue to the Irish Parliament; and there have been violent clashes between police and IRA supporters in Dublin. These developments have led the Irish Prime Minister to complain that the situation in Northern Ireland is destabilising the politics of the Republic.

These developments have to be viewed as further instalments in the continuing saga of Ulster politics, which illustrate once again the iron determination of the Ulster Unionists to keep Catholic politicians out of power, the desperate fanaticism of the IRA and the dogged determination of the British to contain the situation and minimise bloodshed.

Index